NEW YORK WOMEN OF WIT IN THE TWENTIETH CENTURY

Humor in America

Edited by
Judith Yaross Lee, *Ohio University*
Tracy Wuster, *The University of Texas at Austin*

Advisory Board
Darryl Dickson-Carr, *Southern Methodist University*
Joanne Gilbert, *Alma College*
Rebecca Krefting, *Skidmore College*
Bruce Michelson, *University of Illinois at Urbana-Champaign*
Nicholas Sammond, *University of Toronto*

The Humor in America series considers humor as an
expressive mode reflecting key concerns of people in
specific times and places. With interdisciplinary research,
historical and transnational approaches, and comparative
scholarship that carefully examines contexts such as race,
gender, class, sexuality, region, and media environments,
books in the series explore how comic expression both
responds to and shapes American culture.

NEW YORK WOMEN OF WIT IN THE TWENTIETH CENTURY

Sabrina Fuchs Abrams

The Pennsylvania State University Press
University Park, Pennsylvania

Library of Congress Cataloging-in-Publication Data

Names: Fuchs Abrams, Sabrina, 1967– author.
Title: New York women of wit in the twentieth century / Sabrina Fuchs
    Abrams.
Other titles: Humor in America.
Description: University Park, Pennsylvania : The Pennsylvania State University
    Press, [2023] | Series: Humor in America | Includes bibliographical
    references and index.
Summary: "Examines the work of pioneering female writers who used humor
    as an indirect form of social protest to challenge traditional gender norms
    and social expectations in interwar New York"—Provided by publisher.
Identifiers: LCCN 2023034339 | ISBN 9780271095714 (hardback)
Subjects: LCSH: American wit and humor—History and criticism. | American
    literature—New York (State)—New York—Women authors—History and
    criticism. | American literature—New York (State)—New York—20th
    century—History and criticism. | Women humorists—New York (State)—
    New York—History—20th century. | Women and literature—New York
    (State)—New York—History—20th century.
Classification: LCC PS438 .F83 2023 | DDC 817/.509928709747—dc23/
    eng/20230915
LC record available at https://lccn.loc.gov/2023034339

The Pennsylvania State University Press is a member of the Association of
University Presses.
It is the policy of The Pennsylvania State University Press to use acid-free
paper. Publications on uncoated stock satisfy the minimum requirements of
American National Standard for Information Sciences—Permanence of Paper
for Printed Library Material, ANSI Z39.48-1992.

Cover illustrations (*clockwise from top left*): Edna St. Vincent Millay, 1917,
from *Vassar Encyclopedia*, Vassar College Special Collections; Dorothy
Parker, ca. 1919, from Harpo Marx, *Harpo Speaks!* (1961); Tess Slesinger,
courtesy of The Jacob Rader Marcus Center of the American Jewish Archives,
Cincinnati, Ohio, americanjewisharchives.org; Jessie Redmon Fauset in 1923,
IA Collections, Library of Congress; Mary McCarthy from *The Vassarion*, 1932,
Vassar College Special Collections; and Dawn Powell, ca. 1914 (Wikipedia).

to my family

Contents

Acknowledgments

New York Women of Wit in the Twentieth Century is the culmination of my scholarly interest in modern American literature; American women writers; humor studies; gender, racial, and ethnic studies; and the literature and cultural history of New York. My first book, *Mary McCarthy: Gender, Politics, and the Postwar Intellectual* (2004), led to an interest in Mary McCarthy as a satirist and female voice on the New York intellectual scene. This was followed by the edited collections *Literature of New York* (2009) and *Transgressive Humor of American Women Writers* (2017). I am grateful to my students at SUNY Empire in courses on women and humor, literature of New York, and American women writers for lending their insights and enthusiasm to the subject.

I would like to acknowledge the editorial team at Penn State University Press, including HA! Humor in America series editors Judith Yaross Lee and Tracy Wuster and former acquisitions editor Ryan Peterson for their interest in the project and for expertly guiding me through the process. I am grateful to editorial assistant Josie DiNovo and managing editor Alex Ramos for deftly overseeing the project after Ryan's departure. This project was made possible by grants from the National Endowment for the Humanities and Millay Arts. Any views, findings, conclusions, or recommendations expressed in this publication do not necessarily reflect those of the National Endowment for the Humanities. I have further benefited from funding from SUNY Empire Faculty Development Awards, SUNY Empire Sabbatical Awards, and UUP Individual Development Awards that afforded me the time and financial support needed to pursue this book.

Thanks to the anonymous readers at Penn State University Press, whose thorough and incisive comments and words of praise helped make this a better manuscript. I also appreciate the expert feedback from Larry Howe and Darryl Dickson-Carr on the chapter on Jessie Redmon Fauset and thank Penn State University Press for permission to reprint parts of my essay "The Power of Laughter: Jessie Redmon Fauset and the Racial and Gender Politics of Humor," *Studies in American Humor*, ser. 4, 8, no. 2 (2022): 360–80. Parts of the introduction and my essay "Embattled Embodiment: The Sexual/Intellectual Politics of Humor in Mary McCarthy's Writing," which appeared in *Transgressive Humor of American Women Writers*, edited by Sabrina Fuchs Abrams (2017), have been reproduced with permission of Palgrave Macmillan.

I am grateful to my friends, colleagues, and mentors in the field who have inspired and supported me throughout my literary career. Thanks to Sacvan Bercovitch of Harvard University and Ann Douglas and Andrew Delbanco of Columbia University for cultivating my interest in American literature and modern American women writers. I am grateful to Gina Barreca, Wendy Martin, Linda Morris, Margaret Stetz, and Nancy Walker, for forging the path in the field of women's humor and for supporting fellow female scholars along the way. Special thanks to Judith Yaross Lee, who brought me in as book review editor of *Studies in American Humor*, where I found a wonderful community of fellow humor scholars, including James Caron, Chris Gilbert, Joanne Gilbert, David Gillota, Maggie Hennefeld, Larry Howe, Beck Krefting, Gretchen Martin, Teresa Prados-Torreira, and Tracy Wuster. I am fortunate to have found supportive colleagues and friends at SUNY Empire, notably Barry Eisenberg, Diane Gal, Dana Gliserman-Kopans, Mark Soderstrom, Peggy Tally, and Miriam Tatzel, who have been by my side throughout this journey.

My deepest gratitude belongs to my family: my father, Dan Fuchs, my mentor in literature and in life; my mother, Cara, a consummate New Yorker and a beacon of love; my sister and lifelong friend, Margot; my beloved husband, Dave; and our daughters, Natasha and Susannah, our pride and joy and the next generation of bright, bold women.

Introduction
The Female Satirist in the City

Seen as too smart, too sassy, too sexy, and too strident, female humorists have been largely resisted and overlooked. This book looks at the foremothers of women's humor who used satire, irony, and wit as an indirect form of social protest, setting the stage for future generations of feminist humorists. New York women of wit in the interwar period go beyond the domestic realm to address larger question of political and social reform while questioning assumptions about traditional gender roles. Moving beyond the "unthinking laughter" and physical excess of the unruly woman, this book focuses on the "thinking laughter" of women of wit who stood on the periphery of predominantly male New York intellectual circles. I further undertake the feminist project of uncovering the contribution of lesser-known female satirists in a new light. These writers include Edna St. Vincent Millay, who wrote satiric sketches under the pseudonym Nancy Boyd; Tess Slesinger among the *Menorah Journal* group; Dorothy Parker among the Algonquin wits; Jessie Redmon Fauset among the Harlem Renaissance writers; Dawn Powell of the Lafayette Circle; and Mary McCarthy among the *Partisan Review* crowd.

While most studies of women's literary humor focus on the domestic humor of nineteenth-century writers like Frances Miriam Whitcher, Fanny Fern (Sara Willis Parton), and Marietta Holley or the post–World War II writers of domestic fiction like Erma Bombeck, Betty MacDonald, and Jean Kerr, this book looks at the distinct body of humor of New York women of wit that emerged in the interwar period. These women writers developed a more urban and urbane form of humor that reflects the increasingly cosmopolitan and sophisticated time and place in which they lived. The advent of modernism, the women's suffrage movement, the emergence of the New Woman and the New Negro Woman, and the growth of urban centers in the 1920s and '30s gave rise to a new voice of women's humor, one that was at once defiant and conflicted in defining female identity and the underlying assumptions about gender roles.

Satire, which is often written by an outsider, offers women and other marginalized groups an ideal way to voice their social protest through the socially acceptable form of laughter. "Satire is usually written by powerless people; it is an act of revenge."[1] So wrote Mary McCarthy, a female satirist associated with the anti-Stalinist liberal magazine *Partisan Review* in the 1930s. As Gilbert Highet observes, satire is often motivated by a "sense of personal inferiority, of social injustice, of exclusion from a privileged group."[2] This marginalized identity offers a perspective from which to critique the society to which one partially belongs. The female satirist is in a unique position as somewhat of an outsider operating within mainstream society; this dual perspective shapes the often ironic, double-voiced, or dialogical nature of much of women's humor. The aggressive posture of the satirist, however, is often seen as being "unfeminine" and is one reason why women's humor has been overlooked and even resisted.[3] For many of these women writers, the double-voiced irony of humor as well as the female self-fashioning of their appearance offers a necessary masking of their subversive message. Nonetheless, being a sharp and shrewd woman led to being labeled a "modern American bitch" or a "bitch intellectual."[4] These pioneering women of wit broke boundaries for the more overtly feminist humorists of today, who have turned bright, bold, and bitchy from a stigma into a rallying cry for future generations.

The New York Milieu

The cultural shift in the 1920s and '30s that gave rise to the modern women of wit was focused on urban centers, most notably New York City. The growth of New York revolved around several different neighborhoods, each with its own character. The Greenwich Village bohemia of Lower Manhattan included such writers and intellectuals as Edna St. Vincent Millay, Floyd Dell, Max Eastman, Edmund Wilson, and Dawn Powell. The area around Union Square was also home to leftist intellectual and cultural journals like the Communist-affiliated *New Masses* and the anti-Stalinist *Partisan*

Review, whose editorial board included Philip Rahv, William Phillips, Dwight Macdonald, and Mary McCarthy. The magazine and publishing industry of Midtown Manhattan was home to self-consciously urban, sophisticated magazines such as *Vanity Fair*, the *Smart Set*, and the *New Yorker* and was the site of the heralded Algonquin Round Table, including members Dorothy Parker, Robert Benchley, George S. Kaufman, Alexander Woollcott, Edna Ferber, and F. P. Adams. Midtown Manhattan was also the location of the *Menorah Journal*, a predominantly Jewish, leftist literary and cultural magazine founded by Henry Hurwitz and including editors and contributors Elliot Cohen, Lionel Trilling, Herbert Solow, Clifton Fadiman, Felix Morrow, Tess Slesinger, and Anita Brenner, many of whom were educated at Columbia University in Manhattan's Morningside Heights. Harlem was the Uptown social and cultural center of the New Negro Movement with the founding of the NAACP and African American literary and cultural magazines like the *Crisis*, the *Messenger*, and *Opportunity*, featuring such prominent female figures as Jessie Fauset, Nella Larsen, and Zora Neale Hurston, as well as W. E. B. Du Bois, Langston Hughes, and Countee Cullen. It was further the locus of the jazz movement, including venues like the Cotton Club, the Apollo Theater, and the Savoy Ballroom featuring talented artists like Duke Ellington, Louis Armstrong, Ella Fitzgerald, Bessie Smith, and Josephine Baker.

In Ann Douglas's literary and cultural history of Black and white New York in the 1920s, *Terrible Honesty: Mongrel Manhattan in the 1920s* (1996), she identifies the mythical import of New York City as a city of dreams, a liminal place of possibility that is a product of the imagination more than a reality. The reference to "mongrel" is taken from Dorothy Parker's projected memoir (which was never written) and speaks to the racial, ethnic, class, and gendered heterogeneity of New York City and what was to become its rich and diverse cultural heritage. After World War I, argues Douglas, New York emerged as a center of urban modernity and irreverent spirit in a movement away from the New England morality and propriety of Victorian America. Writers and artists were drawn to New York to make something of themselves. "You might do the work of 'making' outside the city, but you 'made it' in New York, and everyone who was anyone knew it," notes Douglas.[5] As E. B. White observes in his 1949 tribute *Here Is New York*, it is the "settler" to New York, "who was born somewhere else and came to New York in quest of something," who gives the city its passion.[6] Dawn Powell considered herself a "permanent visitor" to New York and took as her subject the midwestern transplant to New York in search of an idealized past or future. Dorothy Parker similarly laid claim to her New York identity, despite the chance misfortune of being born in New Jersey while her family was on summer vacation.[7] For Parker, says Douglas, New York is less a physical location than a state of mind: while most of Parker's stories are set in New York City, "she gives no details of the scene; she never describes a building or a street. One senses that she doesn't need to; in her work New York is not a place but a world, even a world order, and her stories are embedded there as in the inevitable."[8]

This mythic and transformative quality of the city is captured by the former *Village Voice* cultural critic Ross Wetzsteon in *Republic of Dreams: Greenwich Village: The American Bohemia, 1910–1960* (2002). Wetzsteon identifies Greenwich Village in the 1920s and '30s as a "mythic place" in the American imagination and a "revolution of consciousness" associated with romantic rebellion, sexual emancipation, nonconformity, and an anti-bourgeois bohemianism of the marginalized outsider. In particular, it was associated with the post–World War I modernist need to "make it new," to paraphrase Ezra Pound, in the face of the failure of belief of the "lost generation," which ushered in "the New Freedom, the New Woman, the new theater, the new art, the new psychology, the new morality."[9] As early as 1916, the Greenwich Village intellectual Floyd Dell lamented the loss of the authentic bohemian past—"the Village isn't what it used to be"—and this sense of adolescent rebellion and freedom in relation to adult, bourgeois responsibility is the essence of Greenwich Village bohemia.[10]

The shift in the landscape of New York bohemian life from the 1930s through the 1950s, and Greenwich Village café culture in particular, is the subject of much of Dawn Powell's New York fiction. Termed the "doyenne of the village" by Gore Vidal and known for holding court at the Lafayette Hotel café near Washington Square, Powell is described by the critic Edmund Wilson as the consummate chronicler of Greenwich Village bohemian life from its height in the 1920s to its displacement by "bearded beatniks and abstract painters" in the 1950s.[11] The spread of high-rise apartments and office buildings along with Robert Moses's plan to expand highways, bridges, and tunnels in the 1930s and '40s was seen at once as progress and a threat to New York neighborhoods. Female activists, led by Jane Jacobs, mounted the successful opposition to Moses's plans to build the lower Manhattan Expressway through the West Village, which threatened to destroy an already changing bohemian café culture. Despite the decline from the "golden age" of Greenwich Village, the dream of bohemia lives on. As Wetzsteon observes, "The Village is dead, long live the Village."[12]

In the aptly titled *The Unfinished City: New York and the Metropolitan Idea* (2001), Thomas Bender describes New York as "a paradoxical modern metropolis" whose "very essence is to be continually in the making, to never be completely resolved."[13] Colson Whitehead's *The Colossus of New York* (2003) similarly captures the constant state of change that typifies New York City. And while Whitehead and E. B. White might feel nostalgia for "my lost city," to borrow a phrase from F. Scott Fitzgerald, they recognize New York to be in a constant state of reimagining that both shapes and reflects the changing identity of its inhabitants. The contrast between the pastoral, agrarian ideal of the country and the paradoxical nature of the city as a potential site of cultivation/civilization and the threat of corruption/decay is captured by Raymond Williams in *The Country and the City* (1975): "On the country has gathered the idea of a natural way of life: of peace, innocence, and simple virtue. On the city has gathered the idea of an achieved centre: of learning, communication, light. Powerful hostile associations have also developed: on the city as a place of noise, worldliness and ambition; on the country as a place of backwardness, ignorance, limitation."[14]

The more rational and orderly side of urban life is associated with masculinity, while the chaotic and disorderly side tends to be associated with the female principle (and female sexuality in particular). The conservative theorist Le Bon says "crowds are like the sphinx of ancient fable"; you must find the solution or risk being destroyed by them. In Elizabeth Wilson's study *The Sphinx in the City: Urban Life, the Control of Disorder, and Women* (1991), she counters this antifemale narrative with the possibility of the emancipatory city, whereby the movement from the private sphere of the home to the public space of the street offers women at the turn of the twentieth century the possibility of self-actualization.[15] More recent critics have tempered Wilson's optimism regarding urban space and female emancipation with a recognition of the intersectional limitations of race, class, and gender on female liberation.[16]

The New Woman, the New Negro Woman, and the Racial, Gender, and Class Politics of Humor

Through the use of satire, the female humorists of the interwar period capture the ambiguity of the progressive ideals of modernism and the dream of urban possibility, many of which revolve around the figure of the New Woman. Issues of racial, class, and gender inequality in the interwar period are taken up by the Harlem Renaissance writer Jessie Redmon Fauset and by Tess Slesinger in what Paula Rabinowitz terms her "socialist feminist" fiction and underlie much of the irony and satire of Dorothy Parker and Mary McCarthy. The changing role of the New Woman from the turn of the twentieth century through the 1920s and '30s creates both opportunities and conflicts for the modern, educated woman. The New Woman is defined in the *North American Review* in 1894 as "an independent, college-educated American girl devoted to suffrage, progressive reform, and sexual freedom."[17] The figure of the New Woman shifted from the first-generation progressive social reformers and suffragettes of the late nineteenth century, who advocated for legal and economic equality for women, to the second-generation Greenwich Village bohemians of the 1910s and '20s, who were defined by the sexual freedom and personal independence that accompanied the advent of birth control and the passage of the Nineteenth Amendment giving women the right to vote.[18] Rita Felski argues for the breakdown of the gendered division between male and female with the growth of urban culture, the entry of women into the workforce, and the rise of consumer culture: "Divisions between public and private, masculine and feminine, modern and antimodern were not as fixed as they may have appeared. . . . [T]he ideology of separate spheres was undercut by the movement of working-class women into mass production and industrial labor. . . . The expansion of consumerism in the latter half of the [nineteenth] century further blurred public/private distinctions, as middle-class women moved out into the public spaces of the department store and the world of mass-produced goods in turn invaded the interiority of the home."[19]

The New Woman of the Jazz Age and the possibilities of free love, radical politics, and artistic and professional freedom found expression in Greenwich Village in the 1920s. Home of the Marxist magazine *The Masses*; leftist intellectuals like Floyd Dell and Max Eastman; the social activists Mabel Dodge, Margaret Sanger, and Emma Goldman; and writers like Edna St. Vincent Millay and the Heterodoxy Club, Greenwich Village was a nexus for progressive thought and modern morality.[20] The radicalized Greenwich Village New Woman gave rise to a more commodified, commercialized version of the flapper in an age of mass media, consumer culture, and modern publishing and magazine culture, in which the progressive, urban values and styles could be spread across the country. The figure of the flapper was contradictory—while her androgynous bobbed hair, drop-waist dresses, and freedom to drink, smoke, and engage in premarital and extramarital sex offered the promise of freedom and autonomy, it was often in the service of the traditional, heteronormative goal of marriage. The New Woman was personified in the media representation of the Gibson Girl: "While she could hold her own with men in a golf match or with her quick wit, her chief purpose in life was to capture a husband."[21]

The figure of the flapper was at once commodified and satirized in modern magazines like *Vanity Fair*, the *Smart Set*, and the *New Yorker*. There was a self-consciously sophisticated and stylized tone to more middlebrow magazines like *Vanity Fair*, which was meant to appeal to the more independent and educated New Woman; it declared in its editorial statement, "For women we intend to do something in a noble and missionary spirit, which . . . has never been done for them by an American magazine. We mean to make frequent appeals to their intellect."[22] And in the editor Harold Ross's vision statement for the *New Yorker* in 1925, he sought to create a sophisticated humor magazine whose "general tenor will be one of gaiety, wit and satire" and "will assume a reasonable degree of enlightenment on the part of its readers"; that is, "*The New Yorker* will be the magazine which is not edited for the old lady in Dubuque."[23] As such, Ross sought humorists like James Thurber, Robert Benchley, and Dorothy Parker, known for their sardonic humor. Despite Ross's appeal to urban sophisticates (or would-be urbanites), as Judith Yaross Lee observes, the *New Yorker* features its own version of local-color humor that revolves around urban nightlife, fashion, culture, and consumption. "Despite its growing population," says Yaross Lee, "New York was (and in many ways remains) a small town. Consequently, the declaration in Ross's prospectus that the magazine would feature small-town gossip drew on a very real fact of New York life: like small-town Americans, New Yorkers live and work and play in overlapping circles of acquaintance."[24] In Catherine Keyser's notable study *Playing Smart: New York Women Writers and Modern Magazine Culture*, she explores the relationship between New York women writers and modern magazine culture. It is this world of the urban sophisticate and their purported progressive values that is the object of satire for such female humorists as Dorothy Parker, Tess Slesinger, and Mary McCarthy, among others.

The figure of the New Woman is further problematic in that she is seen largely as privileged and white; issues of racial and class equality were subordinated in her struggle for gender equality. The National American Woman Suffrage Association (NAWSA) at the turn of the twentieth century excluded African American women, who formed their own National Association of Colored Women (1895) as well as popular Women's Clubs. While the New Woman embraced free love and individual autonomy, the New Negro Woman was engaged in a project of racial uplift whereby she sought the only avenue available to escape racial and gender exploitation, through bourgeois respectability and the model of marriage and motherhood associated with the "cult of True Womanhood" of the Victorian era. The emphasis on purity or sexual respectability was particularly important in that it combated the stereotype of the lascivious Black woman or "Jezebel," an ironic reputation given the reality that Black women were historically exploited by white slave owners and treated as breeders rather than acting as temptresses. Given the legacy of slavery and sexual exploitation as well as the long history of minority women in the workforce as a financial necessity rather than an assertion of personal autonomy, African American women did not view sexual freedom and professional engagement in the same way as their white, bourgeois counterparts. As Martha Patterson observes, "Under closer scrutiny, a seemingly celebratory term like the New Woman becomes not only a trope of progressive reform, consumer power, and transgressive femininity but also one of racial and ethnic taxonomies, social Darwinism, and imperialist ambition."[25]

The progressive ideals of the modern, independent woman of the 1920s are further called into question by the financial crisis of the Great Depression and the social movements of the 1930s. The 1930s emphasis on class struggle and workers' rights subordinated issues of gender equality, both in life and in literature. With the rise in unemployment (25 percent of the workforce was unemployed by 1923), women who were seen as vital to the workforce during World War I were being sent back to the home, and the focus on self-fulfillment characteristic of the 1920s was replaced by a sense of collective social responsibility for the poor and unemployed. Feminist issues of sexual freedom, gender equality, and reproductive rights were subordinated to more pressing and widespread issues of workers' rights at home and the rise of fascism abroad.[26] The Great Depression exacerbated conditions of segregation, discrimination, and looming poverty in Harlem, contributing to the historic race riots of 1919 and 1935.

The changing role of the modern woman was crucial to the development of women's humor in the 1920s and '30s, since theories of humor have traditionally identified the aggressive, intellectual, and sexual tendencies of humor to be largely "masculine" and thereby inaccessible to women. From eighteenth-century conduct manuals to Victorian ideals of the "cult of true womanhood," women were bound by feminine ideals of "piety, purity, submissiveness, and domesticity." In "The Cult of True Womanhood," Barbara Welter identifies how the image of ideal womanhood emphasized emotion over reason and intuition over rationality and intellect. Women were seen to uphold the spiritual and moral foundations of the domestic sphere, while men would become educated, go out in the world, and secure a financial future. Sexuality for women was in the interest of procreation, not pleasure, in perpetuation of the goals of motherhood and marriage. As Virginia Woolf warned, "Killing the Angel in the House was part of the occupation of a woman writer" and by extension a necessity for the Victorian woman to find herself.[27] With access to higher education beginning in the nineteenth century, an increasing role in the workforce during World War I, and the advent of birth control, women began to enjoy a financial, intellectual, and sexual freedom that defied traditional gender roles.

This newfound freedom was seen as a threat to the existing patriarchal power structure, leading some to demonize the figure of the independent woman, creating a split between the domestic "Angel" and the liberated "Monster."[28] This defiant figure is associated with female empowerment, wit, and humor, which, according to Hélène Cixous, is falsely identified by men as a threatening, monstrous figure because they cannot see her for who she is. "You only have to look at the Medusa straight to see her. And she's not deadly. She's beautiful and she's laughing."[29] In the Greek myth, Medusa's power is deadly whenever someone looks directly at her; however, Cixous's interpretation suggests that if Perseus could see Medusa from the proper perspective, he would find her beautiful, not monstrous. Likewise, if men (and women themselves) could see women in all their capacity and not through the distorted male gaze, they would not appear threatening and monstrous but beautiful and enlightened. This laughter can be seen as castrating and emasculating, a sign of intellectual and sexual potency. Laughter can be seen as a physical release, like a kind of orgasm, especially when originated by a woman, as opposed to the "faked" laughter of a woman at a man's joke of which she or some other subordinate person is the butt. But it can also be seen as an assertion of female sexuality, knowledge, and ultimately power. The laughing Medusa, says the feminist theorist Susan Rubin Suleiman, is a "trope for women's autonomous subjectivity and for the necessary irreverence of women's writing and rewriting."[30] The relation of humor to knowledge and of knowledge to power is at the root of the female claim to humor and the denial especially among male critics of women's humor.

Theories of Humor and Interrogating the Category of Women's Humor

To understand the unique place of female humorists of the interwar period, it is important to interrogate the categories of women's humor, humor in general, and satire in particular, as well as the ways in which these categories have been complicated with more contemporary, intersectional, and multidisciplinary approaches to the subject. As the humor scholars Joanne Gilbert, Linda Mizejewski, and Rebecca Krefting, among others, have observed, while the category of women's humor is useful, it has its limitations, and it is a fluid term that has changed meaning over time. In the 1970s, '80s, and early '90s, in the wake of second-wave feminism and the women's movement, the field of women's humor emerged with the publication of pioneering works by Nancy A. Walker, Regina Barreca, Emily Toth, Judy Little, and Linda A. Morris, as well as important collections of essays on women's humor by Barreca, Morris, Gail Finney, and June Sochen. Add to that valuable anthologies of primary source material by female humorists like Nancy A. Walker and Zita Dresner's edited *Redressing the Balance: American Women's Literary Humor from Colonial Times to the 1980s* (1988), and women's humor began to gain a place as a serious field of study. These works reflect the second-wave feminist emphasis on reviving and uncovering works by and about women and have likewise been criticized for reinforcing what some see as an essentialist, largely white, heteronormative point of view. Emphasizing a unique and unified category of "women's humor" tends to overlook the differences among types of women's humor as well as the affinity among humor by women and by people from other marginalized groups, regardless of gender. It also tends to see humor in a monolithic way as subversive of existing patriarchal authority by a marginalized, oppressed category of women. This raises the question of whether humor can be seen as progressive or conservative, as subverting or reinforcing the status quo, or whether it assumes a more ambiguous position dependent on the intention and reception of humor. Related to the question of intention is that of the *efficacy* of humor: To what extent can or should humor translate into political action and social change?

In analyzing the category of women's humor and the place of female humorists in the interwar period, it is useful to examine the broader context of theories of humor. Theories of humor have often been divided into three dominant approaches—the relief theory, the incongruity theory, and the superiority theory—and while these or any categories have their limitations, they offer a good starting point from which to complicate our understanding of women's humor.

The relief or release theory is a psychoanalytic theory of humor that draws on Freud's 1905 work *Jokes and Their Relation to the Unconscious*. In this theory, laughter functions as a release of excess nervous energy, like the relief valve used to vent pressure in a steam boiler. Freud identifies the pleasure in jokes as the "economy of expenditure upon inhibition" of psychic energy ordinarily used to repress sexual and aggressive tendencies. He distinguishes between jokes, the comic, and humor, which he sees as expressions of the economy of expenditure of feeling, thought, and emotion, respectively.[31] For Freud, "tendentious jokes," or jokes with purpose, are like dreams, an outlet for hostile or obscene thoughts and feelings that are temporarily uninhibited and released through laughter. In keeping with the superiority/disparagement theory, these jokes are often used by people in positions of greater authority with the purpose of insulting or wounding those in subordinate positions, thereby reinforcing the status quo (note the many sexist and ethnic jokes used by Freud as illustrations). Beyond this, Freud also notes the potential subversive value of jokes in their capacity to invert the existing power structure by allowing for expression of otherwise-forbidden hostility by people in subordinate positions against those in authority: "Tendentious jokes are especially favored in order to make aggressiveness or criticism possible against persons in exalted positions who claim to exercise authority. The joke then represents a rebellion against that authority, a liberation from its pressure." Freud elaborates that through the masked form of humor, jokes can thereby be directed against people in authority, hallowed institutions, and the social conventions themselves that underlie such injustices: "The object of the joke's attack may equally well be institutions, people in their capacity as vehicles of institutions, dogmas of morality or religion, views of life which enjoy so much respect that objections to them can only be made under the *mask of a joke* and indeed of a joke concealed by its façade."[32] This notion of humor as a masked form of social criticism or even rebellion by people in subordinate positions against injustices perpetuated by existing power structures is at the root of much of women's humor and a response to a hierarchy that is socially contingent.

The superiority theory of a *phthonic* or malicious element in humor as an expression of contempt or hostility, usually directed against people of perceived social inferiority, is elaborated by Henri Bergson in his study *Laughter: An Essay on the Meaning of the Comic* (1911). Bergson identifies laughter as a social corrective used to mock eccentric or deviant behavior in the interest of preserving the status quo. A vitalist who appeals to intuition over the mechanistic and overly rational, Bergson considers laughter to be a corrective for the "mechanical inelasticity" of character that is a hazard of modern life. Bergson emphasizes the social aspect of laughter as a reflection of communal beliefs as well as the moral function of laughter as a social corrective with the intention "to humiliate and . . . to correct our neighbor" in the interest of "preservation of a social norm."[33] Like Bergson, Freud recognizes the social aspect of humor and of jokes in particular in that they require an audience of three parties: the teller, the listener, and the object of the joke.[34] Conversely, the superiority-disparagement theory often has an aggressive component similar to that underlying the relief theory, in that it often involves the intention to humiliate as a kind of "social ragging" in the interest of social conformity. Women and other marginalized groups often find themselves to be the object of this type of humor rather than the initiator.

Unlike the relief theory and the superiority-disparagement theories of humor, which emphasize the sexual/aggressive tendencies and the social nature of humor, the incongruity theory of humor is less emotional and more cognitively based on the perceptual and verbal aspect of humor, in particular, of irony and wit. Incongruity theory, which is considered the dominant theory of humor in philosophy and psychology today, is based on the "assumption that human experience works with learned patterns and expectations. When a thing violates our expectation or mental pattern, it is incongruous."[35] Incongruity theory can be traced back to Aristotle, who identified laughter as being caused by a violation of expectation, and Immanuel Kant, who famously identified laughter as "an affection arising from the sudden transformation of a strained expectation into nothing."[36]

The incongruity theory has aspects of the superiority theory in that the perception of incongruity or disparity between two normally incompatible or disparate things implies a certain knowledge or superiority on the part of the perceiver (the one who "gets" the joke) and also requires a shared assumption or cultural frame of reference to recognize the subversion of expectations (implying an "in" group and an "out" group). While some theorists, like Arthur Koestler, emphasize the aggressive tendency underlying "bisociation" or the perception of two self-consistent but normally incompatible or disparate ideas (e.g., a pun that brings together two different meanings of a word to subvert expectations), later theorists of incongruity downplay the "tendentious" (sexual and aggressive) tendency of humor while emphasizing the cognitive aspects.[37] The incongruity theory of humor, with its emphasis on the verbal presentation and cognitive perception of a double or ironic meaning (of a socially accepted and an underlying subversive meaning), is central to an understanding of women's humor.

Early theorists of women's humor, like Nancy A. Walker, identify certain distinctive characteristics of what she terms "women's humorous writing" that emphasize a more communal purpose and a deeper sense of empathy behind women's humor, which comes from being in a more subordinate position in society: "Women tend to be *story* tellers rather than *joke* tellers. Humor functions for them more as a means of communication than as a means of self-presentation, a sharing of experience rather than a demonstration of cleverness. . . . Women's humorous expression is almost never purely comic or absurd. . . . It carries with it not the lighthearted feeling that is the privilege of the powerful, but instead a subtext of anguish and frustration."[38] Conversely, traditional "male" humor would tend toward jokes and put-downs directed against people of perceived lower social standing, what has been termed "punching down," as an expression of hostility and a demonstration of one's own cleverness and an affirmation of one's social superiority. Such categories of male and female humor are increasingly troubled by our understanding of gender-queer or nonbinary humor production.

Emily Toth elaborates on this sense of difference in women's humor in identifying what she terms the "humane humor rule" in much of women's writing in the twentieth century—namely, "the belief that a writer should not make fun of what people cannot change, such as social handicaps, race, sex, or physical appearance. . . . Rather, women humorists attack— or subvert—the deliberate choices people make: hypocrisies, affectations, mindless following of social expectations."[39] By contrast, "male" humor would be perceived as a more aggressive attack on people of perceived inferiority due to innate difference such as race, gender, physical appearance, and the like. While much of women's domestic humor tends to be more self-deprecatory and to emphasize a shared sense of frustration and at times indignation, categorical differences between men's and women's humor do not apply as well to the more overt feminist humor of the so-called heterodoxy writers of the 1920s, like Florence Guy Seabury and Alice Duer Miller, or to the more complex and ambivalent works of the female satirists of the interwar period.

The categorization of "women's humor" is complicated by the complex nature of female group identity. In Nancy A. Walker's essay "Toward

Solidarity: Women's Humor and Group Identity," she explores the problematic nature of group identity or the social foundation of humor for women, who do not form a unified group with a shared identity. "Unlike other oppressed groups," says Walker, "women do not constitute a group in the usual sense but instead are isolated from one another by their intimate relationships with men, and, traditionally, by their habitation in the private sphere of homemaking and child rearing."[40] That is to say, some women— that is, heterosexual women of privilege who are wives and mothers—are at once insiders and outsiders in society. This further explains the "us/them" mentality of much of minority humor, given the blurred lines for women between "us" and them."[41] While women may be a numerical majority, they stand in the somewhat marginalized position of a minority given their traditionally subordinate status in society. A unified, "group identity" is further problematized by the diversity among women of race, ethnicity, class, and sexuality. This lack of social cohesion, along with the traditionally socially prescribed role of subordination for women, has complicated the notion of women's humor as a category.

The nature of group identity is more complex in that it can be used at once to reinforce social hierarchy by people in positions of power and to challenge existing power structures by those excluded from mainstream society. While a number of theorists of women's humor acknowledge Bergson's identification of the social value of humor and group solidarity, they see this group solidarity among marginalized groups like women and minorities as functioning not as a means of preserving the status quo but as a basis for challenging certain social assumptions. In "Social Cognition, Gender Roles, and Women's Humor," Alice Sheppard applies Bergson's theory of humor as a means of social or group control to the issue of gender, stating that women humorists are ridiculed for deviating from the expected social behavior in asserting their wit and control through humor and are pressured to conform to the social norm. In developing a cognitive-social theory of humor, she elaborates on Bergson's belief that since humor is based on shared cultural assumptions and women are not perceived as being funny, women's humor has been overlooked and even dismissed. "The expectation that women are unlikely to use humor, the limited knowledge and value of women's experience, the low status of women in society, and the characterization of women's gender roles," says Sheppard, have predisposed many people to consider women to lack a sense of humor.[42] The sociologist Paul McGhee traces these differentiated gender roles back to early childhood, where social assumptions are made and perpetuated:

"Because of the power associated with the successful use of humor, humor initiation has become associated with other traditionally masculine characteristics, such as aggression, dominance, and assertiveness. For a female to develop into a clown or a joker, then, she must violate the behavior pattern normally reserved for women."[43] This identification of humor with knowledge and ultimately power or social control is at the root of much resistance to women's humor.

The gendered hierarchy of society has historically necessitated a masking of critical female voices through a double discourse. In "Towards a Feminist Poetics," Elaine Showalter identifies the dual text found in much of women's writing: "The feminist content of feminine art is typically oblique, displaced, ironic and subversive; one has to read it between the lines, in the missed possibilities of the text."[44] Sandra M. Gilbert and Susan Gubar further describe the necessity of women and other marginalized groups to use a double-voiced or "palimpsestic" discourse in order to mask the subversive intent of their words, in "works whose surface designs conceal or obscure deeper, less accessible (and less socially acceptable) levels of meaning. Thus, these authors managed the difficult task of achieving true female literary authority by simultaneously conforming to and subverting patriarchal literary standards."[45]

Such "double-voiced discourse," says Judy Little, is common in comic writing by women, which "deconstructs or exposes the ideologies of authority and power, often by juxtaposing the male voice of solemn formality and the female voice of buoyant hysteria."[46] This "carnivalization" of dialogue is traced by Little to Mikhail Bakhtin's notion of "heteroglossia" or the "dialogic" voice found in "the Menippea" (Menippean satire), which, according to Bakhtin, displays "dialogical parody."[47] While Bakhtin sees the multivoiced discourse as expressing the spirit of "carnival" as a temporary state of transgression or challenge to the status quo, Little suggests that women use this carnivalesque spirit to pose a more lasting challenge to the status quo through a masked, double-voiced discourse. This double meaning can take different forms: the voice of a narrator commenting on the actions of a character, the voice of one character over another, or a split within a single character commenting on their own thoughts or actions.

Bakhtin's application of the concept of the carnivalesque in *Rabelais and His World* (1965) has been influential on feminist humor studies in its celebration of the transgressive and liberatory power of humor, even if it is only temporary. Bakhtin traces the concept of the carnivalesque back to medieval festivals—such as the "feast of fools" and the "feast of the ass," as well as other church and civil festivals—which allow for institutionally sanctioned expressions of laughter. This folk humor is rooted in the concept of "grotesque realism" and finds expression in "the material bodily principle" through images of "the human body with its food, drink, defecation, and sexual life." This "degradation" is not only negative and destructive but is ambivalent in its sense of regeneration and renewal, associated at once with "acts of defecation and copulation, conception, pregnancy and birth."[48]

Bakhtin's concept of the carnivalesque is adapted by theorists of female performative humor like Kathleen Rowe Karlyn with her concept of the "unruly woman," Linda Mizejewski with her critique of the pretty-versus-funny false binary, and Maggie Hennefeld in her discussion of the female grotesque and abjection. The carnivalesque allows for a topsy-turvy reversal of established hierarchies in a temporary release of carnal and subversive thoughts and actions. This celebration of the physical over the rational and location in the nether regions associated with birth, sexuality, and blood/menstruation have been associated by feminist theorists with the female grotesque. While Bakhtin's concept of carnival is temporary, with an ultimate return to the status quo and existing hierarchies, feminist theorists emphasize the subversive potential or at least the ambivalence of the carnivalesque in challenging social hierarchies. In *The Unruly Woman: Gender and the Genres of Laughter* (1995), Rowe Karlyn draws on Mary Russo's concept of the "female grotesque" and Natalie Zemon Davis's feminist reframing of Bakhtin's concept of the carnivalesque to ask *why* "the old hags" that Bakhtin references are laughing and to "investigate the power of female grotesques and female laughter to challenge the social and symbolic systems that would keep women in their place."[49] Using examples from narrative cinema as well as the model of the comedian Roseanne, Rowe Karlyn shows how the physical and verbal excess of the figure of the unruly woman, deemed "too fat, too funny, too noisy, too old, too rebellious," can in fact be a source of empowerment that "unsettles social hierarchies."[50]

In *Pretty/Funny: Women Comedians and Body Politics* (2014), Linda Mizejewski builds on the work of Rowe Karlyn in a feminist reframing of Bakhtin by exposing the false duality of pretty versus funny, female versus male, body versus mind, and heart versus head that has served to reinforce the gender expectation that women should be pretty and demure, not sharp-witted, outspoken, sexual, aggressive, *unruly* beings. Mizejewski shows how the female comedians Kathy Griffin, Sarah Silverman, Tina Fey, Margaret Cho, Wanda Sykes, and Ellen DeGeneres challenge this false binary and ideals of "femininity" through their transgressive and controversial comedy. Maggie Hennefeld reframes the concept of the "unruly woman" in light of abjection theory, arguing that the unruly woman is a collective figure who subverts social or cultural prohibitions, while abject feminism is rooted in primordial taboos and personal psychology. In discussing Bakhtin's conception of the carnivalesque, Hennefeld shifts the focus away from the transgressive versus the conservative debate, "whether an unofficially tolerated, temporary revolution can have lasting effects on the social," to the "gap between *grotesque comedy* and *abject aversion*."[51] In Bakhtin's conception, "grotesque realism" is collective and potentially renewing, whereas in abjection discourse, grotesque realism is related to individual psychology and horror. This ambivalence in the representation of the grotesque female body has implications for contemporary feminist comedians like Amy Schumer and Lena Dunham.

The double voice of much of women's writing and of women's humor in particular is part of the modernist project, which often uses irony to pose a critical, subversive meaning beyond the literal or overt meaning. In Linda Hutcheon's study *Irony's Edge* (1994), she identifies what she terms the "transideological politics" of irony, questioning whether the use of irony is necessarily radical or subversive or if it can be seen as conservative in the literal sense of reinforcing the status quo. According to Hutcheon, "There is nothing *intrinsically* subversive about ironic skepticism or about any such self-questioning, 'internally dialogized' mode; there is no *necessary* relationship between irony and radical politics or even radical formal innovation. Irony has often been used to reinforce rather than to question established attitudes, as the history of satire illustrates so well."[52] The question about the subversive nature of ironic or parodic language is part of a larger debate about the feminist nature of women's humor, or whether women's use of a double-voiced language is subversive or a means of channeling anger and thereby reinforcing the social hierarchy. The "ambiguity" of irony is that it is at once elitist (in that to say one thing and mean another implies a certain privileged or shared knowledge) and subversive (in that it challenges the apparent meaning). A further "problem" of irony is that in the postmodern sense, how can one find a hidden or dual meaning if a primary or singular meaning and language itself are considered unstable?[53]

The double-edged irony or dual meaning underlying much of women's satire is often expressed through a kind of double language. In Robin Tolmach Lakoff's groundbreaking study *Language and Woman's Place* (1975), she identifies what she terms "women's language," that is, the socially accepted and expected polite or "feminine" language, which often belies a more defiant underlying meaning. Published in the 1970s at the start of the women's movement, Lakoff's work reflects what was then a greater necessity to conform to social expectations of female rhetoric. Lakoff identifies the defining characteristics of "women's language," including a questioning intonation, polite forms of language, emphasis and repetition, the use of "intensives" like "so," and, of course, not telling jokes.[54] A stunning example of the satiric invocation of "female language" can be found in numerous sketches by Dorothy Parker, such as "The Waltz," "But the One on the Right," and "The Lovely Leave," in which her speaker engages in a dialogic split between the inner monologue of her ironic, witty self and the outward dialogue of her socially prescribed, polite, "feminine" self.

The performative aspect of women's language and gender identity itself is the subject of the feminist theorist Judith Butler's notable work *Gender Trouble: Feminism and the Subversion of Identity* (1990), in which she writes, "Within the inherited discourse of the metaphysics of substance, gender proves to be performative—that is, constituting the identity it is purported to be. In this sense, gender is always a doing, though not a doing by a subject who might be said to preexist the deed. . . . There is no gender identity behind the expressions of gender; the identity is performatively constituted by the very 'expressions' that are said to be its results."[55] The split between traditional gender roles of "masculine" and "feminine" and the dictates or pressures of "compulsory heterosexuality" are socially constructed. The dichotomy between "masculine" and "feminine" identity and concomitant "masculine" and "feminine" language and behavior harks back to the outmoded, Victorian ideal of true womanhood, which even among twentieth-century women writers continued to create a false binary for outspoken women of wit. This split creates a double bind for women, says Regina Barreca, between the "Good Girl," who does not swear, tell jokes, or engage in sexual or aggressive behavior, and the "Bad Girl," who does all of the above. "Learning to sound like a Good Girl, while half-concealing the text of the Bad Girl," says Barreca, "has been the subject of a great deal of women's humor."[56]

For women, this double-voiced humor is often masked through the invocation of gender stereotypes in order to subvert them. According to Walker, many twentieth-century critics fail to recognize most American female humorists "largely because the *use* of stereotypes is assumed to constitute an acceptance of that stereotype." Women humorists often "employ stereotypes of women for the purpose of mocking those stereotypes and showing their absurdity and even danger," says Walker. Such stereotypes include "the gossipy spinster, the nagging wife, the inept housekeeper, the lovelorn woman, the dumb blond."[57] The negative use of stereotypes is at times so concealed (or the assumption of stereotypes by the reader so strong) that they can be misinterpreted as an endorsement of the social norm, which has led many people to criticize Parker, for instance, for reinforcing the very stereotypes she mockingly invokes. While Parker often uses a kind of self-deprecatory humor, there is a pathos and indignation beneath her use of gender stereotypes. As Suzanne L. Bunkers observes, "Parker is not satirizing women per se; rather, she uses her pitiable, ridiculous women characters to criticize the society that has created one-dimensional female roles and forced women to fit into them."[58]

The question remains whether humor in general, and humor by women in particular, is inherently subversive or conservative or whether those categories are still relevant? In following the Freudian "relief theory," humor can be seen as an outlet for hostile impulses, thereby turning anger into acceptance. Such is the view held by the feminist activist Betty Friedan, who faulted domestic humorists of the 1950s for using humor as a means of sublimating their dissatisfaction with traditional roles as wives and mothers. Domestic humorists like Phyllis McGinley, Jean Kerr, and Shirley Jackson, says Friedan, cause women to "dissipate in laughter their dreams and their sense of desperation."[59] Humor, argues Joanne R. Gilbert in *Performing Marginality: Humor, Gender, and Cultural Critique* (2004), undermines its own revolutionary potential and is "antithetical to action. First, it functions as an 'anti-rhetoric,' always negating its own potential power by being just a joke. More important, humor renders its audience passive. It disarms through amusing. Laughter is not generally a galvanizing force toward political action."[60] As an aspect of the carnivalesque, humor allows for expression of subversive or forbidden impulses but ultimately returns to the existing social order. The paradox of humor, however, is that it allows for this disruptive impulse, this challenging of authority under the guise of social acceptance. So it is, one might say, safely subversive. Other critics of women's humor, like Barreca, find a more overt feminist agenda behind women's humor, seeing a split between masculine humor as "deflective," allowing for the "oh-I-was-kidding disclaimer," and female humor "not as a safety valve but as an inflammatory device, seeking, ultimately, not to purge desire and frustration but to transform it into action."[61] In the introduction to *Pulling Our Own Strings: Feminist Humor and Satire* (1980), Gloria Kaufman makes a distinction between "female" humor and "feminist" humor. "The persistent attitude that underlies feminist humor," says Kaufman, "is the attitude of social revolution—that is, we are ridiculing a social system that can, that must be changed. *Female* humor may ridicule a person or a system from an accepting point of view ('that's life'), while the *nonacceptance* of oppression characterizes feminist humor and satire."[62] Feminist humorists tend toward more overt political action surrounding issues of, say, women's suffrage in the 1910s or women's rights in the 1970s.

But not all women's humor needs to have a feminist agenda in order to be subversive. Nancy Walker makes the important qualification that, while not expressing an overt, revolutionary call for social change, so-called female humor can be quietly subversive by exposing the limitations of gender stereotypes, thereby fostering not revolution but reform. There are two types of women's humor, says Walker: "One, operating subversively within the cultural system of subjugation, acknowledges a woman's subordination while protesting it"; the other "explores the fundamental absurdity of that system and calls for different ways of conceptualized gender definition." So-called female humor "is not merely 'accepting' the status quo but is calling attention to gender inequality in ways designed to lead to its rejection." Thus, she argues, many female humorists "have displayed a feminist consciousness that approaches the problem indirectly."[63] For writers like Mary McCarthy and Dorothy Parker, who did not necessarily have a feminist political agenda, the use of satire and irony allowed for this indirect expression of social criticism through the socially acceptable form of laughter.

The concept of women's humor and its relation to feminist politics have been interrogated and complicated by more recent scholars of humor and feminist theory away from what some see as the essentialist approach of pioneering scholars like Walker and Barreca toward a more intersectional approach, emphasizing differences of race, ethnicity, class, sexuality, national origin, and other defining characteristics. As our understanding of women's humor has expanded, so too has the medium, from a focus on literary humor to multiple media, including stand-up, sketch comedy, television, film, and digital and social media. More recent humor scholars like Joanne Gilbert, Kathleen Rowe Karlyn, Linda Mizejewski, and Rebecca Krefting question the subversive/transgressive binary as well as the efficacy of humor to instigate political/social change.

In Joanne R. Gilbert's influential work *Performing Marginality*, she takes an intersectional approach to women comics "performing marginality," identifying women among a broader group of outsiders marginalized by race or ethnicity, including Black and Jewish stand-up performers. This insider/outsider status affords marginalized comics a certain freedom and perspective from which to critique those in dominant positions of power. Gilbert assumes a more ambivalent position in identifying the effect and efficacy of women's humor. She argues that "through its mockery of social conventions, its laughter at patriarchal norms, women's humor can be seen as subversive," but, she qualifies, this is not unique to women; rather, "it is characteristic of humor by all marginal groups."[64] In considering the performance of humor as a rhetorical strategy, she emphasizes the relationship between the teller, the butt, and the audience in determining the intent and effect of a joke. One may assume more than one position at the same time (for example, teller and butt in the case of self-deprecatory humor), and the same joke may be received differently depending on the point of view of the listener. Gilbert makes an important distinction between the victim and the butt of a joke, which is contingent on "audience identification and interpretation" as to whether one is laughing at someone (the butt of a joke, thereby reinforcing that stereotype) or laughing with someone (the victim of a joke, thereby exposing the absurdity of the stereotype and critiquing the society that created it). In this regard, self-deprecatory humor, in which the female comedian plays the victim, can still have a subversive effect if the audience is in on the joke and recognizes society and social injustice to be the actual target. While Gilbert recognizes the "rhetorically transgressive" intent and effect of humor by marginalized groups in general and by women in particular, she stops short of seeing that humor as "politically transgressive." "No single joke is likely to precipitate the decline of prevailing ideologies," notes Gilbert. "Still, given the inherently subversive power of humor, jokes may be a place to begin."[65] Thus, marginalized humor has a kind of *intellectual* power of consciousness raising that is not equivalent to social action but is a necessary precursor to social change.[66]

It should be noted that much of the recent scholarship on women's humor is focused on stand-up comedy or film/television/media, which puts an emphasis on joke-telling and performative/rhetorical strategies, in contrast to earlier studies that focused on literary humor and more indirect strategies of irony and wit. The satiric mode is especially interesting in that it straddles the written and spoken word—particularly with the proliferation of late-night satiric comedy programs like those of John Stewart, Steven Colbert, Trevor Noah, John Oliver, and Samantha Bee—and has historically been noted for its political/social content.

This issue of the subversive power of women's humor and the relationship between transgressive discourse/ideology and social/political action is widely debated among humor scholars and is central to Rebecca Krefting's influential work *All Joking Aside: American Humor and Its Discontents* (2014).While Krefting builds on Gilbert's emphasis on "performing marginality" with her concept of "charged humor," she is critical of what she sees as a limited emphasis by scholars of women's humor (including Walker, Barreca, and Gilbert) on the subversive power of humor, and she calls instead for humor to move beyond rhetorical transgression to social/cultural/political action. "Charged humor," says Krefting, is "humor challenging social inequality and cultural exclusion" on the basis of gender, race, class, sexuality, ability, or another category of social exclusion. It "springs from a social and political consciousness desiring to address social justice issues" and is "deployed in the service of creating cultural citizenship" for the disenfranchised. Charged humor, argues Krefting, is "intentional," with the goal of "a change in attitudes or beliefs or action taken on behalf of social inequality." Krefting acknowledges that such humor may not have high market value—"there is no economic or cultural incentive for buying into women's perspectives, particularly when they draw attention to their status as marginalized by producing charged humor"—and it depends on a shared cultural citizenship to be well received, but it nonetheless addresses a higher moral purpose to correct social wrongs.[67]

Methods of Humor: Satire and Female Laughter

Of the forms of humor, satire is particularly well suited to women and other marginalized populations in that it is often directed by an outsider, one who is excluded from mainstream society by such factors as gender, race, ethnicity, class, religion, or nationality, against a perceived injustice by those who are in a position of dominance. This marginalized status offers the satirist a perspective from which to critique the dominant society in the hope of reforming or at least exposing its moral weakness. The female satirist is in a unique position; as somewhat of an outsider operating within established institutions, she is in an ideal position to assess and critique mainstream society. Satire, says Gilbert Highet, is often motivated by a "sense of personal inferiority, of social injustice, of exclusion from a privileged group": Alexander Pope was Catholic in Protestant England; Jonathan Swift was an Anglo-Irishman; Lord Byron, George Orwell, and Evelyn Waugh were Anglo-Scots.[68] For these social outsiders, satire was a means of softening "disagreeable truths to tell those in authority" so as not to be suppressed or censored.[69] Satire is further conducive to marginalized populations in that it allows for an indirect form of social critique through the use of irony, exaggeration, understatement, and at times parody and invective.

Satire can be defined as a form of ridicule with a moral purpose—to reform folly or vice by exposing it. It is often divided between Horatian satire, a more benign form of amusement with the intent to reform human vice and folly, and Juvenalian satire, an attack motivated by malice or anger intended to ridicule or malign.[70] Jonathan Greenberg identifies the "canonical model" of satire (sometimes called the "New Critical" approach) that emerged in the 1950s and '60s with such scholars as Northrop Frye, Maynard Mack, Alvin Kernan, Robert C. Elliott, and Ronald Paulson, which considers satire's purpose "to exercise moral judgment." According to this model, "satire does not just identify vice and folly but aims to reform or punish them. . . . Satire thus draws upon norms that are widely shared, and its meaning is fundamentally stable. The enforcement of stable moral norms makes satire culturally conservative, as the satirist speaks on behalf of age-old truths in the face of a decadent modern world."[71] This model is more in line with Bergson's theory, which sees humor in social and ethical terms as preserving social norms of good conduct and rooting out aberrant behavior.

Since the 1960s, argues Greenberg, the stability of satire, along with its moral intent and political/social efficacy, has been called into question in what can be seen as a more *ambiguous* model of satire. This ambiguous model sees satire as both socially disruptive and culturally conservative depending in part on the intention of the humorist as well as the shared reception of the audience. Taking this more contemporary approach to the politics of satire, Greenberg argues that satire cannot be reduced to a single political stance: "There are satires directed against both left and right, new and old, authorities and dissidents. They attack women and men, elites and the populace, the rich, the poor, the bourgeoisie. Rather than viewing satire as simply conservative or liberal then, it might be better to note a tension within satire between enforcing norms and violating them, between restraint and license," stability and instability.[72] While Greenberg's observations move beyond the limitations of the "canonical model" of earlier scholars of satire, it is itself limited in creating a false binary of conservative versus transgressive modes of satire as well as in its primary focus on the politics of satire. There are other approaches to satire that emphasize the "art" of satire—its use of literary techniques of parody, invective, exaggeration, innuendo, irony—as well as the pleasure of satire as a form of play that are deserving of more attention.

Dustin Griffin takes the argument for the ambiguity of satire further in claiming that the conservative and revolutionary impulses of satire are closer than they appear in that both "censure, attack and ridicule; both display their wit, playfully explore a topic, provoke or challenge complacency." In addressing the political efficacy of satire, Griffin makes a distinction between "intellectual and practical subversion." While acknowledging the limitations of satire to effect practical change, he emphasizes the power of satire to be "*intellectually subversive*." "Its effects can rarely be measured in terms of political change or even personal conduct. . . . But satire's real subversiveness operates more stealthily by means of inquiry and paradox. By conducting open-ended speculative inquiry, by provoking and challenging comfortable and received ideas, by asking questions and raising doubts but not providing answers, satire ultimately has political consequences."[73]

James E. Caron applies theories of satire to the contemporary, postmodern condition, acknowledging a new "golden age" of satire in the era of mass media and multimedia (i.e., new media, YouTube, podcasts, social media, etc.). The definition of satire as *lanx satura*, or "a mixed dish," is well suited to the postmodern skepticism of metanarratives and turn to multiple forms of representation. While Caron reiterates the moral intent of satire, he emphasizes the effect of satire as a change in thought rather than action. "Reform," says Caron, "does NOT reference a real-world social or political policy change, but rather entails a potential *metanoia*, a change in thinking, perception, or belief, even a repentance of the old way of thinking, perceiving, believing." He further points to the paradox of satire in expressing a serious, moral intent of social reform through the comic art of ridicule and play. Satire, then, "registers as both serious speech and nonserious (comic) speech—apparently stepping out of and back into its play frame," what Caron refers to as "the satire two-step." He thus reframes the ethical responsibility of satire as "a discourse of comic *parrhesia*," "speaking truth to power" through the art of ridicule. Caron identifies a new type of rhetorical activism, "satiractivism," as a means of performing social change through rhetorical speech acts.[74]

Whether one sees the comic nature of satire—its being "only a joke"— as a strength or a weakness is debatable. This comic framing of serious intent can potentially expand the audience and soften the reception of harsh truths, thereby furthering the recognition of social injustice. Satire in particular, as a targeted expression of anger in the interest of social reform, is seen to be predominantly the domain of white, heterosexual men. Building on Jessyka Finley's observation that "comic soap boxing has been, for the most part, unavailable to black women in the mass media and in political discourse," Krefting notes that "satire has long been the province of men and it has been difficult for women, especially women of color, to deploy it without penalty, in part owing to the angry nature of satire." This brings us back to the original observation about the resistance to women's humor and satire in particular, based on false gender assumptions about masculine versus feminine behavior, and the belief that women and minority women in particular cannot or should not voice a strong and critical opinion. "When women use humor as social critique, it gets labeled as 'angry' and 'humorless,' which means that men's anger counts as humor while women's anger counts as anger."[75] By expanding our understanding of women's humor and satire in particular, we can push the boundaries of what can be said and heard in the hopes of instigating social change.

If satire can be seen as a mode of truth-telling and moral reckoning by social outsiders, then many female satirists of the interwar period are in a doubly marginalized position by virtue of their race or ethnicity as well as their gender. This marginalized identity offers a vantage point from which to critique the worlds to which they partially belong, but it also calls for an indirect form of criticism. For writers like Mary McCarthy, Dorothy Parker, and Tess Slesinger, their (part) Jewish identity was a source of conflict and may have contributed to their self-conscious sense of otherness. An interesting reversal, however, occurs among these women intellectuals whereby being part or wholly Jewish actually made you an insider among intellectual outsiders in New York society. Furthermore, Jewish ethnic humor may itself be a special case, in that Jews tend to be more mainstream than other minorities because they tend to be more assimilated, urban, and middle class, especially female Jewish humorists.[76] African American women writers of the Harlem Renaissance faced further challenges, being criticized at times for conforming to cultural stereotypes of minorities in the interest of social favor from white patrons (an accusation famously launched against Zora Neale Hurston by fellow African American authors from Richard Wright to Langston Hughes) or being conversely criticized for aspiring to bourgeois, "white" values of education and refinement (a charge brought against Jessie Fauset and Nella Larsen both in their personal lives and in their fiction).[77] Many of these women writers faced a double bind in trying to define and at times defy their racial, ethnic, and gender identities within and at times against social expectations, and humor offered a unique vehicle through which to do so.

One of the distinguishing characteristics of female satirists of the interwar period is that many of them move beyond the domestic sphere and beyond male-female relations to write more far-reaching political and social satire. McCarthy satirizes attempts by intellectuals in the 1940s to form libertarian social utopias in *The Oasis* (1949), and *The Groves of Academe* (1952) exposes the hypocrisy of the fellow-traveling liberal faculty in their treatment of a self-proclaimed anti-Communist faculty member at a small, liberal arts college during the Joseph McCarthy era of the 1950s. She addresses the conflicted role of the woman intellectual and the failed idea of progress in the 1920s and '30s in more autobiographical works like *The Company She Keeps* (1939) and *The Group* (1963). Tess Slesinger exposes the antibourgeois idealism of leftist intellectuals in the 1920s in *The Unpossessed* (1934), while addressing the conflicted role of the woman intellectual, trapped between traditional issues of marriage and family and assertion of her independence. Dawn Powell, who aspired to write more sweeping social satire, exposes the false ideals of Greenwich Village bohemians and the hypocrisy of the New York publishing world in the interwar period.

Women's Humor and Public Perception/Reception

Having examined theories and methods of women's humor and humor in general, the question remains, Why does women's humor continue to be overlooked and undervalued? And why did these New York women of wit feel the need to mask their social critique through humor or risk being seen as sharp, shrill, and subversive? The primary resistance to women's humor goes back to false assumptions about feminine versus masculine behavior associated with the expression of intellect, aggression, and humor. Women were not supposed to "get" jokes, and they were certainly not expected to tell jokes. Furthermore, humor was considered a "public" or performative function, usually requiring an audience, while women were traditionally constrained to the "private" spheres of home, church, or other gatherings of women. Walker notes that most nineteenth-century women's fiction tended to take place in such private or domestic spheres and to revolve around domestic subject matter. Thus, if women were acknowledged to have a body of humor, it was dismissed (by predominantly male critics) as revolving around "trivial" domestic or "lady's" matters. In "Why We Aren't Laughing . . . Any More," Naomi Weisstein notes that women are no longer submitting to the nervous, acquiescent laughter when men tell jokes at their own expense; hence they are accused of not having a sense of humor. "So, when we hear jokes against women and we are asked why we don't laugh at them," says Weisstein, "the answer is easy, simple, and short. Of course, we're not laughing, you asshole. Nobody laughs at the sight of their own blood."[78]

Women have traditionally been put in the subordinate role of laughing at others' jokes (and not telling our own jokes) out of a kind of economic necessity. "Whenever men control women's political, economic, and personal lives," says Walker, "humor that makes men the target must be shared in secret."[79] Weisstein similarly concludes, "For most of us our livelihood depends on charming some man, having a provider. . . . Under these circumstances, the development of an open, rebellious humor may not have been an option available to us. . . . For us, the definition of charm depended primarily on our being beautiful, passive, accepting, and mute. . . . But being a funny, nasty clown doesn't go along with the definition of WOMAN that gets us our provider."[80] Though her view is somewhat extreme and dated, Weisstein shows the persistence of "female" stereotypes of quiet submission and lack of humor well into the 1970s. In *The Unruly Woman*, Rowe Karlyn makes a similar point that stand-up comediennes today still combat gender stereotypes of the quiet, demure woman who does not swear or tell dirty jokes and that comediennes like Roseanne Barr and Kate Clinton are seen as defiant in their overt feminist agenda.[81]

In the oft-cited Christopher Hitchens *Vanity Fair* article "Why Women Aren't Funny" (2008), Hitchens reiterates the false assumption that women lack a sense of humor on the basis of an outdated, biological argument of sexual attraction: that men tell jokes in order to appeal to women and that women laugh at (male) jokes in order to show interest and as a form of submission. Inciting laughter in a woman is described by Hitchens in the language of sexual conquest: "If you can stimulate her to laughter—I am talking about the real, out-loud, head-back, mouth-open-to-expose-the-full-horseshoe-of-lovely-teeth, involuntary, full, and deep-throated mirth; the kind that is accompanied by a shocked surprise and a slight (no, make that a loud) peal of delight—well, then, you have at least caused her to loosen up and change her expression." Clearly Hitchens delights more in this orgasmic description of the sexual art of laughter than his objectified female reader does. Seeing women primarily as sexual objects and ultimately as child bearers, Hitchens claims, "Women have no corresponding need to appeal to men in this way. They already appeal to men, if you catch my drift."[82] Aside from the obvious limitations of such a social Darwinist approach to humor, it is blatantly sexist and heteronormative in its assumption that men are the joke tellers and women are the receivers in this sexual game. This "biology is destiny" approach reinforces the false, essentialist split between male/female, mind/body, aggression/submission, active/passive, and, by extension, humorous/humorless. As has been demonstrated, there are a host of sociological factors and cultural conditioning as to why men have historically been initiators of jokes and women have been the object of jokes or passive receivers, based on the false gender assumptions about the perceived aggressive and sexual nature of much joke-telling.

Linda Mizejewski notes how Hitchens's argument reinforces the "male gaze" and the false dichotomy of "pretty vs. funny," as Hitchens notes that there are some funny female comedians, but in his view they tend to be "hefty or dykey or Jewish, or some combo of the three," managing to be racist, sexist, and homophobic in one fell swoop.[83] As Rebecca Krefting points out, there is an alternative, cultural materialist explanation for women's *perceived* lack of humor. In Hitchens's emphasis on biological determinism, he overlooks "cultural explanations of the economy of humor or the way consumption of humor is shaped by the cultural economy, the material incentives shaping popular culture forms in the United States."[84] Simply put, audiences pay to hear male comics affirm their mainstream views, while there is little incentive to listen to female and other marginalized comics challenge the dominant power structures of society through "charged" humor. Marginalized humor by women or other minorities is further resisted because it is seen as a threat to people in positions of power. But this does not mean that such humor does not exist or that it is not funny; it is a matter of perception and access, and increasingly female comedians are finding a venue through multiple media outlets to find an audience for their humor. With the recent proliferation of female humorists on the stage and in the media and with the mantle of the smart, outspoken woman being heralded as a form of female empowerment in the era of Bitch Media, it is time to look back at the foremothers of women's humor with a serious view.[85]

Nancy Boyd and the Greenwich Village Bohemians

The Secret, Subversive Humor of Edna St. Vincent Millay

I.

Edna St. Vincent Millay embodies the spirit of the New Woman of Green-wich Village in the 1920s; she is a freethinker and free lover known at once for her sharp wit and sexual candor as well as her feminine, youthful appeal. This duality presents a double bind for the modern female satirist, who is criticized for not being intellectual or serious enough while at the same time for being too forthright in her ideas and actions and not "feminine" enough. As fellow Greenwich Village woman of wit Genevieve Taggard observes, "When Miss Millay is too sincere and simple for our age, she is called infantile; when she is brave and ironically wise, she is called flip-pant. The critics, usually dismayed gentlemen who are completely incapable of coping with both qualities, have said a good deal under each of these heads, while the world, meanwhile, rises with a roar to receive its poet."[1] In order for a smart, sassy woman to be accepted at the time (and even somewhat today), she had to mask her seemingly "masculine" aggressive, sexual, and intellectual tendencies through the guise of female self-fash-ioning and through humor. While there is an ironic undertone to much of Millay's verse poetry, her satiric sketches under the assumed name of Nancy Boyd provided Millay an outlet for social critique through the seem-ingly benign form of laughter.

Edna St. Vincent Millay was by all accounts the "it-girl" of Green-wich Village in the 1920s.[2] She embodied the sexual freedom, independent spirit, and sharp wit of the New Woman, with her bobbed hair, youthful appeal, witty banter, and sexual experimentation. Upon her graduation from Vassar in 1917, Millay moved to Greenwich Village and soon became a mainstay of Downtown bohemian life. She joined the Provincetown Players, frequented speakeasies, wrote poetry, and took on high-profile lovers from Floyd Dell to Edmund Wilson to John Peale Bishop and Arthur Davison Ficke, many of whom helped further her career. Millay's professional success began at age nineteen with the publication of "Renascence" in the *Lyric Year* as part of a poetry contest and was solidified with the publication of her "light verse" in *A Few Figs from Thistles* (1920) and more serious poetry in *Second April* (1921). In 1923, she was heralded as the first woman to win the Pulitzer Prize in poetry.

Despite her literary success, Millay constantly had to negotiate her status as a woman writer in what was largely a male world of modernist writers. She did this in part by capitalizing on her feminine appearance and at times through the use of diminutive language in her personal correspondence. She used irony, poetic form, and even assumed names to present a public persona and mask her more provocative ideas. Much has been written about the use of masquerade or the masking of identity by modernist women writers and by Millay in particular. Sandra M. Gilbert, Debra Fried, Suzanne Clark, and Nina Miller have all made important contributions on the subject, drawing on the work of the psychologist and Freudian translator Joan Riviere, in her influential essay "Womanliness as a Masquerade" (1929).[3] According to Riviere, the professional woman often needs to assume a flirtatious or "feminine" role in order to assuage the anxiety caused by the assumption of the perceived "masculine" role of a successful professional. This performative feminine role can be seen in Millay's self-presentation and in the representation of her characters through the use of clothing, makeup, "feminine" speech patterns, and flirtatious behavior, often used ironically and for satiric effect.

For Millay, this fluidity of gender roles was defined from the outset of her career. In her early published poetry and in correspondence with her family, she used the name Vincent, derived from her middle name, St. Vincent, after the hospital in New York where her uncle's life had been saved. This masculine nomenclature gave Millay the cover and the freedom with which to write with conviction and authenticity and without regard to female gender expectations. With the publication of her notable poem "Renascence," under the name E. Vincent Millay, Millay seemed to take pleasure in flirting with various gender identities in her correspondence with Arthur Davison Ficke, one of the judges of the contest in which Millay's poem was entered, who became a lifelong friend and part-time lover. E. Vincent Millay finally revealed herself to be a young woman with red, bobbed hair and freckles, much to Ficke's delight. Millay similarly traded on her youthful appearance and feminine appeal at poetry readings, where she wore her red, wavy hair in a fashionable bob and wore long, draping gowns that hid her slight figure.

Millay took on the air and popularity of a celebrity; she was featured in a pictorial spread in *Vanity Fair* in 1920 and had her kitchen featured in *Ladies' Home Journal*. Like her counterparts Dorothy Parker and later Mary McCarthy, Millay was the object of a cult of personality, valued as much for her embodiment of the New Woman as for her bons mots. This proved somewhat problematic for the woman writer, who traded in part on her image in order to gain recognition but paid the price with her literary reputation or body of work, which in many ways seemed secondary to her physical body. This commodification of the New Woman in the age of advertising and popular magazines was as much a product of the times as was Millay's success, and Millay capitalized on the opportunity.[4] The self-projected image of the whimsical, female poet also had its limitations (especially as Millay aged, took on more serious subject matter, and lost some of her flirty, feminine appeal), and Millay found ways to express a more serious, subversive side.

Millay's popularity and early success were built on her expression of the free love and freethinking of the New Woman. In such well-known poems as "First Fig" ("My candle burns at both ends") and "What lips my lips have kissed, and where, and why," Millay expresses the sexual passion and moral indifference ordinarily reserved for men and taken on by the modern, progressive woman. In the lesser- known poem "Thursday," Millay masks the somewhat subversive attitude of the fickle, female lover through the poem's conventional form, nonthreatening sing-song rhyme, and simple diction.

Thursday
And if I loved you Wednesday,
Well, what is that to you?
I do not love you Thursday—
So much is true.
And why you come complaining
Is more than I can see.

I loved you Wednesday,—yes—but what
Is that to me?

With her public persona, her use of conventional poetic form, and her seemingly traditional subject matter of love and nature, Millay did not seem to fit the modernist aesthetic of impersonality, irony, and stylistic experimentation.[5] In the 1930s, New Critics like John Crowe Ransom, Allen Tate, and Cleanth Brooks dismissed Millay as a "woman poet" and a writer of "sentimentality" and "sensibility," lacking in intellect and high seriousness. She is "not an intellect but a sensibility," writes Tate.[6] And John Crowe Ransom, in his telling essay "The Poet as Woman," relegates Millay to the lesser status of "female" sensibility, engaged in pursuit of "the beautiful" rather than the more substantive (male) sense of the "sublime." She is "rarely and barely very intellectual, and I think everybody knows it," he adds with a snide superiority.[7] These predominantly male critics fail to see the ironic undertone to Millay's formal style or the questioning of expected gender roles with her sexually liberated female persona, who undermines expectations of heterosexual love and marriage.

This ironic, subversive voice is most pronounced in Millay's satirical sketches under the pseudonym Nancy Boyd. The assumption of a pen name can be seen as another form of performative identity or masquerading, through which the author can express less conventional or socially acceptable ideas through the double-voiced irony of humor. As Nancy A. Walker, Joanne R. Gilbert, and others have observed, irony and satire are commonly used by women, minorities, and other marginalized populations as a means of expressing subversive ideas in a socially acceptable manner.[8] Sandra Gilbert notes that the name Nancy Boyd resembles the term "Nancy boy," an expression for an effete male and a possible play on gender duality.[9] For Millay, an aspiring poet in the 1920s, the writing of fiction under an assumed name originated as a source of income. At the suggestion of W. Adolph Roberts, the editor of *Ainslee's* and her reputed lover, Millay began writing "potboilers" under the pseudonym Nancy Boyd from 1918 to 1921. Another male mentor and lover, Edmund Wilson, encouraged Millay to bring her talents over to the more respectable but still middlebrow magazine *Vanity Fair*, where he was an assistant editor and arranged for her to make a regular contribution of poetry in her own name and fiction under a pseudonym. As she enthusiastically wrote to her sister Norma, "Nancy is going strong in *Vanity Fair*, isn't she? Isn't she a blessing? Almost two years now the woman has been supporting me."[10] She stopped writing her

Nancy Boyd satires in 1923 once she married Eugen Boissevain and was more financially secure and settled in her upstate New York home, an over five-hundred-acre former blueberry farm in Austerlitz that they named Steepletop after a wildflower that grew there. But her light sketches were more than mere money makers as Millay seemed to take some pride and care in her work. In a 1919 letter to Arthur Davison Ficke, she says of her Nancy Boyd pieces, "they are beautifully written, after a flippant fashion," at once praising their merit and undermining their seriousness.[11] Her satiric dialogues were a commercial success, and Millay was pleased enough with her writing to reprint selected sketches in 1924 as a book titled *Distressing Dialogues*. She wrote an ironic preface in her own name, praising the humorous sketches of Nancy Boyd as "excellent small satires, from the pen of one in whose work I have a never-failing interest and delight."[12]

Distressing Dialogues mostly takes the form of "dialogues," also termed sketches or "playlets," a dramatic form complete with stage direction, as well as some monologues and mock advice-column letters. The dialogue format allows for the use of an ironic, double voice and emphasizes the performative aspect of identity of the characters being played. The sketch or "skit," as Martha Bensley Bruère and Mary Ritter Beard referred to it in their 1934 anthology of women's humor, satirizes the manners and customs of a particular time and place.[13] It can be in monologue or dialogue form, and because of its brief and witty style, it was well suited to the magazines of the day, notably the *New Yorker, Vanity Fair*, and *Ainslee's*. Given the form and the venue, these sketches were often about and for the sophisticated, urban elite, who took pleasure in what appeared to be lighthearted self-parody. (The casual, inconsequential nature of the Nancy Boyd sketches was emphasized by their placement in *Vanity Fair* under the title "Literary Hors D'Oeuvres," implying a prelude to the more substantial main course.)

According to the humor scholar Nancy Walker, male skits or "casuals," as they were referred to by *New Yorker* editor Harold Ross, tended to be "lighter, more frivolous in tone" and comment on "manners, fads and affectations of urban culture" (read: E. B. White, S. J. Perelman), while female skits were "more grounded in the realm of [women's] everyday life" and "express in a more straightforward fashion an immediate discomfort with that life, usually arising from the speaker's experience as a woman."[14] As with Dorothy Parker's satiric sketches, the subject of most of Millay's sketches are male-female relations and the questioning of traditional gender roles and identities. Most are set among an urban, sophisticated elite, some specifically in Greenwich Village bohemia. Through parody and satire,

Millay takes on social expectations of the female artist and the balancing of artistic and sexual freedom with the conventions of female subordination, feminine appeal, and domesticity. While at times invoking female stereotypes, Millay uses humor as a form of social critique to defy and expose the limitations of gendered stereotypes.

The subject of *Distressing Dialogues* and the object of Millay/Boyd's satire can be loosely divided into three types: sketches of the artist woman/intellectual, domestic satire, and satire of Greenwich Village bohemian life. "Distressing" in the title can be taken to mean disturbing, in the sense of both troubling and unsettling the status quo. The title is ironic in that, through exaggeration and parody, that which is "distressing" is contained or released, thereby making it less troubling and more socially acceptable or leading to an indirect form of social change. Some of Nancy Boyd's most powerful sketches (including "The Implacable Aphrodite" and "Madame a Tort!") portray the plight of the artist woman, who can at times be seen as an extension of the author herself. Despite the increased sexual and personal freedom of the New Woman, she was bound by modern expectations of "feminine" beauty fostered by a growing commercial industry of advertising and cosmetics, in which heterosexual love and marriage were often the end goal. This parody of domestic life and male-female relations among the New York elite can be seen in such sketches as "Powder, Rouge, and Lipstick," "No Bigger than a Man's Hand," and "For Winter, for Summer." Millay's satire of the New Woman and Greenwich Village bohemian life can be seen in such sketches as "Art and How to Fake It: Advice to the Art-Lorn," "Tea for the Muse," and "Knock Wood," which are variously written in first-person monologue form from the persona of Nancy Boyd or in dramatic, dialogue form. Through these vignettes, Millay is at once subject and object of satire as she takes part in the very bohemian values of artistic and personal freedom that she exposes through irony and parody.

Millay herself walked a double line, as a successful writer and free lover among Greenwich Village intellectuals and as the wife of Eugen Boissevain, living in their rural home at Steepletop. Even in her role as a woman writer, Millay had to navigate her dual identity as a female, seductive figure and as a serious writer. While critics emphasize the performative aspect of her femininity as a necessary form of masquerade to hide her more threatening, professional identity, one might also see these two sides as authentic representations of a complex, modern woman, who is at once sexual and intellectual, sensual and serious. Millay was a kind of femme fatale of

Greenwich Village in the 1920s, seducing and then dismissing prominent writers and intellectuals of the day, notably Floyd Dell, Edmund Wilson, John Peale Bishop, and Arthur Davison Ficke. She was immortalized by Dell and Wilson, both of whom wrote fictionalized accounts of Millay's sexual charms and seeming indifference in *Love in Greenwich Village* ("The Gifts of the Fourth Goddess") and *I Thought of Daisy*, respectively. Wilson further memorialized Millay in his epilogue to *The Shores of Light: A Literary Chronicle of the 1920s and 1930s*, while Dell's granddaughter Jerri Dell posthumously published a memoir by Dell about his affair with Millay in *Blood Too Bright: Floyd Dell Remembers Edna St. Vincent Millay*. For Millay, an effective way of representing the conflicted identity of the New Woman was through the satiric form of her Nancy Boyd dialogues, thereby allowing her to more brazenly take on a potentially subversive and salacious subject matter under the guise of anonymity.

The title "The Implacable Aphrodite" captures both the temptation and the fortitude of the modern femme fatale. Miss Black, a sculptor who oozes sensuality, at once charms and deflects the advances of Mr. White, a "professional violinist," who seeks in vain to woo her. Written in the form of a "playlet" with dialogue between the two speakers and suggestive stage direction, this sketch emphasizes the performative aspect of sexual identity and the dilemma of the sexually adventurous, independent woman. Miss Black is both seductive and indifferent, capturing the duality of the modern, urban woman. Like Aphrodite, the Greek goddess of love known at once for her beauty and her sexual appetite and infidelity, Miss Black is worshiped by men as the embodiment of modern love and sexuality. The figure of Daphne, whom Miss Black sculpted in a seductive reclining pose modeled on her own form, is also represented in the story. The story of Daphne escaping the pursuit of Apollo mirrors the thwarted advances of Mr. White for Miss Black.

The parenthetical stage directions in italics serve as an ironic comment on the overt dialogue between the man and woman and offer a satiric portrait of the hypocrisy and complexity of modern love. Miss Black is described in beguiling and even menacing terms. She is first seen "*languidly flicking an ash from a cigarette-holder the approximate length of a fencing-foil,*" a representation of the free-spirited New Woman as well as a weapon in the battle of the sexes.[15] Mr. White claims to be different from all the other men; they are drawn to her beauty, while he seeks her "intrepid mind." Unlike the conventional marriage-oriented woman, Miss Black aspires to "a world, a cosmos, where men and women can understand each other, can help each other, where the barriers of sex are like a mist in the air, dissipated with the dawn" (42). Despite Mr. White's lofty words, his actions betray his baser attraction to her physical being. As she prepares tea, she is described in increasingly sensual terms through stage direction: "*Her heavy, loose robe clings to her supple limbs. . . . Her vermilion lips are pouted in concentration*" (44–45). His actions contradict his words: "They don't see you as I do. They do not desire to leave you free, as I do," he protests, "*with aesthetic ferocity*" and "*breathing hard*"(45). In this game of seduction, she continues to tempt him as he tries in vain to resist. Again, through stage direction, she is described in threatening and sensual terms: "*She leans back wearily and closes her eyes, exposing a long and treacherous throat, full of memories*," to which "*he swallows audibly, but meets the look without flinching*" (46), like an embattled soldier. As he argues for her "unparalleled genius" and exhorts her "to go on—to grow—to grow—and to be free!" we are told that "*he shifts convulsively in his chair*," revealing his baser desires (46).

Mr. White becomes increasingly restless as he "*gropes for [his pipe] pitifully*" (49) in his pocket, a potential oral substitute and phallic symbol. Miss Black is engaged in the preparation of tea, which is described using images of castration and violence. In a moment of comedic brilliance, Millay describes this femme fatale as "*cruelly slicing a lemon, by means of a small dagger with which a Castilian nun has slain three matadors*," followed by an image of her "*delicately poising in her hand a sugar-tongs made from the hind claws of a baby gila-monster, and glancing lovingly about the room*" (50). This juxtaposition of violent disruption with domestic action underscores the latent aggression behind traditional gender roles, an irony lost on Mr. Black: "*It strikes him that she looks gentle and domestic. A great peace steals over him*" (50). But his peace is short-lived when she reveals that she is leaving for Europe as she asks how many lumps of sugar he will have with his tea. The gender reversal is complete as the professional woman leaves the infatuated man after indulging in some meaningless flirtation. His pretense of indifference is exposed as he slides from his chair to the floor and kneels before her: "But what about me? What about me?" he importunes, playing the jilted lover (51). He continues the role reversal, declaring his love for her and begging her to marry him. He exposes his latent sexism, claiming, "I don't care how much you work—work your head off! A man's wife *ought* to have some little thing to take up her time" (51–52). Upon leaving at the woman's request, he dramatically declares, "But my heart I leave here," to which she condescendingly replies, "Pray don't. I have room for nothing more in the apartment," devaluing his love as a commodity not worth buying (53). The clever artist woman has won this battle, though she is left "jaded," "restless," and alone (53). There is no positive outcome for this distressing dialogue as the sexes continue to negotiate their way through the modern world of love and liberation.

In "Madame a Tort!" (Madame is mistaken/wrong), the once independent, artist woman is bound by the burden of the ritual of female beauty. The monologue is written from the first-person point of view of a sculptor living in Paris in the 1920s. She asserts, "I was free, and my life was before me" (163). Unencumbered by material objects, by relationships, or by social fashion, she was free to travel and pursue her craft. "I cared but little for the society of men, still less for that of the members of my own sex; I was content to be alone" (163), until the fateful day when a "blue-eyed woman in mink" slipped her the address of an upscale beauty parlor on the rue de Rivoli, "and left [her], smiling" (163). The speaker here suggests a kind of conspiracy among women of a certain stature, who lure nonconforming women into the cult of beauty. The location of the salon, "by the equestrienne statue of Jeanne d'Arc," a symbol of female sacrifice for her independent views, was perhaps a warning to this freethinker (164). What ensues is a mock aesthetic assault, one that recollects Alexander Pope's "The Rape of the Lock." An effeminate hairdresser "with a small waist and smelling of violets" "seized a comb, raked [her] hair violently back from [her] forehead," and proceeded to comb and cut her hair (165). When she thought she was finished, he corrects her: "*Madame a tort!*" he tells her, with a knowing and somewhat sinister determination. He then "pressed [her] head with a heavy hand, and all but drowned [her] in a sudden flow of scalding suds," laughing sadistically (166). The juxtaposition of sadism with scented suds creates an incongruous, comic effect. The assault continues with a manicurist, whose "file stung like a wasp" with intense pain and who "thrust back the cuticle, cruelly, with a hard instrument; she lacerated it with scissors" (168). Despite these images of violence and pain, the once resistant customer becomes increasingly passive and compliant. "It did not occur to me to protest," says the speaker about the manicurist, and like a first-time salon-goer, she admits to having never experienced a facial massage before, "with shame" (169). The events of "that fatal afternoon" culminate in a mock rape scene. The hairdresser (her "tormenter") "savagely" seizes "two pairs of curling-tongs" like a weapon, "glowing red." "I was helpless in his hands," she relates. "I dared not move, for fear I should be branded. I sat fully still and let him have his way" (171). Once the deed is done, she runs from the salon, sobbing, and collapses into a fleeing taxi.

In an ironic reversal, the woman falls in love with her newfound beauty and becomes a slave to her daily beauty ritual, to the exclusion of her artistic pursuits. The woman awakes in her hotel room, surrounded by countless creams and tonics and dyes and powders charged to her account, and she catches a glimpse of herself in the mirror: "No, there was no mistake. I was beautiful," she declares (173). Like Narcissus, who fell in love with his own reflection, this modern-day Narcissus becomes a slave to Beauty at a high cost. "From that day to this I am a slave to the most exacting of tyrants," laments this former artist (173). Where she was once free to travel and to create her own works of art, now she is beholden to a regimen of beauty and has herself become the art object. She is engaged in the idle quest for eternal youth and beauty: "I sit before my mirror, patting steaming, brushing. I will not grow old. I will be beautiful always" (173). The greatest loss, the author implies, is that this modern, artist-woman has sacrificed her creative self-expression for the public image of femininity sold to us by modern advertisers and producers of feminine beauty products. "There comes over me at times a longing for the old free days, a desire to hold damp clay in my hands once more," admits this former sculptor. "But one glance at my nails, so rosy, so roundly pointed, so softly bright, so exquisite from the loving care of years—and I know that I shall never work again" (174). That is, she will never work as a professional sculptor again, though she will be bound by so-called women's work, the eternal "bitter struggle" (174) to subscribe to an unattainable ideal of feminine beauty. Absurd though this sketch may seem, it becomes a parable for the internal and social struggle of the modern, artist- woman in a society that continues to resist changing gender roles.

One of the more autobiographical sketches is the burlesque "Two Souls with but a Single Thought," written in the first person from the point of view of Nancy Boyd—itself an assumed persona. Like Millay, who wrote a satiric column under the pseudonym Nancy Boyd in *Vanity Fair*, the speaker establishes herself as a "screamingly funny" humor columnist, whose literary hors d'oeuvres leave the reader "gasping for breath": "You read me aloud to your best friend's fiancé, and he laughs so hard he nearly falls out of the hammock" (178). Her husband is also part of the New York smart set, who "runs a humorous column in a New York paper, for all the world like F.P.A." (178), the reference here to Franklin Pierce Adams, whose humor column, "The Conning Tower," appeared in the 1920s and '30s. The subject of this sketch, however, is anything but trivial; the narrator tells us that she is on the verge of divorce as their once good-natured battle of wits has turned into an all-out war without words as each fears the other will steal their own jokes. Nancy Boyd sets herself up as a modern woman, who rivals her husband in intellect and professional stature and who is prepared to file for divorce. Divorce, a relatively new practice in the 1920s, signaled the New Woman's willingness to risk social status and financial security for the sake of independence. Even with her desire for a divorce, the independent-minded speaker admits, "It will be difficult to get a divorce," since her husband, Cecil, has not committed what the courts call "misconduct": "His treatment of me has never been cruel and abusive; and he supports me in the penury to which I am accustomed. As for incompatibility,— ha! ha! ha! Pardon my derisive shout" (177). The sardonic tone that Boyd assumes signals a self-ironic knowledge of the absurdity of her situation. For it is not incompatibility that is the problem but the fact that she and her husband are too similar and that there does not seem to be room for two towering wits at the same table. As the title, "Two Souls with but a Single Thought," indicates, it is their very likeness in thought and outlook that has made them unlikeable to each other.

While Nancy Boyd touts her humor, she also sets herself up as a somewhat frivolous writer of lighthearted humor that is the stuff of gossip and innuendo. The speaker establishes intimacy with her audience by sharing her personal news of an impending divorce. "Dear reader," she begins, "by the time you receive this, I shall have left my husband" (177). She continues in the conversational style and tone of salacious gossip that appeals to readers of middlebrow magazines: "No, no, it is useless to try to reason with me. It is useless to throw down the magazine and rush to the telephone and squeak into my ear, 'My dear Nancy! What can you be thinking of!'" (177). Having gained the interest and trust of her reader, the speaker proceeds to elaborate on how the jovial marriage of fellow wits has led to rivalry and distrust, leading to impending divorce. It started off as a marriage of mirth, with husband and wife outperforming each other in what resembles a circus of tricks: "And neither of us could have told you for a new pair of red silk tights, which was the greater fun, to hold the hoop or to jump" (179). But it turns out that neither of them could take a joke, or rather, they start to accuse each other of taking each other's jokes in what devolves into a rivalry or match of wits. What started as "the wedding of the cap and the bells! The comic sock and mask!" (178) has turned into a game of cat and mouse: "We began to watch each other as a mouse watches a cat," hiding any verbal quips for fear that the other might appropriate it as their own (182). Things got so bad that they would go for weeks without uttering a word: "You might think us a pair of undertakers instead of a pair of humorists" (183). Through the metaphor of joke-telling, Millay comments on the dangers of competition and mistrust in male-female relationships of equals. Ironically, in the battle of the sexes, the telling of jokes can be most serious business, and in trying to be funny, they lose their wit(s).

In "Powder, Rouge and Lip-Stick, *or Handsome Is as Handsome Does,*" Millay/Boyd plays with gender roles or the performance of gender identity in a satire of modern, domestic life. Written as a "playlet" or dialogue with scenes and stage directions, Boyd experiments with modes of speech, dress, and makeup as expressions of gender roles. Millay's satire is directed toward the urban elite readers of modern periodicals like *Vanity Fair*, the *New Yorker*, and *Ainslee's* who can view their foibles with a self-ironic grin. Though the flapper was extolled for her independent spirit, sexual freedom, and androgynous style, she also embodied a certain consumerism and conformity to feminine ideals of beauty. The title of Millay's story is an ironic nod to the accoutrements of modern, feminine beauty, while the subtitle, "Handsome Is as Handsome Does," emphasizes role-playing and the subjective nature of beauty.

Millay's ironic tone can be seen both in her depiction of character and through the italicized stage directions, which serve as an ironic commentary on the characters' speech and actions. For Mr. and Mrs. Avery-Thompson, identified by marital title, the act of getting ready to go out for dinner becomes a mock battle over the meaning of beauty, love, fidelity, and identity. The husband insists on his wife's inner beauty in the interest of rushing her toilette in preparation for dinner. What ensues is a satiric battle of the sexes, with lipstick and powder puffs as weapons, complete with hysterical outbursts, gender bending, and an ultimate return to traditional gender norms and social order. The sketch is set at a woman's dressing table, where Mr. Avery-Thompson disrupts his wife's sense of order by asking her to stop using makeup. This sends her into paranoid hysterics, suspecting that her husband is having an affair and seeking to manipulate him through her flirtatious and infantilizing feminine language and behavior. Millay uses what Robin Lakoff identifies as the "feminine" inflections of speech, such as exaggeration and emphasis, to plead her case: "Why, dearest, I don't use *any*! A little tiny box like this lasts me just *ages*!" (112).[16] She further assumes the role of the wounded child, looking at him "*(with a puzzled, childlike stare)*" as she "*sniffs, and lifts her handkerchief to her eyes*" (113) for dramatic effect. Her sympathy tactics and display of feminine vulnerability work on her chivalrous husband, who contritely and condescendingly apologizes, "*kissing the top of her head*" (113).

Mrs. Avery-Thompson's feminine posturing continues, "furiously, flinging the powder-puff wildly across the room, where it perches debonairly in a bowl of roses," as she scolds her husband using baby talk: "Willyouleave-mealoneor*won*chu!" (113). The running together of words with emphasis and the landing of the powder puff in a bowl of roses serve as an ironic commentary on the severity of the crisis. There is a double irony, however, in that there really are serious implications to the necessity of an aging, married woman to look young in order to keep her husband and to act like a damsel in distress to appeal to his male ego. There is the added irony that Millay herself—both in her feminine appearance and her use of baby talk in selected letters—subscribes to the same "feminine" behaviors that are the object of her satire. The wife's underlying insecurity comes to the fore when she confesses, "When you first met me you thought I was wonderful, just as I was, so wonderful that you insisted upon marrying me; and the minute you were married to me you began to want to change me" (114). The pressure of even a modern woman of the 1920s to get and keep a man is real, and the mass-marketed beauty industry capitalizes on this need. After the wife ruins her makeup by crying, she removes and restarts the beauty ritual in a parody of the female toilette—with her cold cream, vanishing cream, rose-water brow paint, and lash liner—until the narrator tells us, "Mrs. Avery-Thompson is someone else again," as she resumes her expected female role (116).

Mr. Avery-Thompson mocks his wife's beauty ritual, literally turning the tables by assuming a place at his wife's dressing table and gleefully appropriating her beauty tools in a play on gender roles. The result is a grotesque parody of feminine beauty, with his "*two apoplectic cheeks, a nose like a tomb-stone, and the morbid eye-sockets of a coal-heaver*" (117). Despite his pleasure at gender bending, the implication is that one should not challenge Mother Nature or at least the social perception of gender difference. After appealing to his ego in an act of weakness—"You don't lu-hu-hu-huv me any more!" (118), she cries—she seems to concede to not wearing makeup. He infantilizes her, saying, "Oh, there's the brave baby! . . . Whose little girl are you?" to which she concedes, "Bobby'th!" (119). The wife, Gwen, takes her husband's directive to an extreme, presenting herself for an outing to the opera wearing no makeup. The shock of her natural appearance and the disruption of social etiquette sends her husband into a literal sweat as he questions whether she is ill. By the final scene, the social order is restored, with the wife resuming her feminine ritual "*in the accepted manner*," the husband patiently waiting for her "*in the accepted manner*," and the husband's ardor restored (121). In a reversal of the end of scene 2, Bob now "savagely" seizes the beautified Gwen in his arms as she whispers in his ear, "Whose little girl am I now?" to which he replies using diminutive baby talk, "Bobby'th" (122). In this battle of the sexes, parody allows for gender play and the breaking of ritual in order to restore the social order. The reader is left wondering who exactly has won this gender duel, as the wife resumes her subordinate, feminine role and they resume their vacuous social rituals.

Another "distressing dialogue" that exposes the miscommunication between men and women through parody and exaggeration is "No Bigger than a Man's Hand." Presented as a skit in four scenes, it follows the decline of a newlywed couple and the severe consequences of pent-up resentment on the part of a seemingly model wife. Once again Millay dramatizes the disparity between ideal appearances of a wealthy, married couple and the harsh reality. In creating the scene, Millay draws on her own knowledge of elite, material culture to show us in vivid detail the privilege (and concomitant ennui) of high society. The characters are presented as types and are decorated like objects representative of the leisure class. According to the stage directions, Joey, the husband, is "*luxuriously upholstered in striped mauve silk, quilted black satin and a pair of red leather lounging shoes*," while his wife, Li'l Elner, is "*exquisitely hung with point-edged handkerchief linen, peacock-blue crêpe de Japon embroidered in festoons of wisteria and one-legged white birds, and a pair of high-heeled, black-satin mules with scream-pink linings*" (73). Millay satirizes the fashionable smart set who indulge in the latest fashions with the most luxurious fabrics, bright colors, and chinoiserie. (Millay's own wardrobe reveals an East Asian influence in her penchant for flowing robes and gowns.) Words like "upholstered" and "hung" emphasize the performative aspect of their identity, with this newlywed couple acting as backdrop to their own play. This role-playing is accentuated by the artifice of their language and their use of clichés and baby talk. Joey and Li'l Elner (themselves diminutive names) conform to expected behaviors of newlyweds in their speech and actions, but their loving platitudes mask an underlying discontent that festers and grows throughout the story. Joey, sensing something troubling his wife, asks, "What is it, my angel?" to which she replies with indirection using the third person to refer to herself and blushing: "Will Joey do something for Li'l

Elner? (73), followed by "I *wish* you wouldn't leave the cover off the tooth-paste tube!" (75). While he laughs at the trivial nature of her request and readily concedes, this seemingly small dissatisfaction is symptomatic of a larger power discrepancy in their relationship, in which she is stuck in the subordinate role of cleaning up his messes and lacks the authority or confidence to directly voice her discontent.

The second scene is eight months later, and the couple's relationship is clearly strained. She maintains a "sour and dyspeptic countenance" and is irritable, a sign of her repressed anger and discontent. The once affectionate, diminutive names have been replaced by the sterner, more formal address of "Joseph" and "Elner." When the husband asks what he has done wrong, she replies "*(bursting into tears and burying her face in the waist-coat)* Le-eave the cover off the tooth-paste tu-ube!" (79). While Millay here satirizes the overwrought, fragile female, there is also an implicit social critique of her powerlessness to assert herself in the face of the thought-less male authority. By scene 3 and eight years later, the parenthetical stage directions indicate that Elner's stony silence has progressed into an "*agonized whisper*" and a "*stifled scream*," as she addresses her husband with exasperation (79). Her pent-up frustration erupts in a declaration that she is going to leave her husband. When he asks in consternation why, she is clearly distraught: "It's not that I don't love you. It's just that I can't stand the sight of you. You've got so you look like a—like a tube of toothpaste to me!" (80). The tube of toothpaste becomes a metaphor for their dysfunctional relationship and his exploitation of her in marriage. By scene 4, Elner's mental state has devolved even further. After obtaining a divorce and remarrying, she discovers an open tube of toothpaste on the shelf above the washbowl and is found with "a smoking revolver" in one hand and a scrap of paper in the other, reading, "THIS IS TOO MUCH." In this melodramatic, short satire, Millay exposes the self-destructive hysteria of the obsessive, compulsive wife, but she also points to a larger issue of the destructive power of a gender hierarchy in which the dutiful wife is trapped in a subservient role.

The image of hands plays a telling role in this short satire. The title, "No Bigger than a Man's Hand," seems to make light of what proves to be a serious situation. According to the stage directions, Elner's husband is repeatedly trying to connect with her emotionally, reaching out his hand to her and then withdrawing it with her rebuke. She, in turn, covers her face with her hands at moments of frustration and anger, signaling repression of her discontent and an inability to face the impasse in their marriage.

Ultimately the situation proves too big for this or any man to handle, as his wife plummets into depression and death.

In "For Winter, for Summer," Millay satirizes traditional gender stereotypes and dramatizes the power play between husband and wife in negotiating a camping trip. The wife, Louise Morton, playing on her husband's jealously and dim wit, manipulates him into inviting her along on his camping trip to Maine. Mr. Morton is portrayed as a manly man, "avidly devouring the racy bits in a bright new gun-catalogue" (147) in preparation for a hunting trip, while she idly fingers the pages of the latest fashion magazine. He dismisses his wife's proposal to accompany him on his camping trip as "crazy" and beyond her feminine capability. "It really isn't fit for a woman, you know, honey," he says with condescension, "'Twould kill you" (149–50). Louise provokes her husband by asking him to deliver a letter to a former suitor of hers, inviting him to visit in her husband's absence. He falls for the bait and is stirred into a jealous rage. He speaks with "*a howl of fury*" and is "*purple with unavailing hate*," while she maintains her composure, "*mildly*" and "*sweetly*" reassuring him that she has no intention of divorcing him "—for years yet" (153). She seems to be enjoying this friendly lovers' quarrel, "*laughing*" and responding "*with a spasmodic giggle*" almost beyond her control (154). While her giggles can be seen as a feminine form of manipulation, laughter is also a way of assuming power, especially for people in a subordinate position.

Millay satirizes the conniving wife and the macho man through the use of exaggeration. The wife's machinations have worked, and the husband refuses to mail the letter or even go on the hunting trip without her. He is seen as "([*manfully*] *springing from the hammock and seizing her melodramatically by the wrist*): You will never write to that man again!" he commands. Like the jealous, chauvinistic Tom in F. Scott Fitzgerald's *The Great Gatsby*, Richard declares, "I'm staying home on account of Mr. Hamlin Jefferies, L.L.D. Ph.D. . . . I want to watch him smoking my cigars, winding my Victrola, making love to my wife" (155). The contrast between the educated ex-lover and the brutish but wealthy husband is clear, and he is readily duped by his wife in this game of wits. Now that she has assumed the upper hand, she dismisses her threat as a joke: "I was only joking!" she says "(*kissing his cheek with many little kisses*)" (156). Instead of him giving up his hunting trip, she slyly proposes that she join him. Forgetting that this was her intention from the start, Richard is duped into believing that this is his idea: "Lou, you don't mean it!" he affectionately exclaims (157). It is only when she starts searching through the catalogue for camping clothes and gear as if she were preparing for a shopping expedition that he starts to show regret. "Show li'l' Lou all the pretty guns," she asks her husband, resuming the subordinate, feminine posture once she has gotten her way. "Oh, dearest, I was *so* afraid you wouldn't let me go!" she reveals, and it is only then that he realizes he has been duped. "By George, that's right, too. You did want to go, didn't you" (159). Though she has won this little battle, the implication is that the war of the sexes is ongoing. When she inquires of her husband what the "cute little baby" gun in the catalogue is for, he replies with clever exasperation, "That cute little baby one's for the tired businessman to commit suicide with" (159). Millay satirically exposes the underlying discontent of the domestic life of leisure and the confines of traditional gender roles.

Millay takes a self-ironic look at Greenwich village bohemia and the role of the New Woman through her satiric monologues and dialogues for *Ainslee's* and *Vanity Fair*. In the mock advice column "Art and How to Fake It: Advice to the Art-Lorn," Nancy Boyd poses as an authority on artistic Village life and gives advice to the next generation of bohemian wannabes on how to look and act like a "real" artist. The first poseur admits to having an artistic inclination without talent and seeks advice on how to attract artists to his studio despite his efforts to make his studio "the very haunt of all that is free, etc. in the Village." He decorates his studio with "a black floor, orange curtains, a ukulele made of a cigar-box, a leaky gas-jet, a back-number of a Russian newspaper, and as many cock-roaches, Chinese back-scratchers, and different shades of paint as anybody," with "ash-trays everywhere," in a parody of the bohemian tendency to decorate cheaply, read Marxist newspapers, cultivate Eastern influences, and smoke excessively (97). The problem, says Nancy Boyd ironically, is that he is trying too hard and instead should show the same indifference and carelessness that will make artists feel at home. She replies:

> The trouble is with the ash-trays; remove them. Get into the habit when alone of crushing out your cigarette against the wall-paper, or dropping it on the floor and carelessly grinding it into the rug. Or tossing it in the general direction of the fire-place. . . . This easy manner on your part will do more than anything else to put your guests at ease. Soon they will be using your studio as if it were their own, going to sleep with their feet in the coffee-tray, wiping paint from their hair and elbows upon the sofa-pillows, making sketches on the walls of unclothed people with small heads and over-developed muscles, and dropping ashes just everywhere. (98)

Millay here mocks not only the pretension of the want-to-be artist but also the affect and irresponsibility of actual artists, with the implication that artistic success in the new Greenwich Village is more about style than substance.

Nancy Boyd similarly mocks an aspiring restaurateur who seeks advice on how to decorate a bohemian Greenwich Village gathering place. The entrepreneur seeks to convert an old stable on Sullivan Street and asks Boyd for suggestions on names. The letter writer (identified as "Ambitious") asks for advice on naming the establishment and offers a number of comically pretentious and obscure suggestions: "*The Topaz Armadillo, The Ultra-Violet Brontosaurus,* or *The Boeotian Swine*" (99). Boyd mocks the whole enterprise by suggesting that he simply call it *The Stable* and leave it unchanged, with stalls and tables made of sawhorses; chopping blocks for seats; walls decorated with old harnesses, bridles, and bits; and a hayloft complete with pitchforks to recline after dinner.[17] She goes even further to suggest that he serve "half-cooked spaghetti, sticky Armenian pastries, and liqueur-glasses of sweetened Turkish mud," thereby satirizing the antimaterialism and antiestablishment spirit of Greenwich Village bohemia, which becomes its own form of conformity (100). There is double irony in that Boyd is mocking not only the naïve advice seekers but also the pretentious readers of her column.

Boyd receives a letter from a frustrated landlord who rents furnished rooms to artists who sit around all day discussing ideas and are loath to pay the rent. Satirizing the Marxist, anarchist sympathies of the bohemian set, Boyd ironically suggests that she place a tin bank in the hall with a placard—"FREE THINKERS! FREE LOVERS! And FREE BOOTERS! If you have any Heathen Pity in your Hearts Drop a Nickel in the Slot for the Starving Baby-Anarchists of Russia! WHO DOES NOT CONTRIBUTE TO THE CAUSE OF ANARCHY IS MID-VICTORIAN!!!" (103)—and watch the donations roll in. Boyd here shows a disdain for the self-indulgence and misguided radical idealism of the artist/intellectual, while she herself is a product and beneficiary of Greenwich Village bohemian life.

Boyd satirizes academic and literary critics as parasites feeding off other people's talents and ideas in a response to another aspiring artist. She writes, "When all else fails, two courses remain open to a man: he can always give lectures on the drama or edit anthologies of verse; for neither of these is either talent or training necessary" (104). Millay here implies the parasitic nature of critics and academics, whose work is seen to feed off the talent of creative writers and artists. This barb is particularly sharp since Millay had relations with several prominent Greenwich Village intellectuals and critics.

Boyd exposes the bourgeois gentrification of the Village in a response to a letter from "A WIFE AND MOTHER" who is looking to decorate a new apartment on Twelfth Street as a haven from her husband. She expects artists to be dropping in, she says, since she knows how to make good coffee. Interior design and artistic taste have become commodified to the point that Boyd suggests that "the safest thing is a Chinese studio; everybody has one, so nobody can criticize yours" (105), mocking the mass consumption of Orientalism. Boyd suggests a standard, Asian décor: "Floor, black; ceiling, blue; walls, lemon-yellow, olive-green, cherry-red, plum-violet, respectively"; put everything on the floor; "everything you can find that is made of teakwood"; "Have something lacquered; doesn't matter what"; "Have a lot of pictures of tom-cats and tigers around" and cheap Japanese prints (105–6). While Boyd's inventory is intended as a parody of the mass consumption of Asian culture that was fashionable in the 1920s, it has offensive racist overtones, as does the final letter from a Chinese Vassar student who writes in broken English to complain about her American roommate's poor taste in decorating their room in a pseudo-Oriental style.

In "Art and How to Fake It," Nancy Boyd satirizes the bourgeois, pseudobohemians who have overtaken Greenwich Village. (It is interesting that as early as the 1920s, Greenwich Village bohemian life was under threat by would-be artists and intellectuals.) In a letter signed "Matisse Picasso" (suggesting that all modernist styles blend together), the writer enlists Boyd to ward off "up-town thrill-hunters" who have taken over Greenwich Village: "Can't you sort of give 'em a hint that the Village isn't fashionable any more? They're thicker down here than garbage-cans" (106). Boyd reassures him that "since the prohibition of spirituous liquors in the States, there has been an ever-increasing migration of the art-just-lovers from Harlem to Montparnasse" (107). While Millay is correct that Paris was the next fashionable destination for expatriate aesthetes, Prohibition did not make the Village any less appealing to Uptown thrill seekers. In fact, the banning of alcohol led to the spread of speakeasies and house parties both in the Village and Harlem, giving rise to a flapper culture that spread across the nation.

In "Tea for the Muse," Nancy Boyd satirizes the pretentiousness of the wealthy art patron. It is set as a playlet at the home of Mrs. Bertha Lang-Jennings, a purported patron of the arts, who is hosting a poetry reading in honor of "the distinguished poet" Cecil Payne (201). Despite the crowds, the refreshments, and the display of priceless *objets* meant to impress, the attendees are more interested in gossiping about the whereabouts of the guests than in the actual reading. Boyd mocks the vacuousness of these supposed patrons of the arts, who can barely identify the poet or his work. Mrs. Lang-Jennings introduces the poet to much fanfare—"(*Murmurs of 'Oh,' 'Ah,' 'Indeed,' 'How interesting,' etc.*)"—though she has to consult a slip of paper to recall the name of the author's collections and generically states, "I'm sure we shall all be delighted to hear Mr. Payne read us a few of his own delightful verses" (203). Mrs. Crane, a caricature of the ignorant art aficionado as collector, admits to buying the author's books but never reading them: "I buy every book of verse that comes out. I don't read 'em, because I don't like poetry. But I buy 'em, because I believe that art should be encouraged" (203). Another guest, Mrs. Loomis, mistakes the title *Cakes and Ale* for the more reductive *Beer and Skittles*, whereby Millay mocks the absurdity and pretension of both the artist and the patron. The poet is a parody of the socially awkward, self-conscious artist, sitting alone near the divan and uncomfortably dressing the part. But the poet need not worry, because the audience is far more interested in each other, and in appearing cultured, than in listening to him. After a hushed scandal in which Miss Ballard lets slip that she saw Mrs. Raeburn at the Biltmore "having break—er—having luncheon with Mr. Dinwiddie" (207), the guests one by one make their excuses for leaving the gathering after having tea and before the start of the reading. After such a humiliating and degrading experience, the poet "*emerges furtively from under the divan, looking very aged and shaken, with wild eyes and working mouth*," and "*exits, sobbing*" (212). Through this parody of a charity event in support of the arts, Millay exposes both the fragility of the artist and the false pretensions and indifference of his patrons.

In the uncollected satiric sketch "The Barrel" (July 1922), Millay exposes the failure of communication between the sexes. The subtitle, "Showing That to a Woman a Man, Even a Philosopher, Is Always a Little Ridiculous, and That to a Man, Any Man, a Woman Is Something More than a Nuisance," sets a flippant tone and a dichotomy between stereotypical male and female behavior. There is a discrepancy between the seriousness of the subject—the philosopher Diogenes's search for an honest man—and the absurdity of the situation, as Diogenes's lover encroaches on his space by sleeping in his barrel. Diogenes, the Cynic, is known for his simple life, reputedly sleeping in a *pithos*, or large ceramic jar, in the marketplace as a show of his asceticism. Millay here satirizes the role of the nagging or controlling woman and the uncommunicative, self-involved man by creating tension when the woman decides to sleep in Diogenes's barrel. After begging her to get out, he ultimately concedes; he "stooped in the barrel and lay down next to her."[18] The feuding couple "turned their backs to each other and lay still. But they hated each other, flesh and bone" (35). Millay here physicalizes the animosity between the sexes as Diogenes seeks to go about his intellectual pursuits unencumbered and the woman seeks to establish her place in the relationship. While he accepts her presence in his life and barrel, he gives a philosophical parody on the inequality of the sexes and foresees a time when men are no longer dependent on women. He says:

Woman is a poor creature, and incapable of abstract thought. She is broad in the buttock and narrow in the chest, and the back of her head is much too near the front. She is unworthy to share the destiny of man; and he has not as yet devised a means of doing without her. That, however, will come. She is today as his left hand, inefficient but useful. Tomorrow she will be as his vermiform appendix, useless and troublesome. The day after tomorrow she will be as his caudal append-age, shriveled up, dropped off and forgotten. And man will go on the more merrily without her. (35)

After this sexist disquisition on the inferiority of women, the woman belit-tles him with a one-line rejoinder: "You don't say" (35).

As Diogenes continues to challenge the woman's place beside him, her tone grows increasingly shrill, and she asserts, "I've got just exactly as much right in this barrel as you have! . . . I'm just exactly as smart as you are! I just haven't had a chance!" When he condescendingly seeks to calm her like a child ("There, there"), she becomes further enraged: "You shut up!" she screams and entrenches herself in the barrel. "'I'm going to stay!' said she" (35). Millay here satirizes the mutual dependence and love/hate relation-ship in the unequal battle of the sexes. She further mocks the controlling female as the woman disrupts Diogenes's search for an honest man with her unsolicited advice. She questions why he is lighting his lantern, and he replies that it is in order to see. She dismissively replies, "But it's daylight, you fool!" He is incensed at her meddling but seems reconciled to try to appease her. "I might as well take it along. I'll need it after dark," he replies (36). This elicits knowing laughter from the woman, who knew that once Diogenes was out of her sight, he would light the lantern. This laugh-ter elicits pleasure and power as she relishes her superior understanding of the man's actions. "And as soon as he was out of hearing, she began to laugh, the sweetest, merriest laughter that had been heard in that valley for a thousand years. And after a while the barrel began to laugh, too. . . . 'Oh! Oh!' squealed the woman again and again. 'Aren't men *funny?* Aren't they *funny?*'" (36). "Funny" refers to the ridiculous nature of man, who insists on having his way. Laughter becomes a way that the marginalized and subordinate assert their indirect authority over the patriarchal establishment. In an ironic twist at the end, however, we learn that the woman is not correct; Diogenes did not deceive her, for "Diogenes did not light the lantern until after dark" (36). He is, perhaps, the honest man that he has been in search of, and the woman is self-deceived in her rightful place beside him. As a woman writer who uses humor to challenge the social order, Millay is able to poke fun at the tendency of women as well as men to deceive themselves in the ongoing battle of the sexes.

How have the satiric sketches of Nancy Boyd been received, and why have they generally been neglected or overlooked in Millay's literary reputation? For the answer to these questions, we need to look first at Millay, who benefited financially from her pseudonymous writing but kept a professional distance. Like Dorothy Parker, who was disappointed when no one seemed to notice her "grand gesture" of giving up the writing of poetry, Millay wanted to be remembered primarily as a serious poet. She even tried to distance herself from her early "light verse" from A Few Figs from Thistles and the first poem that gave her public recognition, "Renascence," while acknowledging their popularity. But the public was enamored with the salacious, young poet of Greenwich Village bohemia, and her more serious, self-described "propaganda poetry" of World War II and even her more melancholy, mature poetry of Mine the Harvest (1954) were generally not well received. While Nancy Boyd's "dialogues" were widely read as a regular contribution to Vanity Fair, they were generally perceived as light throwaways or "literary hors d'oeuvres" in a middlebrow magazine. She received a few appreciative reviews, mostly from critics who probably knew of Boyd's true identity, but Boyd's humorous writings were barely regarded by the scholarly community, that is, until they were rediscovered by feminist critics and more recent scholars of women's humor and women's periodical culture. Millay struggled with the very conflict she dramatized in her satiric sketches—the challenge of being taken seriously as a woman artist/writer in an age that seemed to celebrate women's liberation while simultaneously holding onto traditional gender expectations. Through the masked persona of Nancy Boyd and the indirect form of social satire, Millay found a safe space from which to launch a social critique while still receiving the uproarious approval of laughter.

Dorothy Parker and the "Vicious Circle"

Satire of Modern Love and New York Society

2.

As one of the few women associated with the "vicious circle" of the Algonquin Round Table, Dorothy Parker at once defines and defies the spirit of the New York smart set in the 1920s. As the cultural critic Edmund Wilson observes, "Her wit is the wit of her time and place; but it is often as cleanly economic at the same time that it is as flatly brutal as the wit of the age of Pope; and, within its small scope, it is a criticism of life. It has its roots in contemporary reality."[1] Herein lies the double bind of the female satirist, who is lauded for her sharp wit and lambasted for the "small scope" of her vision. "Parker often weaved her large subjects through small lenses," notes Regina Barreca.[2] This focus on the details of everyday life and women's experiences has led male critics in particular to devalue the contribution of Parker and of female humorists in general. What underlies the resistance to female humorists is the subversive potential of their exposure of gender inequality. Conversely, Parker has been scrutinized by certain feminist critics for her apparent reinforcement of female stereotypes in her satiric sketches. Parker, however, often invokes female stereotypes (the dumb blonde, the forlorn lover, the nagging housewife, the clinging vine) in order to subvert them and expose the hypocrisy and injustice of a society that creates such limited gender roles.[3] Parker makes an important contribution to women's humor both in her style and in her subject matter. She moves beyond the domestic subjects of marriage and motherhood to take on more modern issues of female sexuality, abortion, drinking, infidelity, and divorce. She further pushes the boundaries of women's humor with her witty one-liners and profound and at times profane use of satire, defying gendered assumptions about the propriety and piety of women writers.

Parker's satire is largely directed against people of privilege rather than the exploited: "When Parker goes for the jugular, it's usually a vein with blue blood in it," says Barreca.[4] Parker thereby exposes the hypocrisy and pretentiousness of New York society. Parker's fellow Algonquin Round Table writer and the author of the humor column "The Conning Tower," F. P. Adams identifies the ethical origins of her ironic and satiric outlook: "Nobody can write such ironic things unless he has a deep sense of injustice—injustice to those members of the race who are the victims of the stupid, the pretentious and the hypocritical."[5] This sense of social justice became more pronounced in the 1930s, as witnessed by Parker's political activism and in her later stories like "Clothe the Naked" (1938), "Song of the Shirt, 1941," and "Soldiers of the Republic" (1938) about the Spanish Civil War. Parker displays an empathy that is rare among satirists: "Parker's stories have a sort of two-edged humor-and-pathos. Readers are apt to laugh first, then feel embarrassed for laughing at the naked display of human frailty."[6] Parker's criticism of exploited women is often a form of self-criticism as well as an indictment of an unjust society.

Parker was socially conditioned to devalue her own contribution and that of other female humorists, thereby reinforcing certain gendered stereotypes of women and humor: "I don't want to be classed as a humorist," Parker said in a 1956 interview. "It makes me feel guilty. I've never read a good tough quotable female humorist, and I never was one myself. I couldn't do it. A 'smartcracker' they called me, and that makes me sick and unhappy. There's a hell of a distance between wisecracking and wit. Wit has truth in it; wisecracking is simply calisthenics with words."[7] Call it what you will, but even in denying her own humor, Parker's wit is undeniable. And there is a truth, a veiled but pointed social critique, behind Parker's witticisms and writing. She is similarly self-critical in assessing her verses as "no damn good." "Like everybody was then, I was following in the exquisite footsteps of Miss Millay, unhappily in my own horrible sneakers."[8] The influence of Edna St. Vincent Millay on Parker and Tess Slesinger and the influence of Parker on Dawn Powell and Mary McCarthy are evident, yet they tended to deny any comparison and to deidentify as women writers. Here was a lost opportunity for community building and support among female humorists that is more evident among female comedians today.

In assessing satirists, Parker indirectly reinforces gendered assumptions about women and humor: "They're the big boys. If I'd been called a satirist there'd be no living with me. But by satirist I mean those boys in the other centuries." She dismisses the so-called satirists of her day—George S. Kaufman among them—as topical and temporary. "Their stuff is not satire; it's as dull as yesterday's newspaper. Successful satire has got to be pretty good the day after tomorrow."[9] The humorists she identifies as having lasting value include James Thurber, Robert Benchley, and S. J. Perelman. Part of what makes them valuable, says Parker, is that they have a "point of view," that is to say, there is a purpose or moral message in their writing, as there is in much of Parker's. In her introduction to the work of Perelman, she seeks to define humor: "There must be courage; there must be no awe. There must be criticism. There must be a disciplined eye and a wild mind. There must be magnificent disregard for your reader, for if he cannot follow you, there is nothing you can do about it."[10] By her own standards (though not by her own admission), Parker demonstrates the courage of a humorist by defying traditional gender assumptions and taking a critical stance, consequences be damned. It is in part through identification with the reader that Parker establishes the sense of community or shared knowledge necessary to make a situation laughable.

Parker's satiric outlook and self-doubt are shaped in part by her marginalized, ethnic identity. She was of mixed ethnic origins, with a Jewish father and a Scottish mother. Her ambivalence about her identity can be seen in the projected title of her autobiography, *Mongrel*.[11] Her father, Henry Rothschild, was a successful haberdasher in New York and the family lived mostly on the Upper West Side of Manhattan and summered among wealthy Jewish families in West End, New Jersey—Parker considered herself a native New Yorker and famously lamented being born outside of the city. According to the biographer Marion Meade, Parker quipped, "I was cheated out of the distinction of being a native New Yorker, because I had to go and get born while the family was spending the summer in New Jersey, but honestly, we came back to New York right after Labor Day, so I nearly made the grade."[12] Her father deidentified as Jewish, marrying twice out of the faith and even sending his daughter to Catholic parochial school. Like Mary McCarthy and Dawn Powell, Parker lost her mother, Edna Rothschild, née Marston (of Marston firearms fame), at a young age (six) and was raised by a harsh stepmother who was religiously strict and denied her creative outlet, even destroying her writing notebooks.[13] As with Mary McCarthy, Parker's harsh upbringing helped shape her satiric outlook and use of humor as a coping mechanism. Like McCarthy, the part-Jewish Parker was sent to a parochial school, the Blessed Sacrament Academy, from which she was expelled for her insubordinate, irreverent behavior. "I was fired from [the convent] for a lot of things," jokes Parker, "among them my insistence that the Immaculate Conception was spontaneous combustion."[14] She was the youngest of four children and was left to care for her ailing father, for whom she harbored some resentment, in her teens. Though Parker never finished high school, she developed a love of reading and was exposed to such writers as Swift, Pope, Dickens, Carlyle, Shakespeare, and Thackeray from her father's library, as well as Horace, Virgil, Catullus, Aristotle, Socrates, Goethe, and La Rouchefoucauld while at Miss Dana's boarding school.[15]

For Parker, being a member of the Jewish bourgeoisie, with its concomitant sense of privilege and exclusion, was a source of conflicted identity. She recalled with embarrassment having had servants, which may have influenced her satiric portrayal of the New York elite and her increasing social consciousness in her later years. Parker's class ambivalence is characteristically expressed in an ironic quip. Of the rich, Parker said, "I hate rich people, but I think I'd be darling at it."[16] Though she marched in protest for Sacco and Vanzetti and became more politicized in her writing and her life, she also gladly accepted invitations to vacation on the "Gold Coast" of Long Island (Great Neck) at the home of the award-winning newspaper reporter Herbert Swope and his wife, Maggie, and on the French Riviera with Sara and Gerald Murphy.[17] Yet she felt her own sense of social inferiority as a Jewish woman. In her early autobiographical poem "The Dark Girls' Rhyme," she shows a certain Jewish self-hate in describing herself as "folk of mud and flame" and implying that she is not worthy of her gentile partner. While other women were fighting to keep their maiden names, Parker notably did not join with Ruth Hale (wife of Heywood Broun) and Jane Grant (wife of Harold Ross) in the formation of the Lucy Stone League, an organization established to protect the right of women to keep their maiden names. Instead, Parker eagerly gave up her Jewish birth name to take and keep the name of her first husband, a gentile, Edwin Pond Parker II.[18] A stockbroker at Paine Weber, he descended from an established line of Protestant ministers in Connecticut, who viewed her as "a stranger within our gates."[19] It was a clear mismatch—with Parker's sharp wit and his dull, good looks, not to mention his battle with morphine and alcoholism after his return from service in World War I. She also masochistically continued to have a string of affairs with attractive, gentile men who were for the most part unfaithful and indifferent, until she met the writer and actor Alan Campbell, himself half Jewish and half Scottish, with whom she had a tumultuous marriage in later life.

As a part-Jewish woman, Parker was doubly marginalized among the Algonquin wits of the 1920s. Some scholars have argued that to be a Jewish outsider was to be somewhat of an insider among New York Jewish intellectual and cultural circles in the interwar period.[20] This may have been the case among the more serious, politically leftist intellectual circles associated with the *Menorah Journal* in the 1920s (of which Tess Slesinger was a part) or the largely male, Jewish circle of anti-Stalinist intellectuals associated with *Partisan Review* in the 1930s, from which Mary McCarthy was somewhat marginalized as a woman of mixed religious and ethnic origins. In the case of the more middlebrow theater and publishing crowd associated with the Algonquin Round Table, there were fewer Jews and even fewer women. The Algonquin Hotel was located at 59 West Forty-Fourth Street near the theater district and the burgeoning magazine publishing industry (notably *Vanity Fair*, *Vogue*, the *New Masses*, and later the *New Yorker* and *Life*). It became a regular gathering place for playwrights, actors, producers, publishers, and journalists who met at a round table in the Rose Room from about 1921 to 1931 and who became known as the Algonquin wits Notable among them were the journalists Franklin P. Adams and Heywood Broun, the drama critic Alexander Woollcott, the critic and humorist Robert Benchley, the playwright George S. Kaufman, the journalist Marc Connelly, the film critic and playwright Robert Sherwood, the editor and founder of the *New Yorker* Harold Ross, and Dorothy Parker. One of the few fellow Jewish members, George Kaufman, upon being insulted famously exited the hotel and asked the half-Jewish Parker if she would leave with him, halfway. Parker, however, was doubly marginalized by her ethnicity and gender. While there were several other women affiliated with the Algonquin Round Table—including the novelist Edna Ferber, the painter Neysa McMein, and the playwright and social activist Alice Duer Miller—Parker was the only woman among the core of the Algonquin wits. Parker deftly navigated her gender difference, finding a self-conscious balance between what was perceived as her "masculine" wit and her female persona.

Living and writing in New York in the 1920s, Parker at once embodied and parodied the role of the New Woman. New York became the center of a cultural shift among youth and women in particular, with its urban sophistication, sexual freedom, access to speakeasies, and jazz culture. There was a split, however, between the early suffragists, who fought for legal rights for women while still supporting more traditional domestic values, and the next generation of New Women, who pursued self-fulfillment and personal freedom. In the age of mass production and consumption perpetuated by the growth of publishing, the magazine industry, and advertising, the image of the "flapper," with her bobbed hair, her thin frame, her drop-waist dress, rouged lips, and "ain't we got fun" attitude, at once represented liberation and its own form of conformity.

Parker learned to mask her caustic wit through the guise of her genteel, "feminine" appearance. She was known for her ladylike hats and fashionable suits, often carrying one of her small dogs as a kind of accoutrement. She was also known for her precise diction and proper use of grammar, perhaps to compensate for her free use of obscenities. She insisted on the formality of being called "Mrs. Parker," even among fellow *Vanity Fair* columnists, whom she addressed as "Mr. Benchley" and "Mr. Sherwood." While there was a clear irony in her using the traditional married, formal address, especially after her divorce, she may have been deliberately assuming the public role of the married woman. Her witticisms were a form of both social critique and self-deprecation. Her noted quip "Men seldom make passes / At girls who wear glasses" implies that smart women who read and wear glasses are not appealing to men.[21] Parker, who was herself nearsighted and wore "thick horn-rimmed glasses," avoided wearing them in social situations. Was this part of her conscious feminization to appeal to men, or at least to appear nonthreatening/nonintellectual?[22] In an interview, Parker downplays her own wit: "It *was* the twenties and we had to be smarty. I *wanted* to be cute. That's the terrible thing. I should have had more sense."[23] Being "smarty" or cute is here distinguished from being smart or sensible. For Parker, humor was a way of masking her intelligence under the guise of feminine appeal.

Some critics see Parker's feminized appearance as a self-conscious manipulation of her public persona in a culture of celebrity as an act of self-promotion.[24] As Nina Miller puts it, Parker "entered the public eye as a sexualized woman or not at all."[25] Parker was not necessarily "performing femininity"; her feminine appearance and genteel manner may have been a genuine expression of her complex female identity. Alexander Woollcott famously said of Parker, "She is so odd a blend of Little Nell and Lady Macbeth, . . . a lacy sleeve with a bottle of vitriol concealed in its folds."[26] Wyatt Cooper remembered two sides of Parker's identity: "Her desire to be a lady (and she *was* a lady and a great one), soft-spoken, gracious, delicate, charitable, and well-mannered, was constantly at war with her incredible mind, a critical mind, brilliant, precise and to the point."[27] Parker was also known for her sexual promiscuity and alcoholic excess, often associated with masculine behavior. According to Ellen Lansky, "The alcoholic woman . . . transgresses her traditional role as accomplice [codependent], a position marked female—and occupies the male-marked alcoholic position." Lansky goes further in identifying Parker's drinking companion Robert Benchley as typical of the "homosocial" drinking relationships among men.[28] The culture of excess and indulgence is symptomatic of both a cultural moment—the Jazz Age of the 1920s—and a personal crisis for Parker, whose self-destructive behavior and relationships ended more than once in attempted suicide.

If Parker presented a ladylike exterior, her wit reveals a clearly aggressive and often explicit side. Freud considered the sublimation of aggressive and sexual tendencies through humor to be more common among men than women. This echoes the prevalent assumptions about women in late Victorian and early modern times that have misguided our understanding of women and their relation to humor. Women's humor is often seen as focusing on domestic subjects of marriage and motherhood as a form of bonding or community building through narratives or anecdotes rather than as a mode of self-presentation or superiority, putting down others or showing off through joke-telling. Women's humor is seen as more self-deprecatory and self-directed, while men's humor is considered more aggressive and hostile toward others. Parker defies the traditional gender divide in humor by often assuming an aggressive, "male" stance and clever display in her witty one-liners and put-downs of others. While her stories may at times be self-deprecatory in identifying with the victims of social injustice, this can be seen as an indirect form of protest in exposing the limitation of traditional gender roles.

Woollcott paints an intimidating portrait of Dorothy Parker's dual/duel persona: she was "sweet to your face, lethal behind your back," thereby instilling fear of exposure in the people around her. This double-edged wit is typical of the covert form of critique necessitated by female humorists. "A girl's best friend is her mutter," observes Parker, playing on the traditional notion of a girl's dependency on her mother while suggesting that she hide her defiant thoughts through the muted indirection of muttering.[29] She assumes a more assertive, at times even "masculinist" voice in her suggestive put-downs often of women. When asked to use "horticulture" in a sentence in a typical Round Table game, she famously said, "You can bring a horticulture but you can't make her think." Regarding Parker's use of profanity in her witty observations, Nina Miller observes that Parker felt a certain pressure to conform to the prevailing "masculinism" of the Algonquin Round Table.[30] Parker here plays into stereotypes of women as sex objects without minds. Parker was not shy about using profanity or making risqué jokes. Of the Yale prom, she is reported to have said, "If all the girls attending it were laid end to end, . . . she wouldn't be at all surprised." And of a female acquaintance injured in London, Mrs. Parker insinuated, "This poor lady injured herself sliding down a barrister."[31] Such wordplay and double entendre clearly defy traditional expectations of female humor.

Parker's stories express a masked form of social critique, both through the invocation of female stereotypes and through the use of irony and a double voice. This social critique reveals a modernist outlook. As Alvin Kernan observes, the modern condition, with its sense of hypocrisy and false ideals of progress, demands satire.[32] New York in the 1920s was the locus at once of Jazz Age excess and the moral skepticism and ironic sensibility that characterize modernist writers. The post–World War I disillusionment that Gertrude Stein says typified the writers of the "lost generation" was a reaction to the failure of traditional ideals—heroism, family, God—and the breakdown of values in the face of the absurdity and chaos of the first mass, mechanized war. Like the modernist writers and Parker contemporaries Hemingway and Fitzgerald, Parker dramatizes the vacuousness of the Jazz Age indulgence in drinking and sexuality as well as the miscommunication between the sexes.[33] While more of a social realist, Parker does use modernist techniques of interior monologue and multiple narration in a number of her stories. The use of irony in exposing the discrepancy between social expectations and reality further typifies the modernist sensibility.

Parker's stories tend to take two different forms: first are monologues and dialogues, and second are more conventional narratives that focus primarily on the battle of the sexes. In a 1956 interview, Parker said, "I think narrative stories are the best, though my past stories make themselves stories by telling themselves through what people say. I haven't got a visual mind. I hear things."[34] This tendency to reveal characters through a voice, or at times a double voice of social propriety and inner desire, as well as the focus on the particulars of social experience—a dance, a dinner party, a drink, a date—lends itself well to the popular form in the 1920s of the "skit" or what Harold Ross termed "the casual." The "skit" is a light form or sketch usually written in the first person, tending toward self-deprecation.

It is well suited to newspapers and magazines and was commonly used by male writers like James Thurber, E. B. White, Robert Benchley, and S. J. Perelman in their depiction of the "little man" for the *New Yorker* as well as by female writers like Dorothy Parker, Edna St. Vincent Millay in her Nancy Boyd sketches, and Tess Slesinger. As Nancy Walker observes, the skit was a departure for women writers from the "domestic saga" of the nineteenth century, which focused on domestic issues and was centered around the home, toward more sophisticated, urban issues of heterosexual love, self-doubt, and self-actualization.[35] The skit used humor, irony, and at times self-irony to show the plight of the modern man and woman in the face of a changing social landscape.

The use of a double voice is common among modern women writers as a means of obscuring their subversive intent. This "humoring the sentence" can be used at once as a means of "humoring" or appeasing people in authority as well as "humoring" or distorting the apparent meaning through a hidden or underlying meaning, using what Mikhail Bakhtin describes as the "dialogic imagination" or a polyphonic voice.[36] This dualism can be displayed within a single character, between two characters, or between a character and a narrator, and the irony can be between narrator and audience or made aware by the speaker. The self-ironic, double voice in monologue and at times dialogic split within a single character is characteristic of some of Parker's best-known stories, notably in "The Waltz," "A Telephone Call," "The Lovely Leave," and her lesser-known autobiographical sketches "The Garter" and "But the One on the Right." All of these stories revolve around female anxiety in heterosexual, social relations and reveal a level of self-doubt and self-deprecation common among women at the time in navigating between their socially prescribed roles and their authentic selves. Most of these women show a superior level of wit, self-irony, and intellect, which is masked before their dull, male counterparts. Herein lies the serious social critique behind Parker's apparent lighthearted sketches, which expose the pressure on women to suppress their authentic selves to maintain the gender status quo.

The use of the double-voiced public and private self is on display in the brilliant monologue "The Waltz" (1933). Parker's heroine finds herself at a dance where she is expected to play the passive role of the lady, grateful for the attention of her unappealing dance partner. The woman is of advancing age, and the waltz is a metaphor for the social games a woman must play in search of a mate: "Here I've been locked in his noxious embrace for the thirty-five years this waltz has lasted."[37] Her partner is a physical oaf, who is continually kicking and stepping on her. Nor does he seem to hold any intellectual appeal—"what could you say to a thing like that! Did you go to the circus this year, what's your favorite kind of ice cream, how do you spell cat?" (51). Regardless, the speaker politely accepts his advances. The humor derives from the disparity between the speaker's outward social speech and her inner, bitterly ironic and sarcastic musings. Parker satirizes proper women's speech by having her heroine ironically invoke expected "women's language" in addressing her potential suitor. Robin Tolmach Lakoff observes in her 1975 landmark study *Language and Woman's Place* that stereotypical "women's language" tends to be polite and self-depreca-tory, using "empty" phrases, a questioning intonation, hedging ("well," "you know"), qualifiers, intensives ("so"), superlatives, emphasis, and repe-tition.[38] In the speaker's limited verbal interaction with her partner, she is ingratiating and self-deprecatory, using superlatives ("*I'm simply thrilled. I'd love to waltz with you*"), repetition, questioning, and empty phrases ("*Yes, it's lovely, isn't it? It's simply lovely. It's the loveliest waltz. Isn't it? Oh, I think it's lovely, too*"; 49). She makes excuses for all of his missteps, blam-ing herself instead: "*Oh, no, no, no. Goodness, no. It didn't really hurt the least little bit. And anyway it was my fault. Really it was. Truly. Well, you're just being sweet, to say that. It really was all my fault*" (48–49).

As the speaker outwardly appeases her partner, she is ruthless in her inner monologue, using satiric methods of hyperbole, irony, and sarcasm. The authentic speaker comes off as a seasoned, straight-shooting, intelligent woman who recognizes the injustice of her situation but is powerless to change it. She makes literary references (comparing her withering appear-ance to something out of Poe's "The Fall of the House of Usher") and psychoanalytic references ("I don't want to be the over-sensitive type, but you can't tell me that kick was unpremeditated. Freud says there are no acci-dents"; 49). The dance becomes a metaphor for sexual experience, and the abuse she suffers takes on sadomasochistic overtones as a form of physical violation.[39] "I've led no cloistered life," says the speaker. "I've known danc-ing partners who have spoiled my slippers and torn my dress; but when it comes to kicking, I am Outraged Womanhood" (49). Her feminist outcry and inner rage are tellingly masked by an outward *smile*.

The options for a woman are limited to being "left alone in [her] quiet corner of the table, to do [her] evening brooding over [her] sorrows" or to dance with this loathsome partner. She imagines possible excuses using hyperbole—"I'll see you in hell first. Why, thank you, I'd like to awfully, but I'm having labor pains. Oh, yes, *do* let's dance together—it's so nice to meet a man who isn't a scaredy-cat about catching my beri-beri" (48)—and sarcasm: "I'd love to waltz with you. I'd love to have my tonsils out, I'd love to be in a midnight fire at sea" (48). She compares her partner to a criminal or undesirable—"How do you do, Mr. Jukes?" (47)—and makes repeated reference to their waltz as a kind of brutal football game with him as the boorish athlete: "For God's sake don't *kick*, you idiot; this is only second down," "Two stumbles, slip, and a twenty-yard dash" (50), she says, trying to follow his impossible dance moves. She compares him to an animal with the "heart of a lion, and the sinews of a buffalo" (49) and goes further in comparing him to a degenerate beast to whom she is bound by social convention: "I hate this creature I'm chained to. I hated him the moment I saw his leering, bestial face" (50). She can barely mask her rage at being kicked and stepped on, thinking, "Die he must, and die he shall, for what he did to me" (48). And yet, in the ironic reversal and final insult of the story, when the music stops and the dance is over, the speaker outwardly demurs and agrees to another dance: "Oh, they've stopped, the mean things. They're not going to play anymore. Oh, darn. Oh, do you think they would? Do you really think so, if you gave them twenty dollars? Oh, that would be lovely. And look, do tell them to play this same thing. I'd simply adore to go on waltzing" (51). Again, the speaker uses weak, effeminate questioning intonation and empty phrases ("lovely") and exaggeration ("simply adore") to defer to her partner, who is presumably in the dominant position to pay the musicians for another dance. That such a critical intelligence would suffer repeated personal degradation and physical harm at the hands of an ignorant brute rather than suffer the public humiliation of sitting alone is a negative comment on the limited options for women in society.

"A Telephone Call" (1928) is another notable monologue that shows the split between what a woman is supposed to say and do and what she really thinks or feels. The woman is again relegated to the passive role of receiver rather than initiator of attention as she waits in vain for her lover to call. As in "The Waltz," the social interaction, a telephone call, becomes a metaphor for sexual relations between men and women and illustrates the constraints of gender expectations. Much of the monologue is tellingly written as a supplication to God, the "blessed Father in Heaven," a paternal authority with whom the speaker pleads for her lover to call. "Please, God, let him telephone me now. . . . Please, God. Please, please, please."[40] "Are You punishing me, God, because I've been bad?" she asks. "Are You angry with me because I did that?" (121), implying that she is being punished for having sexual relations with a man. The "good girl /

bad girl" split is elaborated on, when she tries to appease him, saying, "I'll be good, God. I will try to be better, I will, if You will let me see him again," and later, "It was bad. I knew it was bad. All right, God, send me to hell" (120). The double standard here is apparent: sex devalues the woman while it makes the man more desirable. Like the title character of "Big Blonde," the unnamed narrator here recognizes that she must play the role of the "good sport" to keep her man: "I would be sweet to him, I would be gay, I would be just the way I used to be, and then he would love me again" (121). In a moment of honest self-awareness, Parker's heroine admits to the necessity of masking one's true emotions to get ahead in the game of love: "They don't like you to tell them they've made you cry. They don't like you to tell them you're unhappy because of them. If you do, they think you're possessive and exacting. And then they hate you. They hate you when-ever you say anything you really think. You always have to keep playing little games" (122). The speaker vacillates between deferential supplication and uncontrollable anger at the humiliation she must suffer, at one point displacing her aggression toward her silent lover against the phone itself: "You damned, ugly, shiny thing. It would hurt you to ring, wouldn't it? Oh, that would hurt you to ring, wouldn't it? Oh, that would hurt you. Damn you, I'll pull your filthy roots out of the wall, I'll smash your smug black face in little bits. Damn you to hell" (120). Recognizing her own irrational behavior, she jolts herself back to a proper course of action.

While seeming to mock the emotional instability and dependency of the possessive female, Parker (and the reader) shares a degree of sympa-thy and identification with the speaker. Despite the unwritten code of conduct—that a woman should wait for the man to call or risk losing his interest—the speaker has already called her lover once and is at great pains to resist calling again. "I know you shouldn't keep telephoning them—I know they don't like that. When you do that, they know you are thinking about them and wanting them, and that makes them hate you" (119). The speaker here generalizes from her particular lover to all men, making this a representative power struggle between men and women. The story ends with the woman invoking God to make her lover call and counting to five hundred by fifties before she will give in and make the call. This portrayal of a weak, dependent woman who is powerless to act on her true feelings is another indictment of the social constraints put on women in the unequal battle of the sexes.

Parker displays her sharp wit in two lesser-known monologues, "The Garter" (1928) and "But the One on the Right" (1929), which are reprinted in her *Complete Stories*. The self-named narrator is bound by social circumstance—one at a house party, another at a dinner party—and finds herself divided between an outward display of propriety and an inner expression of anger and resentment. "The Garter," written during the height of the Jazz Age era of the flapper, is fittingly named after a confining piece of women's lingerie. A modern variation on the corset, the garter is at once a symbol of female constraint and female sexuality. It serves the practical function of holding up a woman's stockings but can also ironically serve as a form of female empowerment and objectification used to seduce men. The garter here serves the doubly restrictive function of being broken, thereby confining the partygoer to a seat in the corner of the room.

In a mock-epic style reminiscent of Pope's "The Rape of the Lock," Parker satirizes the apparent gravity of a broken garter through hyperbole and allusion. The speaker compares her plight to the crash of a wave in Tennyson's poem "Break, Break, Break": "I would get that kind of break. Break, break, break, on the cold gray stones, O sea, and I would that my tongue could utter the thoughts that arise in me. . . . Thank God I was sitting down when the crash came," she comforts herself.[41] She compares her predicament to a military battle requiring a deliberate strategy: "What would Napoleon have done?" she conjectures. "Wounded? Nay, sire, I'm healthy," she says (99). She exaggerates the gravity of her situation, imagining herself confined to the chair for eternity: "I expect my clothes will turn yellow, like Miss Havisham's in *Great Expectations*, by Charles Dickens, an English novelist 1812–1870" (100). There is a disparity between her deliberate display of erudition and her subordinate role as a woman in a compromising position. Like Miss Havisham, the quintessential "old maid" who wears a yellowing wedding dress after being left at the altar, the speaker is in danger of being rendered a social outcast. In what she ironically refers to as "An Evening with Dickens," she compares her inert body to "a demd [*sic*], damp, moist, unpleasant body" from Dickens's *Nicholas Nickleby* (100), thereby turning the feminized body into a potential site of death and decay. But beneath the humor lies her serious concern of appearing to be alone or, worse, ending up alone.

The moment the speaker's garter breaks, her sense of social isolation begins: "Here I am, a poor, lone orphan, stuck for the evening at this foul party where I don't know a soul" (99), she says in a mock exaggerated tone. And again, she compares herself to "a poor, heartsick orphan, alone in the midst of a crowd. That's the bitterest kind of loneliness there is, too" (99). Her physical isolation at the party betrays a deeper anxiety about the more permanent isolation of spinsterhood. The speaker's compromised physical state, however, does not inhibit her quick wit: "Once they wouldn't let me in the Casino at Monte Carlo because I didn't have any stockings on. So, I went and found my stockings, and then came back and lost my shirt" (100), she quips, playing on the double meaning of losing her money and her literal garment. She is concerned, however, that her public reputation as a wit will be damaged by her compromised state at the party. "Oh, have you met Dorothy Parker?" she imagines people saying. "What's she like? Oh, she's terrible. God she's poisonous. Sits in a corner and sulks all evening—never opens her yap. Dumbest woman you ever saw in your life" (101). Parker tellingly uses her own name, revealing the pressure on the female celebrity to uphold her dual appeal of wit and femininity. Parker fears that her witty remarks will be attributed to a male ghostwriter. "You know, they say she doesn't write a rod of her stuff. They say she pays this poor little guy that lives in some tenement on the lower East Side, ten dollars a week to write it and she just signs her name to it. He has to do it, the poor devil, to help support a crippled mother and five brothers and sisters; he makes button-holes in the daytime. Oh, she's terrible" (101). The implication is that she not only does not write her own work but exploits a needy Jewish man to write for her. We are left, however, less with a public concern for her reputation as a wit than with her personal anxiety over meeting a man. She assures us, with typical female sentiment, that she is "all full of tenderness and affection, and just aching to give and give and give" (101). She admits, "When I was getting dressed, I thought, 'Maybe this will be the night that romance will come into my life'" (101). And the story ends with the speaker hoping that the approaching man will take pity on her and empathize with her dire situation. The reader is left wondering why such a witty and intellectually superior woman seeks validation from your typical bourgeois man, looking "a little too Brooks Brothers to be really understanding" (101). Though the deck seems stacked against this independent woman of wit, Parker gets the last laugh by writing her clever story.

"But the One on the Right" is another double-voiced monologue in which Parker splits the clever, self-ironic inner voice of the self-named narrator and the outer voice of the social self at a dinner party. In this case, Mrs. Parker finds herself seated next to a total bore at a dinner, a real "Trojan horse," while the one on the right, who is otherwise engaged, appears to be an Adonis. The reference to Greek mythology suggests a hyperbolic gravity of mythic proportions that the speaker attributes to a commonplace social anxiety. She further uses exaggeration and sarcasm to describe the severity of her situation: "I'm here against my better judgment. . . . Mrs. Parker vs. her better judgment, to a decision. That would be a good thing for them to cut on my tombstone. . . . I should have stayed at home for dinner. I could have had something on a tray. The head of John the Baptist, or something" (132). Parker shows the disparity between her sharp wit and the dim wit of her dinner companion, whose topic of conversation seems to be limited to the menu. "Let's see, where were we? Oh, we'd got to where he had confessed his liking for fish. I wonder what else he likes. Does he like cucumbers. Yes, he does; he likes cucumbers. And potatoes? Yes, he likes potatoes, too. Why, he's a regular old Nature-lover, that's what he is. I would have to come out to dinner and sit next to the Boy Thoreau" (133).

In a mock argument, Parker tries to liven up the conversation by disagreeing with the man over the trivial subject of food likes and dislikes: "He's asking me if I'm fond of potatoes. No. I don't like potatoes. There, I've done it! I've differed from him. It's our first quarrel" (133). The speaker uses sarcasm to describe how she should have been warned before being seated next to such a bore, "so you could bring along some means of occupation": "Dear Mrs. Parker, do come to us for dinner on Friday next and don't forget your drawnwork. I could have brought my top bureau drawer and tidied it up, here on my lap. I could have made great strides towards getting those photographs of the groups on the beach pasted up in the album. I wonder if my hostess would think it strange if I asked for a pack of cards" (133). The reader identifies with the speaker, for who has not been seated next to a boring dinner companion, and is amused at the incongruity of her proposed solution. There is a hint of seriousness, however, when the speaker considers drinking as a way of escaping her social woes. Parker was known for her excessive drinking to mask an underlying sense of loneliness and isolation. "He doesn't care if I get *vin triste*," she says, referring to the melancholy of drunkenness. "Nobody cares. Nobody gives a damn. And me so nice. Alright, you baskets, I'll drink myself to death, right in front of your eyes, and see how you'll feel" (133). Though this is an idle threat, it is not so amusing given Parker's penchant for drinking and history of suicide attempts.

While the autobiographical speaker feels a sense of superiority over her dull dinner guests, there is an underlying loneliness and a certain desperation in her search to make a social connection: "I'm better than anybody at this table. Ah, but am I really? Have I, after all, half of what they have? Here I am lonely, unwanted, silent, and me with all my new clothes on. Oh, what would Louiseboulanger say if she saw her gold lamé going unnoticed like this? It's life, I suppose. Poor little things, we dress, and we plan, and we hope—and for what? What is life, anyway? A death sentence. The longest distance between two points" (134). Here Parker characteristically takes a seemingly trivial situation (a dinner party) as an occasion to entertain grand philosophical musings. While the speaker is being self-ironic, there is an underlying truth to the sense of alienation and discontent that she reveals. With her designer clothes, her superior attitude, her witty remarks, and her penchant for drinking, this New York sophisticate masks a deeper insecurity and restlessness. In typical Parker fashion, there is a reversal at the end of the story, and the clever, cynical musings of the inner monologue are replaced by the charming public social voice, here in italics. After enduring an evening of dull conversation with the man on the left, the speaker is finally treated to an encounter with the desirable "Greek God" on the right: "*Well, I thought you were never going to turn around. . . . You haven't? . . . You have? Oh, Lord, I've been having an awful time, too. . . . Oh, I don't see how we could. . . . Yes, I know it's terrible, but how can we get out of it? . . . Well. . . . Well, yes, that's true. . . . Look, right after dinner, I'll say I have this horrible headache, and you say you're going to take me home in your car, and—*" (135). The speaker has her chance with the more appealing man on her right, and she assumes an uncharacteristically assertive role with him. They come up with a plan to escape the oppressive party together, but there is a certain desperation in this witty woman's preoccupation with finding a man. Parker's monologues use a seemingly trivial social situation (a boring dinner companion, a broken garter, a telephone call, a dance) to expose at once the limitations of her characters and of the social situations that have created them.

In another lesser-known monologue, "The Little Hours" (1933), Parker uses the self-ironic voice of her autobiographical heroine to show the dilemma of the intellectual woman in a social world that has left her behind. "Now what's this?" asks the insomniac speaker. "What's the object of all this darkness all over me? They haven't gone and buried me alive while my back was turned, have they? Ah, now would you think they'd do a thing like that! Oh, no, I know what it is. I'm awake" (204). "They" are the partygoers and socialites who are returning from a night on the town while she is home alone reading at four in the morning. She implies that she is reduced to staying home and reading after having been jilted by a lover. In a display of her own erudition, the speaker refers to the French author La Rochefoucauld: "He said that if nobody had ever learned to undress, very few people would be in love" (204). She then comes to her own cynical conclusion: "I wish I'd never learned to read." She says, "I wish I'd never learned to take off my clothes. Then I wouldn't have been caught in this jam at half-past four in the morning. If nobody had ever learned to undress, very few people would be in love. No, his is better" (204). The plight of the New York woman of wit, she concludes, is not laughable.

Her clever puns, however, do merit a good laugh: "First thing you know, I'll be reciting *Fleurs du Mal* to myself, and then I'll be little more good to anybody. And I'll stay off Verlaine too: he was always chasing Rimbauds" (205). A real source of her sleeplessness is her anxiety over her literary success: "Produce, produce, produce, for I tell you the night is coming. Carlyle said that," she observes, paraphrasing another literary icon (205). The speaker is clearly conflicted between her literary aspirations and the subordinate role that a woman is expected to assume in society: "If that isn't the woman of it for you! Always having to do what somebody else wants, like it or not. Never able to murmur a suggestion of her own" (206). She further reveals her anxiety about her literary reputation: "I'm never going to accomplish anything; that's perfectly clear to me. I'm never going to be famous. My name will never be writ larger on the roster of Those Who Do Things. I don't do anything. Not one single thing" (206). She immediately undercuts the gravity of her remarks through characteristic humor, punning, and understatement: "I used to bite my nails, but I don't even do that anymore. I don't amount to the power to blow me to hell. I've turned out to be nothing but a bit of flotsam. Flotsam and leave 'em—that's me from now on." "Oh, it's all terrible," she concludes, with mock seriousness (206). In a final effort to put herself to sleep, the speaker recites "a list of quotations beautiful from minds profound" in a tour de force of literary parody (207). She ultimately gives up on trying to fall asleep and, by implication, on conforming to social norms and defiantly stays up reading: "I'm going to turn on the light and read my head off" (208). In a double irony, Parker exposes not only literary types but a society that ostracizes women for their scholarly and literary aspirations.

Parker satirizes the hypocrisy and superficiality of the New York elite in such monologues as "From the Diary of a New York Lady" and dialogues like "Mrs. Carrington and Mrs. Crane." Written in 1933 at the height of the Depression, "From the Diary of a New York Lady: During Days of Horror, Despair, and World Change" emphasizes the disparity between the self-indulgence and vacuousness of the titular New York lady and the suffering and deprivation of the people around her. The subtitle is ironic in that the crisis and despair of the ignorant first-person narrator revolves around broken nails, broken dates, and the latest gossip. Its exaggerated speech and focus on New York City nightlife and fashion resemble the self-ironic magazine writing of Lois Long, who followed Parker as drama critic at *Vanity Fair* and later at the *New Yorker* under the provocative alias "Lipstick." Parker's New York lady, however, lacks the self-awareness to see her own excess and limitations.

The distinctive diary form of "From the Diary of a New York Lady" allows the reader to enter the mind of the character while emphasizing the daily monotony and meaninglessness of her incessant and aimless pursuit of the latest fashion, food, and fun. The New York lady reveals the ennui and excess of the postwar Jazz Age, which appear vulgar and irresponsible in the face of the social crisis of the 1930s. "MONDAY. Breakfast tray about eleven; didn't want it. The champagne at the Amorys' last night was *too* revolting, but what *can* you do? . . . TUESDAY. Joe came barging in my room this morning at *practically nine* o'clock. *Couldn't* have been more furious. Started to fight, but *too* dead. . . . WEDNESDAY. The most terrible thing happened *just this minute*. Broke one of my finger nails *right off short*. Absolutely *the* most horrible thing I ever had happen to me in my life" (191–92). Parker satirizes so-called women's language through the New York lady's exaggerated use of hyperbole, emphasis, questions, repetition, and empty phrases. The disparity between the emphatic, hyperbolic words and the trivial actions reinforces the superficiality of the New York lady, and the repeated phrase "but what *can* you do?" points to a kind of resignation and a disavowal of personal responsibility. There is an underlying sense of desperation and pathos in the New York lady's almost frenetic pursuit of a good time and of a companion with whom to share it. Like the jilted lover in "A Telephone Call," the unattached New York lady searches in vain for a connection in this alienating city. She repeatedly calls and even telegrams one eligible male suitor to accompany her to the latest theater opening in vain and goes instead with her gay standby, Ollie Martin. "He *couldn't* have more poise, and what do *I* care if he *is* one?" (191), she says with a homophobic slur. She similarly relies on and belittles her manicurist, Miss Rose, who serves the all-important function of supplying gossip to and from the society ladies, indirectly exposing those she serves. The erratic New York lady vacillates between praising and damning Miss Rose, thereby revealing her own sense of social superiority in exploiting others. The excess of the nights of drinking, dancing, and entertaining masks an underlying sense of depression and disaffection of the New York socialite, made all the more distasteful in contrast with the genuine suffering of the Depression era. After failing to find a date for the opening of the ironically named "White Man's Folly," the speaker bemoans her fate: "*Couldn't* feel more depressed; never should have gone *anywhere near* champagne and Scotch together. Started to read a book, but too restless. . . . Absolutely *walking the floor* like a *panther* all day" (194). Stuck in her own cycle of self-indulgence and dissatisfaction, the unnamed "New York lady" represents a type of the ennui and malaise of the lost generation.

In the dialogue "Mrs. Carrington and Mrs. Crane," Parker again paints an ironic portrait of the self-delusion and superficiality of New York high society. These two aging society women embody the values they critique, with their aimless pursuit of the latest fashion, beauty trends, and cultural fads and their incessant gossip (the cultural economy of the social climber). Criticizing their fellow New Yorkers from their "must have" summer retreat in the "country," Mrs. Carrington ironically complains about the superficiality of the New York elite without recognizing her own complicity. "The emptiness. And the silliness. And the eternal gossip, gossip, gossip. And all the talk about the clothes they have and the clothes they're going to get, and what they do to keep thin. Well, I'm fed up with it, that's all," she says, gossiping and refusing another sandwich: "No, thanks, dear, I don't dare take another sandwich; I'll have to roll all day tomorrow as it is" (200). Parker here uses the figure of the *eiron* or the ignorant narrator who unwittingly exposes her own weakness. The ladies display the cultural superiority of many of the New York elite and long to return to the city, where they will partake in the mass-marketed consumption of high culture and knowledge. In New York, they say, you can "do something really worthwhile—picture galleries, and the Philharmonic, and, oh, exhibitions of paintings, and concerts, and things like that" (200). Mrs. Carrington shows a vague interest in higher learning as a form of conspicuous consumption—"I'll take some sort of course or other at Columbia" (202), she says—but is easily distracted when Mrs. Crane tells her that Mary Morton lost twelve pounds taking up tap-dancing. The idle pursuit of the New York society women to keep up with the cultural and intellectual fashion is heightened by the context of the Depression and the knowledge (on the part of the author and the reader) of how the other half lives. Beneath the ironic mockery of the New York elite lies a more serious social message.

Parker attempted to move away from the more dramatic form of the monologue and dialogue to what she considered the superior form of the third-person narrative, in which the writer needs to show rather than to tell the story. "I think narrative stories are the best," observed Parker in a 1956 interview, "though my past stories make themselves stories by telling themselves through what people say. I haven't got a visual mind. I hear things. But I'm not going to do those *he-said she-said* things anymore, they're over, honey, they're over. I want to do the story that can only be told in the narrative form, and though they're going to scream about the rent, I'm going to do it."[42] Parker seems to overlook her natural gift for the spoken voice and the power of her witty monologues and dual-voiced dialogues, particularly when assuming the personae of her autobiographical heroines. In her third-person narratives, Parker uses humor to take on such taboo subjects as abortion in "Mr. Durant" and "Lady with a Lamp," racism in "Arrangement in Black and White," and sexism in "Big Blonde." In these satiric stories and sketches, Parker often invokes gender, class, and racial stereotypes in order to subvert them.

Parker has a complicated relationship to feminism, at once defending women's rights and reinforcing the sexist stereotype of sentimental women writers. "I am a feminist," says Parker, "and God knows I'm loyal to my sex, and you must remember that from my very early days, when this city was scarcely safe from buffaloes, I was in the struggle for equal rights for women. But when we paraded through the catcalls of men and when we chained ourselves to lamp posts to try to get our equality—dear child, we didn't foresee *those* female writers" (referring to Faith Baldwin, Edna Ferber, and Kathleen Norris, whom she considered writers of "fantasies").[43] Whether Parker's judgment comes in part out of jealousy for the relative success of other women writers, Edna Ferber in particular, or whether she considered many women writers of her time to be "lightweights" is unclear. With the exception of "Big Blonde," which won the O. Henry Award in 1929 for the best short story, Parker's narrative stories tend to lack the intimacy, quick wit, and memorable one-liners of her monologues and dialogues. In assuming a more serious tone and relying more on irony and pathos, these narrative stories deliver a poignant satire and an incisive social critique with a more sardonic tone.

Parker takes on the taboo subject of abortion in two lesser-known stories, "Mr. Durant" (1924) and "Lady with a Lamp" (1932). I focus on the former since it also offers a scathing portrait of the self-focused, misogynistic male character and various female types, from the self-abnegating young mistress to the doting, oblivious wife. Parker uses her hallmark irony bordering on parody to show the unwitting callous and calculating behavior of the male bore in Mr. Durant. The subject is all the more raw for Parker, who made the conflicted decision to abort her love child with Charles MacArthur, a charming Chicago journalist who became a part of the Algonquin circle, after her affair with him had soured. Like Mr. Durant, MacArthur, in a failed gesture of gallantry, offered to pay for only part of the procedure. Parker used humor to diffuse the situation, blaming herself "for putting all [her] eggs in one bastard."[44] But the wounds were deep, and in characteristically masochistic behavior, Parker attempted suicide for the second time.[45] For Parker, Mr. Durant embodies the male chauvinist, concerned only for his own pleasure and annoyed by the inconvenience of his mistress becoming pregnant. He is a midlevel businessman at a "rubber works" factory, described in phallic terms as "the solid red pile, at the six neat stories rising impressively into the darkness" (23).

Mr. Durant has a smug sense of self-importance, returning nightly to his solicitous wife and two children. When he starts having an affair with a young, virginal secretary in his office, aptly named Rose, whom he deflowers, he considers it a privilege for this plain, inexperienced girl (she is only twenty, compared with his forty-nine) to be the object of his affection. In fact, he chooses her primarily for the convenience and her "desperate timidity" and obsequiousness. "She was never one to demand much of him, anyway. She never thought of stirring up any trouble between him and his wife, never besought him to leave his family and go away with her, even for a day" (25). Parker here presents the typical sadomasochistic relationship, in which the innocent, self-abnegating, insecure female is victimized by the egotistical, self-deluded, and entitled male. It is not until Rose becomes pregnant and in need of Mr. Durant's support that he cuts her off. He views her pregnancy with "deep bitterness" and resentment: "And then everything had to go and get spoiled," he describes passively, as if he had no part in impregnating her, and he blames her for "getting in trouble" (26). When she comes crying in his office, he shows no compassion for her "blubbering, . . . as he sweepingly put it, all over the place" (26), as if even her tears were her own mess that threatened to disrupt his orderly desk and life. He is concerned more with appearances (and with getting caught) than with her fragile state: "The main thing was to get her out of sight, with that nose and those eyes," swollen from crying; such things could be "fixed up" he said, as if it were a broken deal or gambling debt (27).

The individuals are seen as exaggerated types of a social system that is broken and in need of reform. Sadistic men need to take responsibility for their actions, and exploited women need to stand up for their rights as individuals of worth. Mr. Durant throws money at the problem (he "gallantly insisted" on paying the $25 for the abortion) and walks away—"'Well, that's that,' he said to himself. He was not sure that he didn't say it aloud" (28).

While Rose is left alone and irreparably damaged, Mr. Durant returns home to his family with a little extra energy left to ogle some young girls passing by: "He had often lingeringly noticed their fresh prettiness. He hurried, so that he might see them run up the steps, their narrow skirts sliding up over their legs" (29). He continues to view women as objects for his own pleasure and delights in the return of his libido. In a sadistic fantasy, he recalls another young woman he saw on the bus: "Her tight little skirt slipped up over her thin, pretty legs as she took the high step. There was a run in one of her flimsy silk stockings. . . . Mr. Durant had an odd desire to catch his thumbnail in the present end of the run, and to draw it on down until the slim line of the dropped stitches reached to the top of her low shoe" (24). The tear in the young girl's stocking, which he imagines ripping further, becomes a metaphor for his desire to deflower another young virgin. We are given another glimpse into his sadistic nature when he callously casts aside a stray dog that his children have brought home when he discovers she is female. For Parker, who loved animals and had a dog as a constant companion, this act of callous indifference is all the more loathsome. In tackling the sensitive "female" subject of abortion, Parker highlights the chauvinism and irresponsibility of the sadistic husband while showing a certain complicity of the solicitous wife and weak-willed mistress.

In Parker's 1927 *New Yorker* story "Arrangement in Black and White," she satirizes the racism and hypocrisy of the New York society woman. A guest at a house party in honor of the acclaimed African American musician Walter Williams, the unnamed "woman with the pink velvet poppies" reveals her unconscious bias by invoking racial stereotypes and revealing her unease at meeting this celebrity. She defends her southern husband, claiming, "He had this old colored nurse, this regular old nigger mammy, and he just simply loves her" (78), inadvertently revealing her own prejudice by using a racial slur in her stereotyping of the woman. She claims that her husband "hasn't got a word to say against colored people as long as they keep their place" (78), unaware of the contradiction of his position. She tries to differentiate herself from her husband, saying that it makes her sick to hear him say that he "wouldn't sit at the table with one for a million dollars," but she feels "terrible" for reprimanding him, as if the moral violation is in contradicting him, not in his racist beliefs (78).

Although the speaker repeatedly claims, "I haven't the slightest feeling about colored people" (78), meaning that she holds no negative feelings or prejudice, her speech and actions reveal otherwise. While claiming to be a fan of Walter Williams, she stereotypes him as having a talent typical of his race: "Oh, can't he sing! Isn't it marvelous, the way they all have music in them? It just seems to be right *in* them" (79). Although she is eager to show her progressive values by meeting the musician and shaking his hand, her discomfort is apparent. While she extends her hand "at the length of her arm and [holds] it so for all the world to see," she talks down to him "with great distinctness, moving her lips meticulously, as if in parlance with the deaf" (79). She catches herself in a racial slur, commenting negatively on the dark complexion of the actress Katherine Burke: "I thought she was much better-looking," says the woman with the pink velvet poppies. "I had no idea she was so terribly dark. Why, she looks almost like—" (80) and she later reveals to her host that she nearly said the "n" word. While praising the singer's civility to the host, she remains unaware of her own incivility and prejudice in her attitude toward the honored guest. "Why, he's awfully nice," she observes with some surprise. "Nice manners, and everything. You know, so many colored people, you give them an inch, and they walk all over you" (80). She is here no better than her husband, who tolerates African Americans so long as they stay "in their place." She seems less interested in meeting the Black musician than in the public display of meeting him and can hardly wait to tell her husband about what she sees as her transgression in calling him "Mister" as an equal. For Parker, who identified with the oppressed, this typical New York society woman reveals the moral failing of the white, urban elite.

In Parker's most acclaimed story, "Big Blonde" (1929), she uses satire to expose the disparity between the illusion and the reality of the freedom of the sexually liberated New Woman. The power of Parker's story lies in her ability to stir the pathos of the reader in seeing the protagonist, Hazel Morse, as a frustrated product of a society that expects her to play the role of the good-time girl, the "good sport," or the "dumb blonde," a role for which she is no longer suited. The aging Hazel Morse tries in vain to assume another traditional role for women—that of the devoted wife—and finds herself abandoned by her husband and betrayed by a society that has little use for her. Thus, Parker invokes gender stereotypes in order to expose them; we feel sorry for Hazel Morse and do not laugh at her but laugh with her at her self-ironic awareness of the plight of the aging blond bombshell. As Nancy Walker observes, Parker's text operates on two levels, "one that appears to endorse popular stereotypes of women, and another that points to the origins of those stereotypes in a culture that defines women in terms of their relationships with men."[46] While on the surface Parker may appear to be endorsing cultural stereotypes, a closer look at the "double text of women's humor challenges cultural assumptions" on which these stereo-types are based. While some of Parker's monologues and dialogues show a self-awareness on the part of the speaker, who recognizes the injustice, albeit the inevitability, of her situation, in "Big Blonde," Hazel Morse seems more an unwitting victim of circumstance, adding to our pathos.

Hazel Morse appears to be the type of the "dumb blonde" or female sex object; her primary concern is with pleasing others or being the "good sport" or companion. She is described as "a large, fair woman of the type that incites some men when they use the word 'blonde' to click their tongues and wag their heads roguishly," but we get a hint at some defect or decline with the description of her hands as "strange terminations to the flabby white arms splattered with pale tan spots," which have, perhaps, been some-what disfigured by an attempt to enhance them with jewelry.[47] She was a model in wholesale dresses in her twenties, known as much for her conge-nial nature as her full figure. In typical "feminine" behavior, she learned early to ingratiate herself with the opposite sex, "laughing at their jokes and telling them she loved their neckties" (187) and in effect marketing herself to get attention from men, ultimately, in hopes of landing a husband. She learned to play the game and played it well: "Men liked you because you were fun, and when they liked you they took you out, and there you were. So, and successfully, she was fun. She was a good sport. Men liked a good sport" (187). As she approached her thirties and her looks began to decline, she felt a certain urgency to get married and find security. Her convivial nature "had come to be more conscientious than spontaneous" (188), and she felt a certain relief upon getting married and letting her guard down, often complaining and crying. The reader gets a hint at some underlying discontent in Hazel, perhaps a tendency to depression, which is increas-ingly masked with drink. She resembles Parker in her depressive nature and turn toward alcohol and later attempted suicide. Parker, however, main-tains her wit and her writing as personal outlets.

For Hazel, marriage offers a safe haven where she thinks she can reveal her inner fears and insecurities; her husband, however, "is not amused." He expects to continue to be served and entertained by his wife, and when the marriage becomes work, he abandons her: "Crab, crab, crab, crab, crab, crab, that was all she ever did. What a lousy sport *she* was" (191), Herbie complains. While Herbie is the stereotypical self-focused, unsupportive husband, their relationship points to a broken system whereby men and women are set up to have false expectations of marital bliss and the woman, in particular, is expected to sacrifice her needs to save the marriage. Trapped in what becomes a progressively abusive and unfulfilling marriage, Hazel turns increasingly to alcohol to numb the pain of her condition. Her name, Hazel, takes on symbolic meaning as she devolves into the haze of alcohol: "She commenced drinking alone, little, short drinks all through the day. . . . She lived in a haze of it. Her life took on a dream-like quality. Nothing was astonishing" (193). Hazel is very much a product of the times, in which alcohol and sexual promiscuity mask the inner loneliness and despair of the urban isolato. Hazel is one of many aging, abandoned women, like her new neighbor, Mrs. Martin (she "had no visible spouse; you were left to decide for yourself whether he was or was not dead"; 193) or the inter-changeable string of women who go to Jimmy's place, one of the transient, shabby speakeasies in Midtown Manhattan, seeking companionship. "They were all big women and stout, broad of shoulder and abundantly breasted, with faces thickly clothed in soft, high-colored flesh. They laughed loud and often, showing opaque and lusterless teeth like squares of crockery. There was about them the health of the big, yet a slight, unwholesome suggestion of stubborn preservation. They might have been thirty-six or forty-five or anywhere between" (198). Parker vividly captures the pathetic persistence of the "has-been," the middle-aged mistress/divorcée who relies on her dwindling looks and forced charm to hold onto whatever male companion-ship and financial support she can sustain. The women's loud and frequent laughter barely masks the desperation of their lovelorn lives. These outcasts are reduced to selling their bodies and their adoring, cheerful attitude for financial security. "The aim of each was to have one man, permanently, to pay all her bills" (199). The catch, however, is that they must appear always cheerful and gay, must play the "good sport." "I got worries of my own," one patron tells her. "Nobody wants to hear other people's troubles, sweetie. What you got to do, you got to be a sport and forget it. See?" (199). Sadness, authentic feeling, becomes a "privilege," a luxury, that Hazel cannot afford.

Parker powerfully invokes the exploitation of a whole class of women, who are forced in effect to prostitute themselves, to ingratiate themselves to their male supporters, laugh at their jokes, compliment their appearance, constantly play "the good sport," at the expense of authentic feeling and self-expression. Hazel goes from suitor to suitor, from Ed, the married man who put her up in an apartment near Grand Central for maximum conve-nience, to Charley. "There was nearly a year of Charley; then she divided her time between him and Sydney, another frequenter of Jimmy's. . . . Then Sydney married a rich and watchful bride, and then there was Billy. No— after Sydney came Fred, then Billy" (200). Hazel is left in a "haze," in which "she never recalled how men entered her life and left it" (200). Like so many people during Prohibition, Hazel turns to drink to dull the pain of her lonely, desperate existence: "She was never noticeably drunk and seldom sober. It required a larger daily allowance to keep her misty-minded. Too little, and she was achingly melancholy" (197).

For Hazel, the pressure of keeping up the appearance of fun and masking her inner suffering becomes too much of a burden to bear, and she considers suicide an inviting and her sole possibility of escape: "She dreamed by day of never again putting on tight shoes, of never having to laugh and listen and admire, of never more being a good sport. Never" (201). She identifies with the downtrodden, exploited horses on Sixth Avenue—beautiful, massive creatures that have been run down by mistreatment and neglect—and is overwhelmed by melancholy. In Parker's description, one can barely distinguish between Hazel and the horse: "As she slowly crossed Sixth Avenue, consciously dragging one foot past the other, a big, scarred horse pulling a rickety express-wagon crashed to his knees before her. The driver swore and screamed and lashed the beast insanely, bringing the whip back over his shoulder for every blow, while the horse struggled to get a footing on the slippery asphalt" (204). Like Parker, who empathized with dependent and vulnerable animals, Hazel is overwhelmed by the horse's brutal mistreatment. With an uncharacteristic sense of purpose and eagerness, Hazel obtains veronal (the same method Parker used for her second attempted suicide) and takes the pills with "the quick excitement of one who is about to receive an anticipated gift" (205). With a sardonic wit more typical of Parker than Hazel, Hazel sees the irony of going to sleep to die: "'Guess I'll go to bed,' she said. 'Gee, I'm nearly dead'" (205). She becomes the joke teller, and she is no longer forced to laugh at others' jokes: "Gee, I'm nearly dead," she repeats, chuckling, "That's a hot one!" (205). But even in death, Hazel's attempt at self-assertion is thwarted. Her Black maid, Nettie, one of many devoted, caring servants portrayed by Parker, finds Hazel the next day, gets help, and "saves" her life. Doomed to a life of unhappiness, Hazel can only hope that alcohol will continue to dull the misery of her ongoing cycle of drinking, despair, and feigning fun. She has nothing left to believe in, except the power of alcohol to make her not feel. Her trusted maid joins her in a drink and prays: "Maybe whisky would be her friend again. She prayed without addressing a God, without knowing a God. Oh please, please, please, let her be able to get drunk, please keep her always drunk" (210). With a final self-ironic toast, Hazel raises her glass with the familiar salutation, "Here's mud in your eye" (210). While Nettie is able to muster a cheerful giggle, Hazel offers a sarcastic dismissal: "Yeah. . . . Sure" (210). This ironic self-awareness does little to improve the aging divorcée's situation, but it does show a certain insight and the power of laughter to endure.

Parker was all too familiar with the desperation and despair that led to drinking and attempted suicide. She similarly failed in her attempt at suicide with sleeping pills. She made light of another suicide attempt with a razor, decorating her wrists with bows.[48] And she was well known for the dark humor of her morbid poetry, as noted by the morose titles of the collections (*Enough Rope, Sunset Gun, Death and Taxes*) and most notably in the often quoted poem "Résumé," in which the poet opts for life over the inconvenience of death by suicide: "Razors pain you; / Rivers are damp; / Acids stain you; / And drugs cause cramp. / Guns aren't lawful, / Nooses give; / Gas smells awful; / You might as well live."[49] Where death and depression became a source of creativity and self-irony for Parker, her characters like Hazel Morse were not so clever or capable. For many of Parker's female protagonists, there was no escape from the socially prescribed roles of the "dumb blonde," the "good sport," the "clinging vine," the jealous girlfriend, or the shrewish wife, and they were bound by gender expectations. While Parker took on the limitations of traditional gender roles, she offered few alternatives for her ignorant characters and only a frustrated self-awareness for the self-ironic ones. The reader primarily feels pathos for the former and can appreciate the humor and muted protest of the latter.

While recognizing Parker's more direct style and modern subject matter, some critics see her as not going far enough to change women's conditions. Emily Toth identifies Parker as ultimately a "feminine" rather than a "feminist" writer in that she points to problems in women's lives without offering a solution or alternatives, say, through communities of women or social action, as did her feminist counterparts in the 1970s.[50] Others consider the value of female humorists of Parker's generation as bringing "recognition, not resolution," to the issues of gender inequality. Regina Barreca argues that women use comedy "not as a safety valve" according to Freudian relief theory "but as an inflammatory device, seeking, ultimately, not to purge desire and frustration but to transform it into action." She acknowledges, however, that such "rage" must be masked: "Like a handgun hidden in a handbag, the woman writer often obscures her most dangerous implements by making use of her most feminine attributes."[51] Through the indirection of satire and wit, Parker challenges traditional gender norms, thereby setting the stage for more overt feminist humorists to follow.

Tess Slesinger, the *Menorah Journal* Group, and the Feminist Socialist Satire of 1930s America

3.

Witty, daring, experimental, radical—these are some of the words used to describe Tess Slesinger and her famed first novel, *The Unpossessed: A Novel of the Thirties*. Slesinger is one of the few women intellectuals affiliated with the secular, leftist Jewish literary and cultural magazine the *Menorah Journal* in the late 1920s and early 1930s. Her writing satirizes the ineffectuality of the radical New York intellectual and the conflicts of the progressive ideals of the New Woman. Her first and only novel, *The Unpossessed* (1934), based loosely on her own experiences with the *Menorah Journal* circle, exposes the failure of radical intellectuals to put their ideas into action both personally and politically. In particular, she reveals the false dichotomy between what was seen as the bourgeois values of marriage and family and the radical idealism of the public intellectual. Slesinger's novel takes on the then controversial subjects of abortion, free love, divorce, and infidelity using modernist techniques of stream of consciousness and multiple narration. She dramatizes the quest of the modern woman for personal and intellectual fulfillment in a sexist world of leftist intellectual idealism. Slesinger also satirizes the failure of progressive values in New York society in the Depression era and the limitations of class, gender, and race in her collected stories, *Time: The Present* (1935), reprinted and expanded as *On Being Told That Her Second Husband Has Taken His First Lover and*

Other Stories (1971).[1] Through her use of humor, modernist literary form, and marginalized perspective, Slesinger pushes the boundaries of so-called social protest fiction to blend the personal with the political in a form of feminist, socialist satire.

Slesinger is a product of New York Jewish progressive education, and she at once embodies and critiques the bourgeois lifestyle and liberal values in which she was raised. The daughter of Jewish Hungarian and Russian immigrants, Slesinger was raised on New York's Upper West Side and was schooled at the progressive Ethical Culture Society (which was considered by some New York intellectuals to be "a means by which Jews of a certain class carried forward their acculturation").[2] She attended Swarthmore College and the Columbia University School of Journalism, where she received a master's degree in 1927. Her father attended City College and dropped out of Columbia Law School to work in his father-in-law's garment business, while her mother was self-educated as a lay analyst (she was a patient and student of Erich Fromm and Karen Horney) and helped establish the New School for Social Research. While Slesinger lived in an upper-middle-class environment, her father lost money in business (making the misjudgment to invest in fur coats for chauffeurs on the brink of the Depression), and her parents separated on their fiftieth anniversary.[3] Her upbringing and family dynamics figure into Slesinger's own views on male-female relations, psychology, social values, politics, and gender roles, as seen in her fiction.

As somewhat of an outsider, Slesinger offered a satiric look at both the New Woman of the 1920s and the leftist intellectual of the 1930s. In 1927, at the age of twenty-two, Slesinger married Herbert Solow, then managing editor of the *Menorah Journal*, and she was one of two women (along with Anita Brenner, who studied anthropology at Columbia University and was a historian of Mexican art) to be associated with the *Menorah Journal* group. The *Menorah Journal* was a secular, leftist Jewish magazine of the New York intellectuals devoted to Jewish history and culture with a broad, cosmopolitan outlook. It was founded in 1915 by Henry Hurwitz, a Jewish immigrant from Lithuania, who remained editor in chief until his death and the dissolution of the magazine in 1962. The *Menorah Journal* was the outgrowth of the Menorah Society, founded in 1906 by Hurwitz as an undergraduate at Harvard University, as a student group devoted to the cultivation of "Jewish humanism" and cultural pride at a time of rising antisemitism in the academy in the US and worldwide. The Menorah Society gained in popularity across university campuses, and in 1913, the Intercollegiate Menorah

Association (IMA) was formed; by 1930, there were as many as eighty chapters on college campuses in the US and in Canada.[4]

As stated in the Menorah Society's founding document, *The Menorah Movement: For the Study and Advancement of Jewish Culture and Ideals* (Ann Arbor, MI, 1914), the organization was "devoted to the study of Jewish history, literature, religion, philosophy, jurisprudence, art, and manners, in a word, Jewish culture."[5] This revival of interest in Jewish culture was intended in part to combat Jews' sense of self-consciousness on college campuses as a result of antisemitism and "even of a desire to forget or to hide their Jewish origins" and to foster instead a sense of Jewish belonging and self-acceptance.[6] In a 1966 essay, "Young in the Thirties," the literary and cultural critic and *Menorah Journal* affiliate Lionel Trilling observes that the Menorah Society was intended to make Jewish students "aware of the interest and dignity of the Jewish past, to assure them of, as it were, the normality of the Jewish present." Trilling defines the *Menorah Journal* group in secular terms: it was bound together by "the idea of Jewishness": "This had nothing to do with religion; we were not religious. It had nothing to do with Zionism; we were inclined to be skeptical about Zionism and even opposed to it. . . . Chiefly our concern with Jewishness was about what is now called authenticity."[7] Authenticity here recalls the title of Trilling's essay collection *Sincerity and Authenticity*, in which "authenticity" refers to a kind of moral authority inherent in the liberal imagination, as well as a respect for skepticism, ambiguity, complexity, irony, and a multiplicity of points of view that is a distinction of the modernist sensibility.[8]

One of the founding members of the Menorah Society, Horace M. Kallen, a German Jewish immigrant and philosopher, defines "the Menorah Idea" in terms of secular humanism and cultural pluralism. One of the society's stated objectives was "the study and promotion of Hebraic culture and ideals." Kallen traces the reference to "Hebraic" rather than "Jewish" culture to "the English tradition of comparing and contrasting Hebraism with Hellenism," emphasizing Hebraism's "concern with a comprehensive humanism which would take in every aspect of the Jewish heritage, not the religious alone."[9] The distinction between Hebraism and Hellenism is associated with Matthew Arnold, for whom "Hebraism was defined by a proclivity for morality and religious knowledge, Hellenism by intellectual knowledge and, by extension, politics, art, philosophy, and science." The symbol of the menorah is associated with "Jewish enlightenment"—"to spread the light of Hebraic culture"—though the Menorah ideal connoted a broader dedication to cultural humanism.[10]

Kallen recounts the conflicted identity of the Jewish student facing antisemitism at the turn of the twentieth century and the pressure to assimilate: "I entered college and desired to escape the handicaps laid upon one by being known as a Jew, and I was disposed not to be so known. . . . I regarded the term 'Jew' as a name for a fear-nurtured error called 'religion' and also as a name for an invidious error called 'race.' Together they automatically imposed a gratuitous penalty upon anyone labeled Jew."[11] In later life, Lionel Trilling similarly recalled "the shame that young middle-class Jews felt [in the 1920s]; self-hatred was the word that later came into vogue but shame is simpler and better."[12] This language of Jewishness as a "handicap" or "penalty" and what Kallen later describes as a "lameness" that did "cripple [his] strivings for a life and a living" draws parallels with the crisis of African Americans being ostracized as Other, as documented by W. E. B. Du Bois and Alain Locke, among others, at the time. Like Du Bois, who describes the "twoness" or "double consciousness" of African Americans, Kallen sees Jews as having a dual identity of being Jewish and American based on the (mis)perception of the dominant white, Anglo-Saxon culture. The Menorah Society's emphasis on Jewish pride and call for a Jewish cultural renaissance is further reminiscent of the Harlem Renaissance emphasis on racial pride and cultural distinction. The feeling of "inferiority and insecurity, together with resentment of the conditions which bred them—Jewish 'self-hatred,' as it came to be called"—led to a suppression of and dissociation from one's ethnic identity.[13]

A number of New York intellectuals experienced antisemitism in academic and professional circles firsthand. Horace Kallen's attempt to "pass" with his appointment as a philosophy professor at Princeton was foiled when his Jewish identity was discovered, and his contract was not renewed. A "friendly" colleague informed him that had the committee known about his Jewish origins, he would not have been hired in the first place.[14] Elliot Cohen reportedly left graduate school because he had no real prospect of an academic job as a Jew; Lionel Trilling, who was considered somewhat of an experiment as an English professor at Columbia University, was highly conscious of maintaining a genteel and what could be considered a "gentile" manner. Despite the relatively large number of (male) Jewish students on college campuses, especially in major cities and at public institutions, there continued to be a limit on hiring among faculty and administration.[15]

The identification of Jewishness with race and religion was something that Kallen and the Menorah idea moved away from in defining Jewishness in more general terms as primarily an ethnic and cultural identity. Under the influence of William James and George Santayana, Kallen advocated for cultural pluralism, whereby Jewish and other ethnocultural groupings contributed to a diverse American identity. Rather than the popular model of assimilation or acculturation, whereby Jews and other racial and ethnic groups conform to the dominant white, Protestant notion of American identity, cultural pluralism allows for cultural difference within a diverse American community. Thus, the metaphor of the melting pot is replaced by Kallen with that of an orchestra, with different instruments creating a harmonious whole.[16]

The *Menorah Journal*, on which Tess Slesinger's satire of leftist, largely Jewish intellectuals of the 1930s is based, was founded in 1915 by Henry Hurwitz in New York City as "a magazine of Jewish culture and ideas," according to its masthead, and as an outgrowth of the Menorah Society. The journal was located in Midtown Manhattan (East Fifty-Ninth Street); however, it is associated with the radical intellectuals of Greenwich Village, where many of its contributors lived, and the Morningside Heights area of Columbia University (West 116th Street), where many of its editorial staff and writers were educated in the 1920s. While Hurwitz remained the longtime editor in chief of the journal, he was older and more conservative than the younger, radicalized intellectuals who were drawn to the journal by Elliot Cohen. Cohen, who served as managing editor from 1925 to 1929, was described by Lionel Trilling as "a Socratic personality, drawing young men to him to be teased and taught."[17] Originally from Mobile, Alabama, Cohen maintained an affinity for "the people" and took a self-ironic view of Jewish politics and ideas. His satiric editorial musings, which appeared as "Marginal Annotations," set the tone of "irreverent vivacity" that character- ized the *Journal* under his tutelage in its consideration of "the complexities of the Jewish situation with an energetic unabashed intelligence."[18]

Among Cohen's coterie were Lionel Trilling, Herbert Solow, Clifton Fadiman, Felix Morrow, Tess Slesinger, and Anita Brenner.[19] Herbert Solow served as assistant editor of the *Menorah Journal* in 1928, the year he and Slesinger were married, and as contributing editor, before turning to the more conservative *Fortune* magazine. Solow was characterized by Trilling as "a man of quite remarkable intelligence, very witty in a saturnine way, deeply skeptical, tortured by bouts of extreme depression," and a great political journalist who never fully realized his potential.[20] After the stock market crash of 1929, in the wake of the Depression, and with the spread of Marxism in leftist intellectual circles, the *Menorah* group under Cohen moved from cultural pluralism and Jewish humanism toward revolutionary internationalism and Marxian socialism.[21] This increased politicization and radicalization (especially by Cohen, Solow, and Morrow), as well as the anti-Zionist viewpoint expressed by Solow and others, led to a split with editor Henry Hurwitz. In 1931, Cohen and Solow resigned from the *Menorah Journal* and were followed by Trilling, Morrow, and others.

Although Hurwitz considered the *Menorah Journal* to be dedicated to "destructive criticism" and a diversity of perspectives, the more polemical, younger generation considered him to show a lack of tolerance for opposing viewpoints and a concession to the more establishment, bourgeois position of the *Journal* donors and the growing Jewish Reform movement.[22] The Jewish Reform movement differed from the *Menorah Journal* point of view in identifying Judaism as primarily a religious movement. It also took a pro-Zionist and antiassimilationist perspective, considering Jewish identity as separate from American identity and supporting the establishment of a Jewish state.[23] Elliot Cohen went on to become founder and editor of *Commentary* (1945–59), a liberal, anti-Communist magazine devoted to Jewish political, social, and cultural issues; Herbert Solow followed the trajectory of many leftist intellectuals, from radical Marxism to anti-Stalinism and Trotsky sympathizer (he helped organize the Dewey Commission inquiry into the charges made against Leon Trotsky during the Moscow Trials in 1937), to a break with radicalism after World War II, when he became an editor at Henry Luce's *Fortune* magazine.

With Slesinger's increasing estrangement from Solow personally and politically, she broke with the *Menorah Journal* group in 1932 after their divorce. She continued to write fiction and publish in the *Menorah Journal*, *Scribner's Magazine*, *Story*, *Mercury*, and *Modern Quarterly*, among others. Her breakthrough novel, *The Unpossessed* (1934), was followed by her collection of stories, *Time: The Present* (1935). Slesinger was considered a literary success with a sharp wit in the tradition of Dorothy Parker and a modernist sensibility that was compared to that of Katherine Mansfield or Virginia Woolf. Some scholars speculate that her divorce was precipitated by her relative success as well as Solow's sullen temper, his absorption in radical Marxist ideology, and his pressuring her to have an abortion, which she later fictionalized. Trilling also considered Slesinger to be estranged from Solow's polemical and radical brand of politics. In a later letter to Slesinger's son, Peter Davis, Trilling characterized her as maintaining an ironic distance from radical politics: "She certainly never made any avowal, and there was always a discernable detachment in her attitude, even an irony.

She was not in the least an ideological person and eventually, I believe, she came to feel that [Solow's] particular ideology was a kind of bullying, from which she undertook to escape."[24] In the 1960s, Michale Blanfort similarly identified in Slesinger a certain sensitivity and aversion to the political infighting of 1930s radicals: "Tess Slesinger was profoundly dismayed and sickened by the political breaking across the days of our lives. It is difficult today . . . to understand how bloody and cruel were the internecine wars of the '30s among the Stalinists, Trotskyists, Lovestoneites, et al. . . . The wars were catastrophic enough to cause sensitive artists like Tess Slesinger to run away from them, from New York, and even from writing itself."[25] This characterization of Slesinger in gendered terms as overly sensitive belies the fact that she wrote a scathing satire of leftist intellectuals shortly before her departure from the scene.

Slesinger chose to leave the world of New York intellectuals and move to Hollywood in 1935 to become a screenwriter; there she was offered a salary of $1,000 per week by MGM's Irving Thalberg.[26] While the intellectual purists of New York City might have seen Slesinger's move as "selling out," she was in good company; Dorothy Parker, Robert Benchley, and F. Scott Fitzgerald were among the literary heavyweights who were transplanted to Hollywood, albeit with ambivalence and some disdain. In Hollywood, Slesinger found personal and financial stability, marrying MGM producer Frank Davis, with whom she had two children and collaborated on a number of successful screenplays. These included adaptations of Pearl S. Buck's *The Good Earth* (1937) and Betty Smith's *A Tree Grows in Brooklyn* (1945), directed by Elia Kazan, for which she and Davis won an Academy Award for Best Adapted Screenplay.[27] She remained politically engaged in advocating for workers' rights while in Hollywood, joining the Screen Writer's Guild and becoming an officer in the Motion Picture Guild. She also supported the Popular Front attack on the Dewey Commission (1937), which her ex-husband Solow had helped initiate, and joined the Communist-supported Anti-Nazi League and the Communist-initiated Third American Writers Congress. Like many other fellow-traveling liberal writers and artists, she became disillusioned with the Communist Party after the Moscow Trials (1936–38) and the Hitler-Stalin Pact (1939).[28] (Her son later defended her against accusations of her being a Stalinist sympathizer.) She was working on a satire of Hollywood, parts of which have been published as "A Hollywood Gallery," when she died in 1945 at the age of thirty-nine of cancer.[29] *The Unpossessed*, which is somewhat ironically dedicated to "my contemporaries," can be seen as a satiric and at times sympathetic farewell to the 1930s leftist intellectual scene surrounding the *Menorah Journal* and an interrogation of the conflicted role of the New Woman in navigating modern, urban culture.

The figure of the New Woman shifted from what can be seen as the first-generation progressive New Women of the late nineteenth century, who were social reformers and suffragettes focused on legal and economic equality for women, to the second-generation, radical New Women of the 1910s and '20s, associated with the bohemian radicals of Greenwich Village and defined by the sexual freedom and personal independence that accompanied the advent of birth control and the passage of the Nineteenth Amendment in 1920, giving women the right to vote.[30] The focus of the New Woman on free love as the key to liberation can be seen as limiting in that it "still defined women in terms of men even while celebrating their erotic powers, . . . [which] ultimately worked to undermine the fight for women's economic, intellectual, and political equality" through legal and social reform.[31] As portrayals of the modern, independent woman by such writers as Slesinger and Mary McCarthy convey, many were conflicted between the traditional values of marriage and motherhood instilled by their mothers' generation and the false promise of sexual and personal freedom. The association of women's liberation with power and autonomy—to beat a man at his own game—further reinscribes essentialist notions of gender difference.

The figure of the New Woman was commodified in the popular image of the flapper, as embodied by the Gibson Girl and represented in middlebrow magazines like *Vanity Fair, Life,* and *Harper's Weekly.* In Slesinger's autobiographical essay "Memoirs of an Ex-Flapper" (1934), she takes a self-ironic look at the performative rebellion of the flapper and her own complicity as an Upper West Side New Yorker of privileged background in the 1920s. The title "Ex-Flapper" suggests her later distancing from what was a stage of adolescent rebellion for herself and metaphorically for a country that was sobered by the economic hardship and social dislocation of the 1929 stock market crash and the Depression that followed. The flappers became a self-conscious product of media and consumer culture, to which they felt a need to conform: "We were growing restless," says Slesinger. "We had a public now, and our public demanded something of us. We read about ourselves constantly in newspapers and magazines. . . . By the world disapproved and of that world disapproving, we learned that we were a wild crowd, and we had to make good our legend." While there is a degree of pathos in Slesinger's self-portrayal of the flapper, there is an overarching ironic awareness of the superficiality and self-indulgence of a class of bourgeois adolescent youth at a time of increasing poverty and suffering, or the diminishing life of "Private School Children in a rapidly strengthening Public School World."[32] In the 1930s, the struggle for sexual freedom and personal autonomy were subordinated to more pressing issues, including unemployment and poverty at home and the rise of fascism abroad.

Slesinger's novel, *The Unpossessed: A Novel of the Thirties* (1934), offers a gendered critique of the ineffectuality of radical intellectuals and the discontent of the modern, liberated woman through its use of satire and irony. While Slesinger exposes the inadequacy of the false dichotomy between masculine and feminine behavior, reason and emotion, public and private, and mind and body, her use of gendered language and stereotypes can also be seen as partially reinscribing the gendered binaries that she seeks to dismantle. Although the novel is set in a particular time and place—New York City surrounding the *Menorah Journal* in the early 1930s—it provides a more broad-based social commentary on human behavior and social interactions in relation to abstract ideology and belief.

The object of Slesinger's satire is based loosely on the intellectuals associated with the *Menorah Journal* group with whom she was associated, both as wife of Assistant Editor Herbert Solow and as a contributor of fiction to the magazine. More specifically, the character of Bruno Leonard has been identified with Managing Editor Elliot Cohen, Miles Flinders and Margaret Flinders are associated with Herbert Solow and Slesinger herself, and Jeffrey Leonard has been associated with Max Eastman, who was a 1920s Greenwich Village intellectual associated with the Marxist *Masses* magazine but was peripherally connected with the *Menorah Journal* and known for his good looks and womanizing behavior. Lionel Trilling refutes Murray Kempton's suggestion that he may serve as a model for Jeffrey Leonard. His wife, the cultural critic Diana Trilling, further claims in her autobiography that the character of Jeffrey Leonard is based on the Hollywood screenwriter Melvin Levy.[33]

Lionel Trilling identifies in Slesinger's "satiric enterprise" a certain restrained aggression, personally against her ex-husband, Herbert Solow, and ideologically against the leftist radicalism of the *Menorah Journal* group. "If there was anger in it, there was no hatred and no malice," he observes, "as I believe, she had not lost her affection for those whom she was judging and from whom she was separating herself."[34] Trilling's assessment is supported by Slesinger's cryptic and somewhat ironic dedication "to my contemporaries." Diana Trilling makes a telling observation that, in separating herself from Solow and the *Menorah Journal* group with her departure for Hollywood, Slesinger "freed herself from what, in her view, [Cohen and Solow] represented in denial of direct feeling and even of biology."[35] It is this repudiation of human emotion and physical connection in pursuit of abstract ideas that is the ultimate cause of the failure of the intellectuals to found a radical magazine and of the breakdown of their personal relationships.

The lasting contribution of Tess Slesinger's novel is that it is more than just a novel of the 1930s. It is what has been termed a "socialist feminist novel" in that it breaks downs the false division between womb and world to present a dual narrative focused around the interrelationship between ideological sterility and emotional/biological impotence. By focusing on female as well as male intellectuals, it subverts traditional gender expectations as well as conventions of modernist and social realist fiction. As Ronnie Grinberg observes in her essay "Neither 'Sissy' Boys nor Patrician Man: New York Intellectuals and the Construction of American Jewish Masculinity," many of the New York (Jewish) male intellectuals assume traditionally "feminine" traits in their focus on cerebral acuity over physical strength and in their sensitivity and passivity. The women intellectuals presented by Slesinger (and later by Mary McCarthy) can also be seen as more androgynous in their display of traditionally "masculine" characteristics of sharp wit and intellect, sexual freedom, and personal autonomy. These progressive women, however, are caught in a double bind, in that they are considered outsiders in the predominantly male world of New York intellectuals, yet they are alienated from the traditionally "female" world of marriage and motherhood. This dual marginalization of the female artist/intellectual can lead to a sense of discontent and alienation typical of the modernist "lost generation."[36]

By using modernist techniques of stream of consciousness, multiple narration, and free indirect narration, Slesinger subverts conventions of social realism typical of proletariat literature and creates a psychological socialist novel. Thus, the focus on communal betterment of proletarian fiction shifts to the inner, psychological struggle and alienation of individual characters. Through the satiric portrayal of character and situation, Slesinger mounts a critique of radical intellectual politics, the constraints of traditional genders roles, and the literary conventions of social realist and modernist fiction. Slesinger's novel was criticized for her interest in so-called women's issues of marriage, motherhood, and female sexuality, as well as her modernist, experimental style, at a time when social realism and issues of class struggle were considered of paramount importance.

As the title of Slesinger's novel suggests, *The Unpossessed* is the story of a group of intellectuals who are uninspired, who are not "possessed," in the positive sense of the word, by an idea or purpose. Or, rather, they are so consumed by an idea in the abstract that they fail to put it into action. As Lionel Trilling observes in his influential 1966 essay "Young in the Thirties," the title "makes reference to Dostoevsky's great novel about radicalism, *The Possessed*"; however, Slesinger's novel ironically implies "that of not being in the service of some great impersonal vital intention."[37] Slesinger uses the word "possessed" in the additional sense of a woman's being "possessed" by a man, and in so doing, she directs her satire at both the public and private failure of the intellectual to consummate his passions. The men of the novel are unable to give themselves fully to a woman sexually, emotionally, or, in what is considered the ultimate concession to bourgeois life, by having children. There is a disjunction in Slesinger's novel between intellectual abstraction and human experience, between idealism and reality, between the imagination and life itself.

Slesinger's novel is about sexual politics, for the conflict between the pursuit of ideas and the reality of experience is often expressed in gendered terms. The novel is organized around three male-female relationships: Miles and Margaret Flinders, Bruno and Elizabeth Leonard, and Jeffrey and Norah Blake. The three male characters are deemed the old "triumvirate," a group of former radical college classmates who seek to revive their ideological ardor with the formation of a leftist intellectual magazine (which significantly remains unnamed). The female characters dramatize the dis-ease felt by the modern, liberated woman in trying to reconcile her sexual freedom with her lack of fulfillment.

While the central action of the plot is organized around the attempted formation of the Magazine, the novel is framed by the intensely personal drama surrounding the relationship between Miles and Margaret Flinders and the decision to abort their baby. The unborn child thus becomes a metaphor for the aborted attempt to form a Magazine, reflecting on the sterility of the intellectuals in both their personal and professional lives. The conflict between the "masculine" pursuit of abstract ideas to the exclusion of feeling and the "feminine" desire for domestic bliss is parodied in the relationship between Miles and Margaret Flinders. Miles, an Irishman of New England descent, was raised with a paralyzing sense of puritanical morality and guilt. Miles resists what he considers the feminine, maternal influence of his wife, Margaret, whose "amoeba-motherly" sensuality and comfort threaten to weaken and consume him. Though Margaret is an urban, educated woman and an agnostic ("She'd had a good malicious wit before she was a wife," Slesinger wryly observes), she was raised to believe that she needs a man to complete her, and she naively asserts the possibility of domestic bliss.[38] "Her message is that we can be 'happy together,'" says Miles with disgust, adding "(my Uncle Daniel used to say his *pigs* were 'happy')" (20). We learn that Miles was traumatized in his youth by watching his primary male authority figure, Uncle Daniel, shoot his dog, the one thing he loved, as retribution for his dog killing the neighbors' chickens. Thus, the young Miles comes to associate love with suffering and denial of happiness—just one instance of the way Slesinger at once invokes and parodies the modern "science" of psychoanalysis. In this time of intellectual progress and sexual liberation, Margaret nonetheless longs for the domestic comfort and human connection of being a wife and mother. The dispute between Margaret and Miles becomes the false dichotomy of womb versus world, as Slesinger reveals the necessity of one in order to have the other. The Marxist idealist Miles views having children as an expression of domestic, bourgeois life that threatens his intellectual freedom, a belief that paradoxically undermines the personal connection and feeling necessary to realize his intellectual ideals.

Slesinger's satire of intellectual passivity reaches its fullest expression with the character of Bruno Leonard. A Jewish English professor and former radical who now teaches at the university he attended (possibly Columbia University?), Bruno is paralyzed in his life and work in pursuit of an abstract ideal. For twelve years, he had been planning a leftist magazine, but when confronted with the actuality of a filing cabinet ordered by Jeffrey Blake, signaling the realization of their plan, Bruno is reduced to self-reflection and self-doubt. He contrasts himself with Jeffrey, a man of action without thought, who was "still at thirty-odd, plunging headlong into whatever offered itself" (33), be it a relationship or a project, while Bruno, a man of superior intellect, was paralyzed by hyperconsciousness. The result is that Jeffrey, who had no idea in his head, had written seven (mediocre) novels. While Bruno, a man of sophisticated ideas and contradictions, says the narrator ironically, "must content himself or not content himself with the knowledge that if he never wrote a book it would still be a better book than any written by his colleague Jeffrey Blake" (34).

Bruno's hyperconsciousness becomes an excuse for avoiding personal relationships, as Slesinger psychologizes the dysfunction of the intellectual.

While Jeffrey plunges into experience—be it the writing of a novel, the taking of a wife, or the pursuit of a lover—Bruno remains unmarried and unpossessed. Instead, he pins his concept of love on an abstract ideal, on a self-created female double of himself, his younger cousin Elizabeth. Bruno is also presented as having frustrated desire for his homosexual student and protégé, Emmett Middleton, portrayed as the weak and effeminate son of the patrons of the incipient Magazine. Elizabeth and Emmett thus become strange compatriots in their love and admiration for their unattainable mentor. Bruno and Elizabeth's relationship is one of "love without lust," a marriage of minds, which, by filial connection, can never be consummated or tainted. Bruno teaches Elizabeth, "You've got to be free, my dear, free as a man, you must play the man's game and beat him at it. . . . Don't get possessed, cruise around kid, see what it's about; listen to me, Elizabeth, I'll make a man of you yet!" (131). With this highly gendered language, Slesinger at once invokes and satirizes the false binary between masculine and feminine behavior, equating sexual freedom and emotional detachment with the male rotter. The result, however, is a life of fast-paced yearning without fulfillment for the modern American woman, who performs the role of intellectual autonomy and sexual liberation at great personal cost.

Slesinger is most brilliant in satirizing the plight of the freethinking, free-loving New Woman on the "fast express" to nowhere, using modernist techniques of stream of consciousness and free indirect narration in the mind of Elizabeth Leonard:

Chain drinker, chain smoker, chain lover, chain rover. . . . Life is the longest distance between two points my good man (even on board my fast express, my rollicking jittery fast express, my twentieth century sex-express). . . . Home is where you hang your hat and drop your skirt. . . . I speak the universal language, the twentieth-century snappy dead language, of no-love loving, of lust without love, I belong anywhere and nowhere. . . . The lady is lost, the lady has boarded the fast express, all aboard ladies and gay modern gents. . . . All aboard the twentieth century unlimited, hell-bent for nowhere, the non-stop through express. (127–32)

Elizabeth displays the 1920s Jazz Age excess and indulgence that masks a sense of alienation of the postwar "lost generation." An expatriate artist who uses the excess of drink and sex to avoid feeling and to escape the meaninglessness of postwar life, Elizabeth is reminiscent of the characters of modernist writers like Hemingway and Fitzgerald. She employs the fragmented, stream-of-consciousness style of writers like Virginia Woolf, William Faulkner, and James Joyce to express a sense of dislocation and loss.

There are strong parallels between Elizabeth Leonard and Margaret Sargent, the autobiographical heroine of Mary McCarthy's stories like "The Man in the Brooks Brothers Shirt" or "Portrait of the Intellectual as a Yale Man," whose intellectual superiority and sexual freedom leave her alienated from herself and others. Elizabeth's litany of men reads like McCarthy's own in her intellectual memoir, *How I Grew*. Free love of the modern woman results in hardening of emotion that finds expression in a sharp wit as a defense against feeling: "My wit is like a razor-blade," declares Elizabeth. "I use it to wound before I can be wounded" (137). Bruno laments having turned Elizabeth into a hardened "traveling salesman," in endless pursuit of "lust without love" (284). The solution for Slesinger is not in a return to traditional gender hierarchies but rather a mutual expression of authentic feeling and vulnerability in both sexes that allows for genuine human connection.

The hardening of feeling of the modern woman masks the repressed anger and aggression that comes out through sarcasm and wit. Without Bruno's blessing to get married, Elizabeth leaves her lover and returns to the US, sharpening her wit and her "hard-boiled" exterior to avoid the pain of authentic emotion. The dialogue is split between her interior genuine thoughts and her unspoken or deliberately hurtful speech:

> "O, it's snowing and maybe this is love and I don't want to leave you," she could not help not saying again not not once but not numberless times as she ran about the room looking for stockings without holes. . . . "Elizabeth, I love you," he did not cry out. . . . "Don't leave me, don't go!" he did not dare to cry after her for he knew she was a girl who craved tenderness so deeply that when it was given her she was smothered and must shake it off to emerge slick like a seal from water. (103–4)

The proliferation of negatives accentuates the negation of thought and action of these modern lovers, whose true feelings remain unspoken. Elizabeth is conflicted in her freedom and suppresses her longing for the traditional domestic life: "'I could learn to mend, I could learn to cook,' she did not call to him. . . . 'I would be your wife,' she did not murmur as she turned and held her breast to the stinging icicles" of the shower (103). Her true feelings remain unspoken, and the cold, sharp barbs of the shower become a metaphor for her icy exterior. Instead of exposing her "feminine" vulnerability, Elizabeth sharpens her aggressive, "masculine" wit: "You're just a parenthesis, darling, in life's long dreary sentence" (110), she proclaims indifferently, meanwhile burying her sobbing eyes in the bed out of her lover's sight. This dual narrative poignantly expresses the ambivalence of the New Woman's search for identity and fulfillment in a shifting social landscape.

Through the figures of Jeffrey and Norah Blake, Slesinger satirizes the egotistical, ineffectual intellectual and the subordinate, self-doubting wife. If Miles and Bruno are paralyzed by the intellectual's curse of skepticism and overanalysis, the more conventional Jeffrey Blake acts without thought, both in his work and in his relationships. His Don Juanism, however, hides a deep-seated insecurity, as evidenced by his constant need to return to the maternal reassurance of his simple, devoted wife, Norah. Among the most comic scenes in the book are Jeffrey's scripted attempts at seduction of Margaret Flinders, of the bourgeois Magazine patron Merle Middleton, and of the purported Socialist revolutionary Comrade Ruthie Fisher. Jeffrey becomes a kind of prostitute in his willingness to sell his body in the service of seemingly antithetical causes. He becomes a parody of the seducer, as we learn that he is more interested in the pursuit than in consummation of his conquests. His repeated stock phrase, "I am something of a lone wolf" (66), makes a mockery of his actions, as it becomes apparent that "he is trying, at bottom, to seduce himself!" (67). Jeffrey is ultimately as ineffectual in his sexual conquests as in his intellectual ones, and he returns repeatedly to the safe harbor of his faithful and forgiving wife, Norah.

Through the character of Norah Blake, Slesinger satirizes the limitations of the self-effacing, subordinate wife who denies her independent identity in service to an undeserving husband. Norah, who is the only character not to receive her own titled chapter in the novel, is an outsider among the circle of intellectuals and progressive New Women in the text. Norah internalizes sexist assumptions about intellect in expressing her own self-doubt: "She was not clever like the rest, like Margaret, who although she was a woman often entered conversation with the men" (88). A throwback to an earlier generation of women, Norah was significantly raised on a farm in the Midwest, where she was trained "to respect the rooster" (305). Norah is described as a "placid harbour" (76) to which the wandering Jeffrey safely returns. Jeffrey objectifies and (de)values her for what he sees as her simple, animal-like nature: "Like a contented cow she looked, he thought. . . . She was always there and always his" (92). Bruno Leonard sees Norah's submissiveness in even more condescending terms: "Like a blissful deaf mute. She walked among them, offering friendship skillfully distilled: friendship in a bottle—tempered by her own dumb warmth" (78). She is further described by Bruno as standing "like an obedient animal in the circle of his arm" (78) and, again, sitting on his knee "utterly pliable, utterly acquiescent, like a female animal being stroked . . . and sure that in the same dumb, kindly, acquiescent way, she would let him make love to her" (81). The objectification and devaluing of women to the point of indifference and even disgust exposes the ongoing sexism and fallacy of free love for women in the modern age.

The men of the Magazine reduce women to their biological, reproductive function in presenting a false dichotomy of womb versus world. Their exaggerated language and personal inadequacy create a parody of the ineffectual male intellectual. "The point about a woman," theorizes Bruno, "the salient point . . . is her womb" (95). Jeffrey proudly adopts this gendered synecdoche, seeing Norah as embodying the ultimate female principle: "By and large the better the woman the bigger the womb," thought Jeffrey. "And Norah's, he thought, proud, affectionate, must be the size of Jonah's whale" (95). While Jeffrey seems to take pride in Norah's female form, the image of Jonah, who was swallowed by the whale, implies that he fears being engulfed by her feminine, nurturing self. There is also a certain irony in these women being defined by their wombs, when the sterile, male intellectuals refuse on principle or in practice to impregnate them. Jeffrey sees himself as the child to Norah's comforting maternal instincts: "A lovely, brown—a great big comfortable home-like womb, a one-room womb; with room for me" (96), he thinks happily. Miles is more overtly hostile to the female procreative function as represented by the womb, a foreshadowing of the split between him and his wife over having children: "He eyed Margaret with resentment; covertly, with suspicion. A womb (unpleasant thought!). She had never told him she possessed one. Was that where women went and sat, to brood, to count their injuries? Miles vaguely hated her" (95). Margaret tentatively identifies the male sense of inadequacy and jealousy at the root of their resistance to female procreation: "'I think,' said Margaret slowly, 'that that's what men are scared of—what they haven't got. . . . They resent it,' she said courageously" (95).

Through a satiric use of free, indirect narration, Slesinger dramatizes the inner conflict of the New Woman, who is caught in a double bind between her independent and maternal impulses: "My God, said Margaret

Flinders to Margaret Banner-that-was; we are sterile; we are too horribly girlish for our age, too mannish (with our cigarettes, our jobs, our drying lips) for our sex. . . . O Economic-Independence Votes-for-Women Sex-Equality! You've relieved us of our screens and embroidery hoops. Our babies and our vertigo; and given us—a cigarette; a pencil in our hair" (93). The symbols of equality and independence of the New Woman seem inadequate for Margaret when faced with the denial of the traditional right to bear children. Margaret's futile question to Norah, "Why don't we have children?" (93), is echoed in the chapter title, "Why Can't We Have a Magazine?," in the parallel narratives of the thwarted magazine and the aborted pregnancy of Miles and Margaret. Margaret's countdown of the months until the magazine's publication—"March, April, May, thought Margaret . . . June, July . . . why, it might be in August!" (99)—parallels the monthly countdown to the impending birth of her baby. But the ominous signs of failure are in the air for both.

The central action of the novel revolves around the planning of the leftist magazine in the chapter "The Inquest" and the fundraising event for the Communist Party–affiliated magazine ironically titled "The Party." The inadequacy of Bruno Leonard as intellectual leader of the Magazine is exposed through exaggeration, ridicule, and laughter as the founders' radical idealism is disconnected from the engaged action of the student Communist sympathizers. The student activist group's name, the "Black Sheep," implies that they are alienated from society. It is, however, the older generation of radical intellectuals who prove to be truly alienated from the Marxist idealism that they profess and from the common workers whom they seek to defend. The former radical intellectual triumvirate—Bruno Leonard, Miles Flinders, and Jeffrey Blake—are forced to compromise the mission of their Magazine to the left and the right, by including the Black Sheep and by seeking funding from the bourgeois patron Merle Middleton. At "the Inquest," Bruno's disquisition on "philosophic truth, artistic integrity, open forum" (210) is disrupted by the harsh reality of economic inequality when Cornelia, one of the Black Sheep, faints of hunger. The irony is not lost on Bruno, who reflects on the absurdity of the intellectual, removed in his abstraction from his subject: "It seemed to him suddenly that he and his friends were ridiculous, doctors who had passed examinations in a correspondence course; that when suddenly they were faced with a suffering patient, the patient had more concrete knowledge than they, for all their learning. . . . Their bodies (his own numb) were paralyzed by this sudden failure of their minds" (212). Cornelia's fainting precipitates the ending of the meeting to plan the Magazine, as the entire project is reduced to a comic spectacle: "The whole thing, the meeting, the Magazine, this roomful of ghosts, his own whole life, seemed to Bruno farce" (212–13). Slesinger here satirizes the inadequacy of the intellectuals' aspirations as well as the failure of Bruno Leonard as the hypercritical, Jewish intellectual.

The anticlimactic climax of the novel comes with Merle Middleton's Hunger March Party and Magazine fundraiser. Born of the unseemly union between the womanizing artist cum pseudo-Marxist intellectual Jeffrey Blake and the wealthy patron Merle Middleton, the Magazine has an inauspicious beginning. The Party for Hunger Marchers, complete with champagne, caviar, a black-tie crowd, a society band, and a designer cake shaped like the Capitol Building in Washington is a parody of the hypocrisy of the bourgeois intellectual in his pursuit of Marxist ideals. When a drunken Bruno Leonard belatedly arrives at the party to deliver his manifesto, he is interrupted by the entrance of Emily Fancher, "our first prison-widow" (317), who "courageously" makes a public appearance after her husband has been imprisoned for embezzlement ("the rich have their troubles too," one sympathetic onlooker observes; 320). Bruno's speech is further mocked when he opens the envelope containing the manifesto and it showers like confetti into a thousand pieces, the product of Emmett's jealousy and rage, causing a contagious wave of laughter to spread across the room. What starts as nervous laughter becomes a widespread communal laughter, both as a form of mockery and as a means of coping with the absurdity of the situation. The laughter reaches an uncontrollable crescendo as a kind of catharsis, relieving the built-up tension of the meeting of opposites that is the Magazine and Hunger March cocktail party: "The laughter was enormous. Laugh collided with laugh; echoed; doubled; crashed; shrilled; shrieked; held its breath and burst again; and held its breath once more and waited, tittering, to be relieved" (324). The laughter is here personified as a kind of socially inappropriate guest, seeking in vain to contain its recognition of the incongruity between the seriousness of the manifesto and the comic absurdity of the confetti speech. Bruno tries to make a self-deprecating joke to contain and control the laughter—"'pardon my dandruff,' he bellowed"—but the crowd "screamed" and "roared" in response (324). The group laughter creates a sense of solidarity among the guests and serves to further alienate Bruno, the object of the laughter.

Bruno delivers an impromptu speech in which he mocks himself and the hypocrisy of his fellow intellectuals in pursuit of their specious, radical ideals: "Our party is of the intellectuals, by the intellectuals, and naturally against them, . . . the only anti-progress program, . . . outcasts, miscasts, professional expatriates. . . . We have no parents and we can have no offspring; we have no sex: we are mules. . . . In short we are bastards, foundlings, phonys, the unpossessed and unpossessing of the world" (325–27). Slesinger significantly uses the term "unpossessed" not only in the ideological sense of not being possessed by an idea but also in personal terms of not being possessed by a relationship and hence not being able to produce any children or lasting works. The intellectuals are described as being alienated from their cause, their relationships, and themselves, without a history or a future, in the ultimate expression of impotence. The young radical activists leave the party in disgust and disappointment to join the actual Hunger March in Washington, and even Bruno's protégé, Emmett, climbs the stairs to his room like a sulking child. Slesinger here satirizes the folly of the intellectual in his fruitless pursuit of ideas, yet there is a poignant note of sympathy for a world of New York intellectuals with whom she was intimately connected, both ideologically and personally.

The public failure of the Magazine is echoed in the private breakdown of the marriage of Miles and Margaret Flinders with the termination of her pregnancy. The coda to the novel is a chapter titled "Missis Flinders," which was originally published separately as one of the first widely circulated stories on the subject of abortion. While abortion narratives are often presented as sites of resistance and tend to revolve around a woman's choice to have an abortion as subversion of the traditional role of motherhood, Slesinger here uses a woman's unwanted abortion as an act of submission to a patriarchal authority that considers parenthood to be an expression of bourgeois, domestic life to be avoided. Other female leftist narratives of the 1920s and '30s—such as Josephine Herbst's *Money for Love* (1929) and Margery Latimer's *This Is My Body* (1930)—similarly follow what can be seen as an inverted abortion narrative of submission rather than resistance. These modern abortion narratives help raise consciousness about reproductive rights as a political and legal debate and draw attention to issues of racial, class, and gender inequality concerning access and quality of care.[39] Slesinger's abortion tale can nonetheless be seen as subversive in its satiric treatment of the limited and self-destructive viewpoint of the emotionally vacant intellectual who is threatened by the prospect of parenthood. As the magazine fails to come to fruition, so the pregnancy of Margaret Flinders comes to an artificial end. For these Marxist intellectuals, parenthood is seen as a bourgeois concession to concerns with material security. Or, at least according to Slesinger's satiric indictment, this was the ideological pretext that unfeeling, chauvinistic intellectuals used to avoid the financial and personal cost of parenting on philosophical grounds.

Lionel Trilling explains in his recollection "Young in the Thirties":

> The intellectuals of the Twenties and Thirties were likely to assume that there was an irreconcilable contradiction between babies and the good life. The fear of pregnancy was omnipresent, and it was not uncommon for young married couples to have a first pregnancy aborted not because they were so very poor but because they were not yet "ready" to have the child. . . . Men were generally presumed not to want children, intellectual men thought of them as "biological traps," being quite certain that they must lead to compromise with, or capitulation to, the forces of convention. There was also the belief that it was wrong to bring children into so bad a world. And quite apart from all practical and moral concerns, the imagination of parenthood was not easily available, or it worked only to propose an absurdity, an image that was at essential odds with that of the free and intelligent person.[40]

While the leftist, male intellectuals of Slesinger's novel echo Trilling's sentiment regarding having children, the women in her fiction present a far more embattled stance, and Slesinger's own choice to leave New York, remarry in Los Angeles, and have two children speaks for itself. Slesinger resisted such stereotypes of parenthood as concession to the bourgeois life, and on the contrary, she exposed the alienation of the intellectual from life in its most fundamental expression as the creation of a life or having children.

In "Missis Flinders," Miles Flinders expresses the intellectual rationalization against having children in his typical unfeeling, New England manner: "We'd go soft," he argues, "we'd go bourgeois" (345). "They would go soft," translates Margaret Flinders. "They might slump and start liking people" (345). Again, the couple express the conflict between what is seen as "feminine" feeling and search for happiness and "masculine" intellect and retreat into ideas. After the failure of the party and of the Magazine, Miles tries to take the moral high ground: "In a regime like this . . . it is a terrible thing to have a baby—it means the end of independent thought and the turning of everything into a scheme for making money" (349). Behind Miles's appeal to principles and his reduction of everything, even marriage, to materialism, Margaret detects a fear, "maybe, of a personal life?" (346). The sterile, intellectual world is contrasted with the fecund everyday world. On the taxi ride back to the couple's Greenwich Village apartment after

Margaret's abortion, she envies the scenes of procreation and family life that overtake the workaday Fourteenth Street: "Down Fourteenth Street they would go . . . while on the sidewalks streamed the people unlike any other people in the world, drawn from every country, from every stratum, carrying babies (the real thing, with pinched anemic faces) and parcels (imitation finery priced low in the glittering stores)" (354).

Reproduction is the great equalizer, as people propagate regardless of class. Margaret expresses a sense of social superiority as she contrasts the unthinking will of "common," immigrant folks to reproduce with the willful decision of the educated classes not to reproduce: "These are the people not afraid to perpetuate themselves (forbidden to stop, indeed) and they will go on and on until the bottom of the world is filled with them; and suddenly there will be enough of them to combine their wild-eyed notions and take over the world to suit themselves. While I, while I and my Miles, with our good clear heads will one day go spinning out of the world and leave nothing behind, . . . only diplomas crumbling in the museums" (354). The literally crumbling diplomas of the educated elite stand in stark contrast to the teeming life among the workaday world. Reproduction as a choice raises the issue of social inequality in access to abortion: wealthier, predominantly white populations have limited access in the 1930s to "therapeutic" abortions, while less advantaged populations have no choice in matters of reproductive rights.

Slesinger takes a more sympathetic view in her portrayal of immigrant populations, showing the humanity of the Flinderses' working-class, Italian neighbor, Mrs. Salvemini, a mother of multiple children, who detects Margaret's pregnancy before she even sees a doctor and offers words of encouragement and support. The German-immigrant taxi driver Mr. Strite also shows his kindness to Margaret on her return trip from the hospital, driving with care and taking a piece of fruit she offers "for luck," presumably in hopes of her getting pregnant again. He, like the other mothers in the hospital who view Margaret as a "funny one," cannot seem to conceive of an intentional termination of pregnancy. As a poignant metaphor for the Flinderses' unborn child, Margaret leaves the hospital with a half-eaten basket of fruit that Miles had sent her out of guilt for pressuring her to have an abortion. Though she resisted her mother's outmoded belief that a man completes a woman, she had turned to Miles in vain to complete her: "Hurt and hurt this man. . . . He is a man and could have made you a woman," she repeats. She concludes, "He was no man: he was a dried-up intellectual husk; he was sterile; empty and hollow as she was"

(248). In Slesinger's use of gendered language and her differentiation of traditional gender roles, she is considered by some critics to be "conservative." However, her presentation of the conflicted identity of the modern woman and the validity of multiple expressions of gender identity—from wife and mother to free lover and independent intellectual—anticipate more contemporary modes of feminism moving beyond a single definition of womanhood. For Margaret, like Slesinger, being a modern woman of intellect does not necessitate a refusal of life, of maternal instincts, and the possibility of domestic happiness. By forcing an opposition between thinking and feeling, between art and life, Slesinger implies through her satiric lens that the 1930s leftist intellectual is relegated to an "unpossessed" life without living.

The publication of *The Unpossessed* was met with overwhelmingly positive reviews, with praise for her "keen mind and cutting wit," "fine satire," "sheer genius," and "poetic insight and wisdom."[41] Where reviewers found Slesinger's novel lacking, however, was in its perceived lack of realism in its portrayal of the radical politics of the day, as well as its purported sentimental representation of "women's issues" of marriage, childbearing, and female sexuality. As Lionel Trilling notes, Murray Kempton, among others, considered it a "document" of 1930s radical intellectuals that he criticized for its lack of accuracy.[42] In what was to become the preface to the 1966 reissue of the novel, Trilling notes that the focus of some reviewers on political accuracy presumes that the novel is a roman à clef intended to portray a particular time and place, namely, the *Menorah Journal* group in the early 1930s. He warns, "As a document of its time, *The Unpossessed* must be used with caution. The characters practice a deception upon themselves when they think of themselves as being political, and that this deception is to be viewed with satiric irony. The situation thus proposed is interesting in itself and it might well be thought to throw some light on the way people act or on the way certain people acted at a certain time. But it does not throw light on the actual group of which some of its members were, as Mr. Kempton infers, the prototypes of the novels' characters."[43] (Trilling may have been in part defending his own reputation in that he was falsely associated by Kempton with the character of Bruno Leonard.) As Mary McCarthy said of her satire of radical intellectuals of the 1940s, *The Oasis* (1949), "What I really do is take real plums and put them in an imaginary cake."[44] Slesinger can similarly be seen as creating a composite of real-life characters put in a fictional frame. The purpose of such satire is less about personal revenge or malice and more about social observation and critique, which has both historical relevance and timeless value.

Beyond historical accuracy, early reviewers faulted Slesinger for not writing a conventional 1930s novel of social protest in the current style of social realism. In a contemporaneous review in the *Menorah Journal*, the leftist intellectual Edwin Seaver criticizes Slesinger for not "giv[ing] a complete picture of the revolutionary intellectual front." Though he admits that this might not have been her intention, he argues, "The author has an obligation beyond the novel, and . . . in a time of crisis . . . like the present these obligations are paramount."[45] This is part of a larger debate in the 1930s and '40s about the aesthetic versus ideological function of art, for which Slesinger was unjustly critiqued. In a 1934 review in the Marxist *New Masses*, the Marxist turned anti-Stalinist intellectual Philip Rahv attacks Slesinger for "a certain psychological spite," saying that the object of her satire is "a special little sub-grouping of hyper-sophisticates," while she overlooks those radicalized intellectuals "who have ceased straddling the fence."[46] In a 1975 interview, the New York intellectual Sidney Hook criticizes Slesinger for her focus on personal psychology rather than serious matters of politics, of which he considered her to be ignorant: "She never understood a word about the political discussions that raged around her. . . . Her book shows that. There is no coherent presentation of any political idea in it. . . . Tess caught the psychological mood of some of Herbert's friends, but she was a political innocent until the day of her death."[47] Irving Howe similarly claims that novelists like Slesinger and Mary McCarthy "cannot focus upon politics long and steadily enough to allow it to develop according to its inner rhythms. . . . Personalizing everything they could not quite do justice to the life of politics in its own right."[48] But it is precisely this melding of the personal and the political that distinguishes Slesinger's (and McCarthy's) writing and subverts conventional gender expectations of both the modernist novel of the 1920s and the social realist novels of the 1930s. It was not until the women's movement of the 1970s, with its renewed appreciation for the distinctive style and subject matter of lesser- known women writers like Slesinger, that literary critics and the reading public could redefine Slesinger's novel as a successful work of socialist feminism rather than a failed example of proletarian realism.

In 1984, Slesinger's novel was reprinted by the Feminist Press with an introduction by Alice Kessler-Harris and Paul Lauter and an afterword by Janet Sharistanian, reframing the novel as a satire of sexual politics and applying to it the feminist motto "the personal is political." These works—along with Paula Rabinowitz's groundbreaking study *Labor and Desire: Women's Revolutionary Fiction in Depression America* (1991), Rita Felski's *The Gender of Modernity* (1995), and more contemporary criticism on the New Woman and urban spaces by Catherine Rottenberg and Meredith Goldsmith—interrogate the masculinist tendencies of 1920s literary modernism and 1930s social realism in order to reclaim a space for works like *The Unpossessed* that do not fit neatly into preexisting gendered categories.[49] Slesinger subverts the false dichotomy between male and female, public and private, urban and domestic, reason and emotion, intellect and feeling, sense and sensibility, and professional and personal by showing the necessity to meld public engagement and private feeling regardless of gender. It is precisely the failure of the leftist intellectuals of the 1930s to engage in personal emotion in their exclusive pursuit of radical ideology that leads to their failure to put their ideas into action and their ultimate alienation both in work and in love. The object of Slesinger's satire is not primarily the male intellectuals in their attempt to start a radical magazine (as early, primarily male critics contended) but the gendered limitations of a certain group of modern men and women in the 1930s in their struggle to find self-efficacy in life and in love.

While Slesinger is best known for her satire of New York intellectuals in *The Unpossessed* (1934), her lesser-known stories from *Time: The Present* (1935)—reprinted and expanded as *On Being Told That Her Second Husband Has Taken His First Lover and Other Stories* (1962)—use satire and irony to expose issues of gender, class, and racial inequality through a modernist lens. A compilation of stories previously published in *Scribner's*, *Story*, the *Forum*, *Vanity Fair*, *Redbook*, and *American Mercury* in the 1930s, Slesinger's short story collection met with critical and popular success following the publication of her widely acclaimed first novel. While being set in "the present" moment of the Depression-era US in the 1930s, Slesinger's stories balance the personal with the political by exploring issues of class and social injustice through the psychology of individual characters. Slesinger is at the intersection of public and private, of traditionally masculine and feminine discourse and themes; she breaks down these boundaries and shows the dangers of these splits to the efficacy of both emotional and intellectual life. This focus on sexual politics—on personal relations of men and women in the context of socialist fiction—is at once a point of distinction and contention for critics of Slesinger.

Like her predecessor Dorothy Parker and her successor Mary McCarthy, Slesinger uses her marginalized identity as a woman intellectual to gain the satiric perspective to critique the world of New York society and left-ist intellectual circles to which she partially belongs. Despite Slesinger's personal connection with Parker—they both moved from New York to Los Angeles to pursue screenwriting and were in similar social circles—she resisted the limitations of such literary comparisons: "I don't want to snap into Dorothy Parker's girdle," she quipped in a 1935 interview.[50] Some of Slesinger's stories employ the double-voiced irony and inner mono-logue similar to that of Parker's autobiographical stories like "The Waltz," "The Garter," and "But the One on the Right." And the socialist message of many of her stories resembles some of the more socially conscious stories of Parker dealing with racial discrimination ("Arrangement in Black and White") and class inequity ("Soldiers of the Republic").

Slesinger has also been compared with Mary McCarthy, who satirizes the ineffectuality of New York intellectuals and the conflicted role of the woman intellectual in post–World War II America. The most common comparison is between Slesinger's satire based on the *Menorah Journal* intellectuals of the 1930s in *The Unpossessed* and McCarthy's satiric roman à clef of the *Partisan Review* intellectuals Philip Rahv and Dwight Macdon-ald in their attempt to form a libertarian socialist community in the 1940s in *The Oasis* (1949). Like Slesinger, McCarthy is noted for combining the personal with the ideological in her treatment of so-called female subjects of female sexuality, male-female relations, abortion, contraception, and free love. While both authors have been criticized for writing from the privi-leged perspective of the New York educated elite, their use of satire exposes the hypocrisy of progressive intellectuals, and Slesinger in particular is noted for her class consciousness. Lionel Trilling considers Slesinger to be less aggressive and more congenial than McCarthy, which he somewhat chauvinistically attributes to what he considers Slesinger's more fragile temperament.[51] According to Rabinowitz, Slesinger and McCarthy express the "doubly alienated" role of the female intellectual who is not seen as polit-ically serious and "cannot reclaim her maternal identity."[52] Slesinger takes on issues of class and race as well as gender alienation in her satire of New York high society, as well as the struggles of working-class and minority populations in the Depression-era US.

Slesinger's short stories can be divided into the more personal satire of traditional gender roles and the conflicted identity of the modern, liber-ated woman, including "On Being Told That Her Second Husband Has Taken His First Lover" and "Mother to Dinner," and the more political and social satire of class and race relations in the 1930s in such works as

"The Mouse-trap," "The Friedmans' Annie," "Jobs in the Sky," and "White on Black." The titular story of Slesinger's reprinted collection, "On Being Told That Her Second Husband Has Taken His First Lover" (1935), is a satire on the hypocrisy of modern love. The female speaker's voice is split between the direct address of "you" and the third-person "she," reminiscent of Dorothy Parker's double-voiced narrative. The tone is sarcastic and ironic as the superior-minded, modern woman finds herself in the subordinate role of the jilted lover. The speaker, Mrs. Dill Graham, née Cornelia North, is split between her social self, who performs the traditional role of the devoted wife, and her authentic self, who recognizes the injustice of the situation and the social bind of the liberated woman. The speaker in this modern love story is jaded, having already suffered infidelity in her first marriage and being told that her second husband has taken "his first lover," the implication being that the pattern will repeat itself. The second time, the speaker sarcastically reassures the reader, is not as severe or shocking as the first time, though it hurts nonetheless. To feign indifference even for this modern woman seems disingenuous: "There's something cheap in painlessness, something too modern-generationish," she observes.[53] The speaker is self-conscious of her own use of wit and cleverness as a defense mechanism: "So it's nice my dear, that you are always so clever; and sad my dear that you always need to be. . . . Pretty nice to be so clever, Cornelia my gal, pretty sad too" (3). Cornelia establishes an informality and intimacy with her jilted self while also universalizing the experience. Her superior intellect and rationality are irrelevant in the battle of the sexes, where the gender roles and outcomes are predetermined: "Implacable logic comes and sits in your head. Your associative processes, like your wits, are functioning brilliantly, you are intensely, even thrillingly alive with the tingling call to battle in all your veins. . . . Oh, you could talk about the thing, in Proustian vein, forever. Show him where he was weak, analyze his emotions for him, tear him to pieces like a female lion" (4). This woman intellectual recognizes that "you cannot handle these things as though you were giving a lecture course" (4); matters of the heart cannot be resolved with the head.

Cornelia's aggression and insight, however, are misplaced, as her cheating husband seeks reassurances, not challenges, to his male authority. Her husband, Dill, seems a brutish simpleton beside her quick wit, much like the male suitors in Parker's fiction. He passively asks whether she is "through" with him and "what are you going to do?" though he insists with an outmoded double standard that she not cheat in kind. "Anything, but no gents," he demands (and demeans); "I don't know why but it's different with a man," he chauvinistically repeats (10). Cornelia copes with this blatant injustice in typical sardonic fashion, comparing her state of infidelity with a preexisting medical condition about which there is no use complaining: "He has the gall to ask you whether you feel 'through' with him now. No, you answer. . . . I'm not one to look back now that I know I've always had t.b. and say God how I have always suffered" (5–6). Again, she turns to humor as a means of coping, yet it masks her underlying hurt and powerlessness. "At the moment I have no desire but to keep my head above water and say funny things" (6), she assures her husband when he asks her intentions going forward. She recalls how at the moment she caught her husband at a party with another woman, she told a joke as a public display of strength before privately vomiting in the bathroom: "Just before being sick in the bathroom you managed a hearty laugh and said, 'O dear Lord, it looks so funny when you're not doing it yourself!'" (6).

Cornelia is aware of the dangers of overthinking and rationalizing her husband's behavior: "If he loves the real you he cannot *love* anybody else; and if, on the other hand, it is not the real you," then it was not love in the first place (7). She resists modern, unfeeling love without consequences: "No, that's painless dentistry again, remote control, the Machine Age and the reflex, the Modern Generation. . . . God send me pain again. God let me feel" (9). Humor and wit are the modern woman's antidote to feeling and acknowledging the pain and injustice of gender exploitation. But she longs to feel and to connect rather than assume this defensive posture. The modern world of free love without consequence necessitates an ironic outlook to stave off the hurt: "Impossible, clearly, to speak without lilting; try a drop of pallid humor first thing in the morning, nothing like it to aid digestion, avoid those infidelity blues, that early-morning tremolo" (9–10). A good joke can at least temporarily stave off the impulse to vomit at her lover's infidelity. But the joke, Slesinger implies, is on the "liberated" woman, who is expected to take her lover's transgression in stride but longs for a more committed relationship.

The double bind of free love for the New Woman is highlighted by Dill's insistence that she not take a lover—"no gents," he repeats. While he benefited from sexual liberation by her "compliance" with him on the first night, he brands her a "bum" and "a bastard" for cheating with him on her first husband (as revenge for her first husband's infidelity) and wants reassurances that she will not do the same to him. She is aware of the double standard of his benefiting from her sexual freedom but insisting on her "staying home and waiting for him" (12). Cornelia recognizes that he wants to assume the traditional role of the male savior and wonders if she should "let him have the joy of reforming [her], of capturing what was free and keeping it in the cage, of owning what used to belong to nobody" (11). She feigns indifference and fidelity: "'nothing is different, why should it be,' you say gayly," like "a fine English play," a "suave English comedy" (12). But her situation is no laughing matter, and when she sees him dressing in his fine spring suit and bow tie and rushing his first cup of coffee, she knows that he is having an affair. The knock on the door is not her returning husband but instead the laundry man, a painful reminder of the subordinate, domestic role of the modern woman, despite her apparent intellectual and sexual freedom.

One of Slesinger's first and most autobiographical stories, "Mother to Dinner" (1929), is a psychological portrayal of newlywed Katherine Jastrow née Benjamin's conflict between her unfeeling, rational husband (who resembles Herbert Solow) and her sentimental, at times overbearing mother. While it can be seen as a coming-of-age narrative of a young woman separating from her mother and finding heterosexual love in marriage, the story highlights the differences and limitations of traditional gender roles in its satiric portrayal of both mother and husband. The autobiographically based Katherine Benjamin is conflicted between her mature, intellectual self and her more domestic, "bourgeois" self, which she identifies with her mother and the generations of women who preceded her. In preparing to host her parents for dinner, Katherine confronts a literal and metaphorical storm between her past (as a dutiful daughter) and her future (as a modern wife). Katherine is overcome with bouts of loneliness and depression as she leaves the nurturing, if controlling, home of her mother for life with her clever but unfeeling and unsupportive husband. The split is exacerbated by the insistence of her husband, Gerald A. Jastrow, that she separate from her mother and his mocking condescension toward his mother-in-law and his wife's resemblance to her.

The protagonist is divided between her two loves (and aspects of herself) and would sooner die than have to choose between them. "Like a human shuttle she wove her way between these two, between Gerald and her mother, the two opposites who supported her web. (Why couldn't they both leave her alone?) When she was with her mother she could not rest, for she thought continually of the beacon of Gerald's intelligence, which must be protected from her mother's sullying incomprehension. And when she was with Gerald her heart ached for her deserted mother, she longed for her large enveloping sympathy in which to hide away from Gerald's too-clear gaze" (98–99). She feels guilt for laughing at Gerald's mockery of her mother, "balancing her stout body" to "navigate like a boat" (97). Upon returning from her honeymoon, Katherine is conflicted between feeling guilty for abandoning her mother and a desire to share all of the details with her. This portrait of the unfeeling, self-absorbed male intellectual in contrast with the more sentimental, domestically inclined female is elaborated in the relationship between Miles and Margaret Flinders and throughout *The Unpossessed*. Amid Katherine's storm of feeling and divided loyalty, she imagines her mother and her husband struck by lightning and is reduced to "passionate tears" (114). The story ends with the doorbell ringing and Katherine paralyzed by uncertainty: "Was it her mother, or was it Gerald? Which, in the midst of storm, did she want it to be?" (115). As she slowly opens the door handle, "she wished that one of them, Gerald or her mother, were dead" (116). Slesinger's mother was reportedly insulted at her negative portrayal as an overbearing, stout, and simple figure, but the story was well received for its psychological insight and its satiric edge and prepared the way for more in-depth exploration of women's roles in modern-day relationships.

Slesinger is noted for her treatment of socialist themes in a modernist style, and the majority of her stories use satire to expose class, race, and gender inequality while maintaining a more personal, psychological perspective. "Jobs in the Sky" (1934) is among Slesinger's social protest stories that expose job insecurity and social hierarchy in Depression-era New York City. Set at the M&J department store during the Christmas season, the story satirizes the hypocrisy of the department store manager, Mr. Marvell, whose magnanimous Christmas spirit masks his self-interested, capitalistic focus on profit. Marvell's universe is an illusion built on dreams at the expense of workers, who compete with one another to meet sales quotas and keep their jobs at a time of economic distress. The title is a reference to the song "The Preacher and the Slave" or "Pie in the Sky" (Joe Hill, 1911), a parody of the Salvation Army hymn adopted ironically by the Industrial Workers of the World (IWW), or Wobblies. The original refrain, "Work and pray, live on hay, there'll be pie in the sky by and by," is discredited in the Wobblies' ironic observation, "You'll get pie in the sky when you die (That's a lie!)." The line is modified by one of the young workers of Slesinger's story to "Work and pray, live on hay, there'll be jobs in the sky by and by" (157). Like the elusive wealth or "pie in the sky," jobs for the unemployed are an illusion perpetuated by the people in power to keep wages low and hours long.

The employees, who were formerly among the "army of the unemployed," are designated by number, like disposable parts in the commercial machine. Among the workers is Joey Andrews (No. 191-23, 167B), a young, temporary worker who is recruited during the Christmas rush and is misled to believe that his efforts will be rewarded with a possible full-time position. He ironically describes himself as one of the "Washington Square gang," who was homeless and living in the "grass hotel" of Washington Square Park before landing this department store job. "Dad said I'd meet swell fellows in New York, but he didn't think I'd find 'em on a park bench" (152), Joey ironically observes. When he learns that his coworker Miss Paley, a retired schoolteacher, will be let go, he distances himself from her, "as if she has been touched for him with some infectious germ" (147). This divide-and-conquer strategy is used to pit worker against worker in a competitive race to keep their jobs in a precarious market.

Mr. Marvell, the department store owner, is presented as a parody of the hypocritical wealthy, Jewish merchant who hails from exclusive Westchester, New York. He gives his "Christmas speech" to rally his employees about having a "spaycial responsibility toward your countray, your fellowmen the femilay of M&J" and how department stores contribute to "the good cheer of this heppy holiday come rich and poor alike gifts for his loved ones differences forgotten all men are equal at Christmas" (149). His fragmented speech, lack of punctuation, and Yiddish inflection indicate his own likely immigrant origins. His speech ends with a rousing call to action, a kind of sloganeering and salesmanship that promises false hope in these dire times: "KEEP ON YOUR TOES ALL DAY OUR PROFIT IS YOUR PROFIT IT MAY BE THAT YOU CAN WIN YOURSELF A PERMANENT POSITION" (159).

Joey embraces the challenge and is exhilarated by the prospect of useful work and helping others. There is an impersonality about the Christmas shopping season and a sense of social determinism. Customers are reduced to a "frenzied herd of cattle" (154) stampeding the lobby as the opening bell rings, and the workers are like automatons in a giant machine: "Feet were like rubber tires now. Bodies were conveyors of books. Minds were adding machines" (163–64). But the most disturbing force is the "invisible electric wires" of the rumor mill, signaling the next in line to be terminated: "Six hat-girls are going to be dropped, three of them old employees, three of them just taken on for the Christmas rush. They don't tell them . . . until the last minute—so they'll keep on selling to the end" (164). When Joey is fired despite making his sales quota, Slesinger emphasizes the injustice and inhumanity of the corporate machine in the Depression-era US.

In another 1934 story, "The Mouse-trap," Slesinger exposes the exploitation and manipulation of workers at an advertising agency. Set in the swanky Fifth Avenue office of Bender, Inc., Advertisements during the Depression, the "mousetrap" set by the employees to protect an individual worker from being fired is turned against the group to collectively ensnare them. Slesinger's characters are reduced to satirical types to convey her moral message. Peter Bender is the classist, sexist advertising executive who gets a sadistic thrill from asserting his authority over his struggling workers. Betty Carlisle is the attractive, unwitting secretary from good midwestern stock who defers to her boss in the false hope of marrying him and bettering her station, only to discover that she is equally dispensable. Mildred Curtis is the social activist and left-wing organizer who seeks to unite the workers in solidarity against the firing of one of the more vulnerable of their rank. Gracie is the young, easily intimidated worker who is subject to the exploitation and manipulation of management. Each character plays their role in the somewhat predictable and disheartening mouse-trap charade of management-worker relations in Depression-era New York City.

When Mildred Curtis, the activist stenographer, learns of the vulnerable "telephone girl" Gracie being let go, she tries to organize a walkout, setting the "mousetrap" for the boss. Betty Carlisle, the loyal secretary from Topeka, Kansas, informs Mr. Bender of a suspected plot among the workers to unite against him. Bender gets a sadistic thrill from turning the trap on his subordinates. "Some people were just born to be mice" (192), he says with a sense of entitlement. "We'll catch the mice in their own trap. . . . I'm going to put on one swell show—and then we'll make whoopie tonight in celebration" (198), he tells Betty excitedly. Slesinger uses exaggeration to expose Bender's deep-seated sense of social superiority and his sexist and classist behavior. He relishes the fight against people he sees as subordinates: "I get rather a kick out of it, to tell you the truth; I like having something to buck. Reminds me of the good old days at college when we went out strike-breaking and had the time of our lives with the scabs' daughters" (198). As the workers are pitted against one another to secure their jobs, so Betty turns against her fellow workers in hopes of securing her own future, blind to the fact that Bender is merely using her for his own pleasure.

Bender takes a divide-and-conquer strategy, requiring each of his employees to meet with him separately to negotiate their terms of employment. He assumes a tone of mocking condescension in opposing their walkout: "Strike! He said, almost baby-talking it, kidding it, turning it round in his mouth like a teething-ring and sticking it between his teeth to show he didn't fear it" (204). The analogy to baby talk and a "teething-ring" reinforces his patriarchal authority over the powerless workers, who are infantilized and disenfranchised. The heartless boss further manipulates his workers by exposing their personal weaknesses and publicly humiliating them. He reminds the most vulnerable errand boys, Jasper and Willy, of their need for employment and deference: "Jasper, your dad is living on city relief, I think? And your mother is having another baby, Willy?" (206).

The boss uses humor as a way of asserting authority and creating an in-group and out-group that further alienates specific workers. He mocks Gracie for causing a stir about her job loss: "Why my God, my dear gal, last week I got socked as hell in the market, but you don't see me picketing Wall Street, do you?" (211). He belittles her with mocking laughter at his own joke, which spreads uncontrollably among the employees. Bender "laughed easily, and then harder, and then allowed himself to shake with his laughter as though he couldn't control it. Betty Carlisle joined in, as heartily as refinement would permit, pretty soon Miss Pierce was laughing too, and Dickinson started coughing till you couldn't tell whether he was laughing or clearing his throat" (211). This display of contagious laughter reinforces Bender's authority and alienates and humiliates the vulnerable Gracie. He further bullies the receptionist and plays on her guilt in causing a walkout: "You don't want all your friends to lose their jobs on account of you, do you, Gracie?" (211), he cajoles, as he reminds her of her responsibility to her sister, who is partially dependent on her. Gracie caves under the pressure, striking Mildred Curtis across the jaw with her displaced frustration and aggression, effectively ending the strike.

Bender relishes in his triumph over his workers in a display of sadistic glee: "Oh my God, I haven't had such a good time since the War!" he tells Betty, and his patriarchal power play quickly channels into masculine, sexual aggression. "Come and kiss papa, honey, quick!" (221–22). He kisses her "with a new and violent passion," and though she is drawn to his appeal of wealth and power—the "scent of his expensive shaving lotion mingling with his country-club tweeds" (222)—she is stopped by her sense of midwestern morality. "No, no, no," she objects, but he persists until she could no longer talk, in an attempted rape (224). "Betty Carlisle, who had never let the Kansas boys take liberties with her, had let the boss take the final liberty with her on the evening of the day they had settled the strike together" (225). Slesinger, however, adds a comic reversal, whereby the sturdy midwestern woman, aided by the forces of nature, ultimately succeeds in repelling her boss's advances. As he attempts to shut the door, a forceful wind, which "seemed to come from the prairies of Kansas," "would develop a sense of humor and fling it back in his face" (226). He becomes the object of ridicule as she laughs at him, fighting back the wind "like a puny giant" (226).

Laughter here gives strength to the disempowered secretary as the roles in this power struggle are temporarily reversed. The weakened boss threatens Betty with the loss of her job if she leaves, but she overpowers him with her superior midwestern, working-class strength and morality: "Kicking and struggling she pitted her good basket-ball muscles against his tennis-and-golf-and-whisky wrists and gave him a kind of half-Nelson that her brothers had taught her in Topeka, before she realized she had lost her job and crept out and down the stairs like a mouse to catch the elevator from the eighteen floor" (227). Although she is caught in the mousetrap of losing her job, she has preserved her dignity and autonomy in this cat-and-mouse game. Thus, Slesinger satirically exposes the power relations between the sexes and the classes during this time of heightened economic insecurity and gender inequality in the US.

Slesinger's story "The Friedmans' Annie" (1930) uses satire and irony to expose the class discrimination of a wealthy, Jewish New York family in the treatment of its German-immigrant housekeeper, Annie Schlemmer. It anticipates Alice Childress's satire of racial and class exploitation of a domestic worker Like One of the Family (1953). The title, indicating possession and depersonalization of its protagonist, shows the widespread exploitation of domestic workers among the wealthy. The "Friedmans' Annie" is one of many domestic workers of wealthy Jewish families defined by their house of employment (the Allens' Bertha, the Goodkinds' Elsa, the Golds' Lisa), reinforcing the social hierarchy of New York society in the 1930s.

Annie considers herself fortunate to hold such secure and respectable employment, unaware of the ways in which her future and her identity are being compromised in the service of another. Even among domestic laborers, there is a kind of hierarchy, and Annie distinguishes herself from newly immigrated "greenhorns" like Elsa in her aspiration to follow the assimilated style and manner of her employer. Annie says she will never go back to Germany and her life on a farm: "Annie is an American now, she will never milk a cow again, New York is her home, and she wears high heels even with her uniform" (263). This sense of class consciousness ironically undermines her own aspirations for independence as she adopts the materialistic values and gendered hierarchy of modern, urban society. The white immigrant workers further display their racial prejudice within the social hierarchy. Another domestic worker, Bertha, tells Annie, "Will I ever forget your face, Annie the first time you saw a nigger—it was only poor old Albert, but you sure thought he was a devil out of hell" (262–63).

Mrs. Friedman exploits Annie's desire to be Americanized by convincing her to rebuff the marital advances of her German-immigrant boyfriend, the plumber Joe Schmidt, and to aspire toward financial independence through her continued employment with the Friedmans. Mr. Friedman shows no consideration for Annie's interest as he flirts with her and requests that she give up her night off (and date night with Joe) so that he and his son can keep their social plans while Mrs. Friedman entertains company. When Joe cautions Annie that she is being mistreated by the Friedmans—"what do they think you are anyway, a horse, do they think they own you?" (259)— she echoes Mrs. Friedman's charge that Joe is not wealthy or respectable enough to be her husband, thereby further undermining her relationship with him and ironically increasing her dependence on the Friedmans for employment. While Annie seeks to assimilate—"she cut off her hair, she bought herself silk stockings, she asked the Allens' Bertha to buy her powder and gloves" (270–71)—Joe has no illusions about social injustice in the US. Joe critiques the social inequality in the US, ironically revealing his own race and class prejudice: "There's a lot of Jews and rich people here the same as any other country and the people that have the money keep it" (271). Jealous of Annie's loyalty to the Friedmans, Joe lashes out with anti-Semitic slurs, describing Mrs. Friedman's sister wearing her long, black cape in winter as looking "like a beetle" and describing Mrs. Friedman as nothing "but a goddam Jew no more American than they were" (273). Slesinger here exposes the racism and discrimination across class lines in the fight for social equality and financial security.

Only Mrs. Friedman's daughter, Mildred, a leftist activist, defends Annie's rights and exposes her family's exploitation of their loyal servant. Mildred ironically describes Annie's servants' quarters "like a palace only a little more like a coffin with your toilet in a closet and your trunk hanging over your head on a shelf" (269). She encourages Annie to get married and have a home of her own and defends Annie's right not to work on her day off. Mildred is mocked by her brother for being a "Socialist" who spends time advocating for the rights of the unemployed and homeless down on Fourteenth Street. When Mrs. Friedman pressures her twenty-three-year-old daughter to get married, Mildred again defends the twenty-eight-year-old Annie's interest in marriage: "Why don't you advise

Annie to get married mother, you don't even have to find a man for her!" (289). When her mother balks at Mildred's comparison of herself with a servant, Mildred sarcastically retorts, "Oh my goodness, no, why Annie's *pretty*—and she's five years older!" (289).

Despite Mrs. Friedman's prejudice against Annie and her desire to keep her as her own servant rather than see her happily married, Annie fools herself into believing that Mrs. Friedman has her best interest at heart. "She told me only today I'm like one of the family," defends Annie to Joe, to which he sarcastically replies, "The one that does the work" (280). Annie realizes that she has cast the final insult on Joe as she echoes Mrs. Friedman's racist and classist language, saying, "You talk like an ignorant foreigner" (288). Her employer tries to compensate her with material goods, passing her old hats and other accoutrements onto her. "That's a pretty cheap trick," observes Mildred, who refuses to do her mother's "dirty work" (289). When Mrs. Friedman tells Annie to help herself to her old black hat, Annie realizes, "It was Mrs. F's old black hat alright, but there were a couple of loose black threads on the side where the flower had been" (290). Evidently Annie is not worthy of the fine floral decoration of her employer's station—like one of the family, indeed. Annie nonetheless accepts her place in the Friedmans' household with perhaps a heightened awareness of its limitations. Slesinger's story is particularly poignant not only for its exposure of the social prejudice among New York society against the immigrant domestic workers but for the bias and desperation among the workers themselves that further reinforce their oppression.

In "White on Black" (1931), which is reminiscent of Dorothy Parker's "Arrangement in Black and White" (1927), Slesinger satirically reveals the racial and class prejudice of the New York elite. Written from the retrospective first-person point of view of a wealthy, white student at an elite, "progressive" school on the West Side of Manhattan, the narrator reveals her unconscious bias despite her sympathetic inclination toward her Black classmates. Slesinger exposes the systemic racism in New York elite society by showing how the accepting elementary school students become increasingly prejudiced against their Black classmates and how the Black students internalize that racism, going from confident leaders to retiring and deferential outsiders.

As a student at a socially progressive private school on the West Side of Manhattan, which followed "not only the liberal practice of mixing rich and poor, Gentile and Jew, but made a point also of including Negroes" (173), the speaker reveals the disparity between her perceived tolerance and her unconscious bias through racist language and stereotypes. Among the well-scrubbed faces of the white students stood "an equally scrubbed black one sticking out like a solitary violet in a bed of primroses" (173), says the speaker, exoticizing and objectifying the Black students. She also sees the integration of Black students from the white student's perspective as having the intended effect of teaching the "well-bred little boys and girls at the least the untruth of the common slander that Negroes have an unpleasant odor" and of affirming the axiom "that all men were created equal" (173–74). She speculates on what has become of those Black students almost as a curiosity or social experiment: "Where are they now? Did they drift back to Harlem, those Wilsons and Washingtons and Whites? How do they look back upon their ten years' interlude with white children?" (174).

What follows is a satiric portrayal of the token Black siblings at her school, which reveals more about the prejudices of the white speaker than the actual experience of the Black students. The brother, Paul, is idealized and objectified as being "exquisitely made, his face chiseled and without fault; a pair of delicately dilated nostrils at the end of a short fine nose, and an aureole of dim black curls" (174). His sister, Elizabeth, fares worse, described as "bigger, coarser, more negroid; darker, her lips were thick, her nose less perfect; but still she was a beautiful child, luxuriously made, and promising to develop into a type of the voluptuous Negro woman at her best" (174). Elizabeth is judged negatively for having what are perceived as more "Negroid" features and is sexualized as becoming a "voluptuous Negro woman." Both children are stereotyped as being "marvelous athletes" and "born leaders" (175), with Elizabeth demeaned as being as "strong as a horse" and displaying "animal strength and fearlessness" (176). The teachers treat them with the extra care owing to a disadvantaged student, "which was always extended to Negro, or crippled, or poverty-stricken children" (175), as if race were a disability. Interestingly, the students value their Black classmates equally to, if not more than, their other classmates, and the eleven-year-old twins become "czars" of the secondary school. The speaker fantasizes about marrying Paul and sexualizes his Black, male body while he is stereotypically playing basketball, revealing "a few inches of coffee-colored skin glistening with sweat, which caused [the speaker] to gasp with delight" (177).

If these racial (and racist) stereotypes were not bad enough, the privileged, white students reveal an increasing prejudice under the influence of their parents and other adults as they grow older. Elizabeth's friends begin to diminish, and the parents of one girl who was particularly close to her transfer their daughter to a boarding school in the South, "rumor said to get her away from the black girl and teach her a proper sense of color" (184). As the siblings sense that they are being ostracized, they start to remove themselves, leaving immediately after school, and by the third year of high school, Paul has dropped out altogether. The white students make no effort to include their Black classmates and instead express relief at not having to confront their own part in their segregation: "We were, I suppose, faintly relieved, in so far as we thought about him at all" (185).

Elizabeth internalizes her white classmates' perception of her and starts to play a subordinate role: "On committees Elizabeth volunteered for unpleasant jobs and carried them out cheerfully and efficiently. She grew generous and sweet-tempered, and a little like a servant; and like a servant, she was thanked for her services and forgotten" (186). The speaker draws an analogy between her deferential Black classmate and a servant without irony, revealing her deep-seated sense of social superiority and racial bias. The speaker seems relatively untroubled by this change in social status of her Black classmates, and though she documents the experience, she does not voice any protest or disgust at the injustice of the situation. The final insult comes at the graduation dance, where Elizabeth is described as "looking rather too burly and black in the prescribed white dress" (186), and though her white classmates were "very nice to Elizabeth and even took down her address as a matter of form," they had no intention of staying in touch after graduation. In a moment of self-awareness, the speaker is overcome "with an overpowering sense of guilt to spare him embarrassment" when Paul returns to pick up his sister, and her eyes burn with tears at his downfall (188). There he stood, "their former god and leader," with his hat over his eyes in a mix of defiance and shame. "This should have been his graduation" (188), notes the speaker, with a poignant, if passing, recognition of the injustice of the situation. For Slesinger, who was socially engaged in fighting for rights for workers, women, and minorities throughout her career, this story is an indictment of the systemic racism and class bias of the self-righteous New York elite. With her particular blend of social consciousness, feminist perspective, modernist literary form, and psychological characterization, Tess Slesinger integrates the personal with the political to satirize the limitations of class, gender, and racial hierarchies in the US in the 1930s.

Jessie Redmon Fauset, the Harlem Renaissance, and the Racial and Gender Politics of Humor

4.

In "The Gift of Laughter," the Harlem Renaissance writer Jessie Redmon Fauset expresses the paradoxical doubleness of African American humor, which originates in the suffering of slavery yet can be seen as a source of resistance and overcoming: "The remarkable thing about this gift of ours is that it has its rise, I am convinced, in the very woes which beset us. Just as a person driven by sorrow may finally go into an orgy of laughter, just so an oppressed and too hard driven people breaks into compensating laughter and merriment. It is our emotional salvation."[1] Here Fauset introduces the concept of laughter as a coping mechanism, as a means of overcoming the suffering of racial oppression, as well as a kind of release or relief of anger and aggression. While Fauset served as literary editor of *The Crisis*, the cultural journal of the newly founded National Association for the Advancement of Colored People (NAACP), from 1919 to 1926, she went beyond her perceived role as one of the "midwives" of the New Negro movement.[2] She was a pioneering female humorist of the Harlem Renaissance and one of its most crucial voices. It is past time to reassess Jessie Redmon Fauset's fiction, which has historically been cast into the sentimental fiction genre, largely due to her gender. Fauset, who had a thorough understanding of African American humor equal to her peers, employs irony to subvert the sentimental romance genre with which she has been associated and satire to challenge gender and racial stereotypes of the time. In so doing, Fauset participates in the ethical project of using humor as an indirect form of social protest in combating social injustices suffered by women and minorities during the Harlem Renaissance.

In Fauset's best-known work, *Plum Bun* (1928), she invokes stereotypes of the New Woman, the New Negro, and the New Negro Woman to show at once their value and their limitations in defining Black female subjectivity. She further challenges conventional narratives of marriage and passing of the New Negro Woman in Harlem in the 1920s. At the time of publication of the novel and in the years following, *Plum Bun* was largely misread as a bourgeois, female novel in the sentimental tradition. This may be in part due to the gentility and education of an elite class of Harlem Renaissance female writers like Fauset as well as the New Negro emphasis on bourgeois respectability at a time when modernist experimentation and challenging of social norms were in vogue. Some proponents of the New Negro project of racial uplift, like W. E. B. Du Bois, praised Fauset for what they perceived as her shift away from the popular representation of Black primitivism and the underclass toward more bourgeois respectability.[3] But even Alain Locke, who valued her contribution to the New Negro movement, ultimately criticized her for being "too mid-Victorian for moving power today" and said that her "point of view falls into the sentimental hazard."[4] Of the contemporaneous critics, only William Stanley Braithwaite recognized an ironic complexity to her writing and praised her writing as "both a tragedy and a comedy of manners" and as showing a "passionate sympathy and understanding of [African Americans'] ironic position in the flimsy web of American civilization."[5] Fauset was misread retrospectively by fellow Harlem Renaissance writer Claude McKay in the 1930s as "prim and dainty as a primrose," with her novels "quite as fastidious and precious," and by Richard Wright in the 1940s as being among "the prim and decorous ambassadors who went a-begging to white America, dressed in knee pants of servility, curtsying to show the Negro was not inferior."[6] More recent critics question the bourgeois sentimental and romantic interpretation of her work and identify a double-voiced irony and satiric bent to her writing. In this chapter, I explore further how Fauset subtly employs the tools of irony and satire to challenge the conventions of the marriage and passing plots. More importantly, I show how the novel uses the socially acceptable form of laughter to expose the limitations of racial and gender expectations of putatively progressive movements of the time.

In "The Gift of Laughter," Fauset anticipates some of the current debates concerning racial representation through humor and its subversive potential. Originally published as "The Symbolism of Bert Williams" in *The Crisis* (1922) and retitled as part of Alain Locke's influential collection *The New Negro* (1925), Fauset's essay addresses the ironic position of the Black "funny man," as embodied in the minstrel performance of Bert Williams, in bringing the "gift of laughter" to white audiences who have been the source of sadness and suffering through the history of slavery and racial oppression. There is further irony in that Bert Williams, a Bahamian-born stage actor, had to learn the dialect and gestures attributed to southern Blacks, thereby wearing the mask of blackface to hide his own educated, cosmopolitan identity. Thus, Williams's racial performance obscured the complexity and authenticity of Black identity and was a source of sadness and anger for the performer and for those whom he impersonated. Fauset quotes fellow comedian W. C. Fields as saying about Bert Williams, "[He was] the funniest man I ever saw and the saddest man I ever knew." "The gift of laughter in this case," observes Fauset, "had its source in a wounded heart and in bleeding sensibilities."[7] For Fauset, this disparity between the man and his performed identity, as well as the shared understanding of the Black audience, is at the root of understanding the ironic double message of African American satire. There is a danger, however, that white audiences will take the buffoonish caricature at face value, thereby reinforcing the racist stereotype. The final irony, Fauset argues, is that the laughter instilled by Black minstrel performers can in some way be seen as a gift, in that it potentially leads to what Fauset sees as more serious, substantial opportunities for theatrical performances, like the contemporary Broadway musicals *Shuffle Along* (1921), *Liza* (1922), and *Runnin' Wild* (1923). What underlies Fauset's discussion of African American humor is an awareness of the ironic power of laughter and its ethical purpose in expressing the underlying melancholy and rage, which exposes the racist stereotypes and social injustice that it exploits.

Fauset's fellow Harlem Renaissance writer Langston Hughes similarly situates the joy of Black laughter—like the blues, spirituals, and other forms of "folk" expression—in the sorrow and pain of slavery and racial injustice. In "The Negro Artist and the Racial Mountain," Hughes describes the "incongruous humor" of the Black artist, "that so often, as in the Blues, becomes ironic laughter mixed with tears," which intersects with jazz music as "a revolt against weariness in a white world, . . . the tom-tom of joy and laughter, and pain swallowed in a smile."[8] Theorists of African American humor take laughter as a coping mechanism a step further by emphasizing the subversive and revolutionary nature of minority humor and of

Black satire in particular. In Darryl Dickson-Carr's seminal study *African-American Satire: The Sacredly Profane Novel* (2001), he identifies the primary purpose of satire as social critique and traces the subversive double message of Black satire back to the subjugation of slavery. "As the literary genre whose primary purpose is to criticize through humor, irony, caricature, and parody," observes Dickson-Carr, "satire is nothing if it does not aggressively defy the status quo." This revolutionary agenda had to be hidden or masked due to the historical realities of racial and gender hierarchies, notes Dickson-Carr, leading to "complex coded languages" by subjugated peoples and "indirect expression of their frustration" through such modes as irony and satire.[9]

Building on Hughes's concept of laughing sad (to keep from crying), Bambi Haggins introduces the idea of "laughing mad," seeing laughter as an expression of anger and a tool for social justice.[10] Danielle Fuentes Morgan further elaborates on Hughes's notion of laughter as a coping mechanism to situate Black satire as a means of survival, expressing sublimated anger but also building community. Black satire further expresses self-identity by exposing and defying the racist essentialism inherent in racial stereotypes. By exposing the absurdity and ridiculousness of racial stereotypes through their ironic invocation, argues Morgan, Black satire enables the questioning of those stereotypes and opens the way to express a more authentic, "multitudinous nature of Black identity," which she terms "kaleidoscopic Blackness." Black satire can thus be seen as an ethical project in that it "moves us toward social justice, or at least toward considering what social justice might look like."[11]

Humor by African American writers and African American women writers in particular has until recently been largely overlooked and undervalued. Dickson-Carr attributes this neglect in part to an assumption about representation that reinforces racist stereotypes as well as to the formal emphasis on satire as a traditionally conservative genre, dating back to Northrop Frye and Henri Bergson's theory of humor as a social corrective or preserver of the status quo.[12] The neglect of African American *women's* satire can be seen as part of the larger resistance to women's humor as aggressive, at times explicit, and "unfeminine." "To put it bluntly," says Dickson-Carr, "readers and critics—often male—seldom expect a woman author to produce satire in any sustained, written form. Satire's tendency to employ aggressive forms of irony tends to be gendered male, a skill afforded those expected to go for the jugular, whether writing in a surgically precise rhetorical mode, or in the type of content to be included."[13]

Satire, as a targeted expression of anger in the interest of social reform, is seen predominantly as the domain of white, heterosexual men. Building on Jessyka Finley's observation that "comic soap boxing has been, for the most part, unavailable to black women in the mass media and in political discourse," Rebecca Krefting notes that "satire has long been the province of men and it has been difficult for women, especially women of color, to deploy it without penalty, in part owing to the angry nature of satire."[14] This brings us back to the resistance to women's humor and false assumptions about gendered behavior, most notably the belief that women, and minority women in particular, should not speak up or out against the status quo. "When women use humor as social critique, it gets labeled as 'angry' and 'humorless,'" observes Krefting, "which means that men's anger counts as humor while women's anger counts as anger."[15] By expanding our understanding of women's humor and satire in particular, we can push the boundaries of what can be said and heard in the hopes of instigating social change.

In order to explore the contribution of Jessie Fauset and female humorists of the Harlem Renaissance, it is important to establish the context of time and place: Harlem and New York in the 1920s and '30s. New York became the nexus for conflicting gender and racial identities of the New Woman, the New Negro, and the New Negro Woman. The Great Migration of African Americans from the South to northern and midwestern urban centers like New York and Chicago beginning in 1915 was spurred by the rise of oppressive Jim Crow laws, as well as Ku Klux Klan vigilantism, a downturn in southern agriculture, and expanding opportunities in the manufacturing centers in the North and Midwest. There were deliberate efforts to advance issues of racial equality and social justice and to cultivate a distinctive African American arts movement by prominent intellectuals like W. E. B. Du Bois with the founding of the NAACP (1909) and its cultural journal, *The Crisis* (1910). *The Crisis* joined *The Messenger*, *The Crusader*, and *Opportunity*, among others, as organs of Black social and political advocacy and cultural expression. As literary editor of *The Crisis* from 1919 to 1926, Fauset was responsible for fostering the careers of Langston Hughes, Jean Toomer, Countee Cullen, Claude McKay, Nella Larsen, and Gwendolyn Bennett, among others. She further hosted an informal salon of predominantly Black writers, artists, and musicians at her apartment on 142nd Street in Harlem, which she shared with her sister Helen Lanning.[16] Despite her own literary distinction, Fauset was identified by fellow Harlem Renaissance writer Langston Hughes as one of the "midwives" of the New Negro movement.[17] She spent many decades trying to overcome the reputation of "literary midwife" to establish her own reputation as one of the Harlem Renaissance's most influential novelists and critics.

The Harlem Renaissance movement and the designation of the New Negro were sustained by prominent intellectuals like Alain Locke, whose anthology *The New Negro* (1925) collected works of art, literature, and culture by upcoming figures like Langston Hughes, Countee Cullen, Claude McKay, and Jean Toomer, as well as established writers and thinkers like W. E. B. Du Bois, James Weldon Johnson, and Walter White and the archivist Arthur A. Schomburg. It included a limited number of works by African American women writers such as Zora Neale Hurston and Jessie Fauset. The anthology was an outgrowth of a special issue of the *Survey Graphic* dedicated to the arts in Harlem, guest edited by Alain Locke, which arose from a gathering of prominent Black artists, writers, and intellectuals as well as several prominent Black and white publishers in New York at the Civic Club in 1924.[18] As Arnold Rampersad observes, while the purported occasion was to honor the publication of Jessie Fauset's first novel, *There Is Confusion* (1924), Alain Locke took the opportunity to promote the New Negro movement and persuaded editor Paul Kellogg to feature a special edition of the *Survey Graphic* devoted to the arts in Harlem, which was later reprinted as *The New Negro* (1925).[19] Rampersad, among others, critiques how Jessie Fauset, a woman writer and editor, was sidelined not only on the occasion of her first book publication but also in not receiving proper credit as a prolific writer of the period and as an influential editor who shaped the literary taste of the times.

Despite the racial progress and opportunity that the Harlem Renaissance and the New Negro movement offered, African American women were subordinated in their quest for racial and gender equality and artistic autonomy. The New Negro Woman was expected to participate in the project of racial uplift of the New Negro movement through the institution of marriage and the cultivation of the role of "race mother." The July 1923 issue of *The Messenger*, designated the "New Negro Woman's Number," outlines her task of racial betterment and support of the New Negro Manhood movement:

The New Negro Woman, with her head erect and spirit undaunted, is resolutely marching forward, ever conscious of her historic and noble mission of doing her bit toward the liberation of her people in particular and the human race in general. Upon her shoulders rests the big task to create and keep alive, in the breast of black men, a holy and consuming passion to break with the slave traditions of the past; to spurn and overcome the fatal, insidious inferiority complex of the present; . . . and to fight . . . for the attainment of the stature of a *full man*, a free race and a new world.[20]

Thus, the New Negro Woman was expected to subordinate her aspirations, personal and professional, for what was seen as the communal betterment of the race. This emphasis on bourgeois respectability and domesticity can be seen as an outgrowth of the Victorian model of femininity that was built around what Barbara Welter termed the "Cult of True Womanhood," as embodied in traits of piety, purity, and domesticity.[21]

In "Afro-American Women and Their Work" (1895), Katherine Tillman reinforces the moral imperative on African American women to be homemakers and perpetuate moral values: "Since home-making is of such great importance, every woman who expects to have one should learn how to make it the happiest on earth. We should remember that there is nothing more serious than a marriage, save it be a birth or death."[22] The unironic reinforcement of such heteronormative, Christian values added to the pressure on Black women to be model homemakers and economically help sustain the family in the interest of supporting the advancement of the race. The emphasis on purity or sexual respectability was particularly important in that it combated the stereotype of the lascivious Black woman, or "Jezebel," an ironic reputation given the reality that Black women were denied the possibility of having their own sexual identities and choices, much less being "temptresses." The latter accusation often came from slaveholders' wives, who cast blame on enslaved women for their husbands' rape and abuse of Black women, to say nothing of other infidelities. The New Negro Woman's emphasis on respectability politics can be seen as conflicting with the more progressive aspirations of the New Woman of Greenwich Village bohemia in the 1920s. Tracing the origins of the New Negro Woman to the late nineteenth and early twentieth centuries, Treva B. Lindsey shows how Black women's suffragists and Black clubwomen strategically "used politics of respectability [and the corresponding politics of appearance and bodily adornment] to counter prevailing racialized gender stereotypes of black women [as being libidinous]. . . . Performing 'ladyhood' offered an aesthetic path to becoming visible and viable within the Negro political culture."[23] Brittney C. Cooper, in *Beyond Respectability: The*

Intellectual Thought of Race Women, contends that Black women intellectuals like Anna Julia Cooper, Mary Church Terrell, Fannie Barrier Williams, and Pauli Murray go beyond the culture of dissemblance (muting the Black female body) and the politics of respectability to center embodied experience in their social theorizing. This reclamation of the Black female body at the center of knowledge production subverts the false binary of male/female, white/black, mind/body and reframes respectability discourse in terms of gender possibility.[24]

By contrast, the New Woman emerged after World War I as an embodiment of sexual, political, and personal freedom in opposition to the restrictions of Victorian womanhood. With the advent of birth control, led by Margaret Sanger, the modern woman was able to enjoy premarital (and extramarital) sex without the consequences of unwanted pregnancy. The passage of the Nineteenth Amendment in 1920 secured women the right to vote. The passage of the Volstead Act, or Prohibition, paradoxically enabled women to engage in social drinking and smoking in speakeasies and at house parties. Greater access to higher education after World War I further broadened women's professional opportunities. As a product of the post–World War I rise of modernism, urbanization, and commercialism, the New Woman came to be associated with the personal and sexual freedom, style, and savvy of urban culture in general and New York in particular. The role of the flapper and the "smart set" was further cultivated by the rise of periodicals like the *New Yorker*, *Vanity Fair*, and *Vogue*, along with the mass production of cosmetics and fashion that could spread and export urban chic from the cities across the US. There was a disjunction between the more manufactured frivolity associated with the flapper and the more radical, intellectual, and political origins of the New Woman associated with Greenwich Village bohemia, but they both shared in a sense of free love and personal freedom that was a luxury that the New Negro Woman could not afford in her responsibility to advance the project of racial betterment.

The New Negro Woman and the African American female writer/artist were often forced into a false binary of bourgeois respectability versus primitive sexuality in their self-presentation and representation of their race/gender. Blues singers like Bessie Smith and "Ma" Rainey and dancers like Josephine Baker capitalized on the vogue of Black exoticism and the fetishizing of the Black female body as sex object through the explicit lyrics, sexual innuendo, and provocative dress (or, in the case of Baker, her notorious state of undress). Harlem became the mecca of forbidden pleasure, where wealthy white patrons could partake in jazz and blues clubs like the Cotton Club and the Savoy Ballroom, which featured the so-called primitive rhythms of Black music, dance, and minstrelsy shows featuring Black performers who were ironically barred from entry as patrons due to racial segregation.

While Fauset has been faulted for representing an elitist, bourgeois perspective, she came from modest origins. Jessie Redmon Fauset was born in a small town outside of Philadelphia (Fredericksville, New Jersey) to a father, Redmon Fauset, who was an African Methodist minister, and a mother, Annie (Seamon) Fauset, who died when Jessie was a child. While her father was an educated professional who upheld conventional morality and family values, the family was on the periphery of the middle-class, urban life that is often depicted in her fiction and with which she is associated.[25] Fauset was raised predominantly in Philadelphia and experienced both the educational opportunities and the discrimination of being biracial in a segregated mid-Atlantic state at the turn of the twentieth century. She excelled as one of the only African American students at the Philadelphia High School for Girls, and after being barred from admission to Bryn Mawr College on account of her race, she attended Cornell University, where she was one of the first African American female graduates and was awarded Phi Beta Kappa. Her education at Cornell was in classical languages and the humanities, and she went on to pursue a master's degree in French from the University of Pennsylvania. Despite her academic distinction, she was prevented from teaching in integrated schools and instead found a job at Douglas High School in Baltimore and the distinguished M Street High School (later named the Dunbar High School), where she met fellow Black women writers Angelina Grimké and Georgia Douglas Johnson.[26] She left teaching to assume the position of literary editor of *The Crisis* from 1919 to 1926. After spending some time in Paris, in 1926 Fauset returned to a teaching position in New York at the DeWitt Clinton High School, where she remained until 1944 and where she actively pursued her own literary career, publishing her most acclaimed novel, *Plum Bun* (1928), *The Chinaberry Tree* (1931), and *Comedy, American Style* (1933). She was married in 1949 at the age of forty-seven to an insurance broker, Herbert Harris. This biographical contextualization is relevant to both the opportunities and obstacles facing African American women in postwar America.

The reputation that Jessie Fauset and fellow Harlem Renaissance writer Nella Larsen represented a bourgeois, educated class of New Negro Woman was based in part on the appearance they cultivated. Fauset and Larsen were among an elite group of highly educated, refined, cosmopolitan, urban career women of mixed race associated with the Harlem Renaissance. In a portrait from the period, Fauset can be seen in a fashionable drop-waist, flounce dress with bobbed hair, a long strand of pearls, seated in an ornate chair beside a window draped with full-length curtains. Critics like Sandra M. Gilbert and Susan Gubar see this self-presentation as a kind of performativity of bourgeois femininity, whereby the Black female artist subverts the racial Othering of the dominant white male gaze.[27] Whether this is an authentic form of self-expression or a performed identity and deliberate subversion of racial/gender stereotypes, the image of the New Negro Woman ironically created its own limitations on the reputation and reception of female Harlem Renaissance writers.

In *Plum Bun: A Novel Without a Moral* (1928), Fauset satirizes the roles of the New Woman and the New Negro Woman and conventions of the marriage and passing plot. The title of the novel can be taken ironically in its invocation of a nursery rhyme, which is used metaphorically to refer to the protagonist's commodification of herself on the marriage market in order to financially secure her future. The nursery rhyme it references serves as the epigraph to the novel: "To Market, To Market, / To Buy a Plum Bun; / Home again, Home again, / Market is done."[28] The innocence implied by the nursery rhyme is disrupted by the biracial heroine's failed quest to pass by marrying a wealthy, white suitor and her return "home" to a recognition of her racial and class origins.[29] The chapter titles are taken from the nursery rhyme and lend an informal structure to the novel, tracing the protagonist's development from her "Home" on the modest Opal Street in Philadelphia; to "Market" as she seeks to establish her artistic and personal value in New York City; to "Plum Bun," which becomes a metaphor for her lost virginity and illusions of romantic love and marriage to a wealthy, white society man; to her return "Home Again" to Opal Street with renewed appreciation for her modest but moral origins; to "Market Is Done" with the end of her hopes of passing in New York City and her choice to pursue her artistic career and her authentic love interest abroad. The subtitle, "A Novel Without a Moral," is further ironic in that Fauset seems to be subverting both the sentimental tradition of Christian morality especially among women writers as well as the convention of social protest fiction that focuses on racial discrimination and social justice. There is perhaps a double irony in that, while not intending to write a moralistic tale, she in fact does convey a moral message of racial, gender, and class inequity through the indirect use of irony and satire.

Fauset's novel tells the parallel but divergent stories of two biracial sisters, Angela and Virginia Murray, whose search for identity and love are conditioned by these conflicting racial and gender movements. The Murrays are raised in a modest suburb of Philadelphia. Their father, Junius Murray, was a former coachman for a white actress, while their mother, Mattie Murray, served as her domestic servant. Junius significantly saved Mattie from a compromising situation with one of her employer's clients, recalling the sordid history of Black women's sexual exploitation by white slave owners. Their marriage is presented as a traditional one of love and devotion, with Mattie serving the domestic role of wife and mother and Junius acting as provider and protector.

The theme of racial hierarchy and inequality is introduced as we learn that the light-skinned Mattie enjoys spending Saturday afternoons with her light-skinned daughter, Angela, by passing at exclusive restaurants, shopping at Wanamaker's, having tea in the Bellevue Stratford, or sitting in orchestra seats at the symphony. Mattie introduces Angela to "the possibilities for joy and freedom which seemed to her inherent in mere whiteness" (14). Angela thus internalizes a sense of racial exclusion and shame and a desire to disassociate herself from what she sees as the encumbrance of race. She also feels a certain sense of racial superiority at the "chance" occurrence of her light-skinned appearance and good looks. "Colour or rather the lack of it seemed to the child the one absolute prerequisite to the life of which she was always dreaming. . . . The mere possession of a black or a white skin, that was clearly one of those fortuitous endowments of the gods. . . . She began thanking Fate for the chance which in that household of four had bestowed on her the heritage of her mother's fair skin" (14). Critics point to this among other passages to show Fauset's sense of racial elitism and bourgeois aspirations, but the protagonist's point of view needs to be distinguished from that of the narrator and that of the author. Through the eventual failure of the passing plot and Angela's change in self-perception, Fauset reveals the falsity and racial bias of her youthful ignorance and the value of her African American heritage.

By contrast, the desire of Angela's mother to pass is somewhat unconvincingly seen through her husband's eyes as "harmless" and "just a little joke"; it is even described in sexist terms as an "essentially feminine" weakness for shopping and attending "fashionable gatherings" (15). Mattie is described as "having a keener sense of humour than her daughter; it amused her" to play the part of a white patron at unsuspecting elite white establishments (15). But laughter is seldom harmless, and a joke is rarely just a joke, as Fauset elaborates in her essay "The Gift of Laughter." Mattie's role-playing has consequences for her dark-skinned husband and for her impressionable daughter and creates a rift within the family and even within Angela's own sense of identity. The youthful Angela comes to the conclusion that "the great rewards of life—riches, glamour, pleasure,—are for white-skinned people only" (17) and starts to "feel a faint pity for her unfortunate relatives and also to feel that coloured people were to be considered fortunate only in the proportion in which they measure up to the physical standards of white people" (18). Such self-hating racist conclusions were considered by early critics as evidence of Fauset's elitism and assimilationist attitude, but they are reflections of Angela's youthful ignorance and unlikability at the beginning of the novel and serve as an opportunity for Angela's self-education as she comes to repudiate these beliefs by novel's end. Such ideas are nonetheless dangerous, and in a pivotal scene that foreshadows Angela's "cutting" of her sister in a train station in Harlem, Angela and her mother, while out on a shopping expedition on the exclusive Walnut Street and standing in front of the Walton Hotel, refuse to acknowledge her father and sister passing in arm's reach "in the laughing, hurrying Saturday throng" (19). Junius and Virginia are associated with the joyous laughter of the everyday African American community, while Angela and her mother are separate and unfeeling in their passing role as imposters. While Mattie is ashamed of her actions, Angela is relieved at not having to expose her true identity and spoil the ruse. Fauset here points to the intraracial prejudice that threatens to destroy familial allegiances as a consequence of an internalized sense of racial inferiority through the white dominant gaze.

Angela yearns to be free of what she sees as the confines of race and leaves her humble home and African American roots in Philadelphia for the opportunity and anonymity of New York City. By contrast, Angela's sister, Virginia, represents the New Negro Woman in upholding the Victorian virtues of piety, purity, and propriety and in her aspirations to marriage, motherhood, and domestic life. The darker-skinned Virginia and her father spend Saturdays on historical excursions in the local community. Virginia further enjoys her Sunday-morning "ritual" (20) of preparing the family's breakfast, dutifully performing the household chores, and playing hymns on the piano to accompany her father's singing before attending church services. Her happiness lay not in the acquisition of material things but in aspirations of marrying, serving her husband, and having a large family: "She would pray very hard every day for five children, two boys and two girls and then a last little one. . . . And on Sunday they would all go to church" (22). This ideal of the "race mother" is part of the New Negro project of racial uplift, whereby the African American woman serves as the moral center of the household in supporting her husband, raising their children, and bettering the race. Although Fauset was faulted for her somewhat superficial depiction of character, these exaggerated types—the passing figure in Angela and the New Negro woman in Virginia—are used by Fauset for satiric purposes of exposing the limitations of racial and gender stereotypes. As the novel progresses, both characters become more complex and realistic representations of African American womanhood.

The Murray daughters also express the New Negro Woman's aspirations toward professional success, though in a limited capacity. Both daughters have artistic talent, Virginia as a musician and Angela as a painter. The Murray daughters are pressured by their parents to find more accessible and secure teaching positions rather than pursue their artistic inclinations, so as to avoid the hardship and suffering that their parents endured. Even then, Angela reminds her sister, "You know perfectly well that there are no coloured teachers of music in the public schools here in Philadelphia" (34), a nod, perhaps, to Fauset's own experience of racial discrimination when seeking a position as a language teacher in the segregated Philadelphia school system. After Angela confronts numerous instances of racism upon being "outed" as Black at her high school and at a Philadelphia Arts Academy, she has a crisis of conscience, reinvents herself as European-sounding Angèle Mory, and decides to try to pass for white in the arts scene and on the marriage market in New York City.

In part 2, "To Market," Fauset offers a satiric portrayal of the opportunities and obstacles confronting the New Woman and the New Negro Woman in New York in the 1920s. Fauset presents three New York locales in the novel—Union Square, Greenwich Village, and Harlem—each reflecting a different racial and class dynamic. When Angela first arrives in New York, she is less interested in the impersonal, professional Midtown Manhattan and chooses instead to go to Union Square, home of the teeming masses. Union Square, the area from Fourteenth Street to Seventeenth Street, was a somewhat eclectic neighborhood, featuring both commercial and industrial buildings like the Everett Building and Consolidated Edison Building and department stores like S. Klein and Ohrbach's as well as a growing artist population housed in the old mansions on the south side of Fourteenth Street.[30] Fauset's opening description of Manhattan conveys the grandeur as well as the diversity, impersonality, and humanity of the city: "Fifth Avenue is a canyon; its towering buildings dwarf the importance of the people hurrying through its narrow confines. But Fourteenth Street is a river, impersonally flowing, broad-bosomed, with strange and devious craft covering its expanse. . . . Fourteenth Street was the rendezvous of life itself, . . . the jostling shops, the hurrying, pushing people with their showings of grief, pride, gaiety, greed, joy, ambition, content" (87).

As a portrait painter, Angela is interested in depicting the life of "Fourteenth Street types" in and around Union Square Park (89). She assumes a certain distance and superiority in her observation of what she considers the "type" of the common urbanite. In watching the pedestrians gathered in front of a storefront with a player piano playing jazz music, Angela detects a certain "wistfulness" of the passersby, at once drawn to the promise of life that the jazz music offered and painfully reminded of the burdens of the workaday world. "The young woman looking at the gathering of shabby pedestrians, worn businessmen and ruminative errand boys felt for them a pity not untinged with satisfaction" (90). Susan Tomlinson notes that the Fourteenth Street School movement of painters like Isabel Bishop and Raphael Soyer chose as their subject "street vendors, resting workers, and, very frequently, window-shopping working women" in the Union Square area, with the aim of "represent[ing] the humanity of an alienated working class and the increasing social commodification which contributed to that alienation" in the post–World War I urban landscape. These artists represented at once the possibilities of feminized occupations like the new class of office workers and sales girls, as well as the alienation of the "emergent urban white female labor force," marginalized by the myth of the New Woman.[31] Angela assumes the role of first the subject and later the object of the Fourteenth Street School of painting, starting as a hopeful professional and ending up identifying with the alienated and dehumanized workforce.

The second New York that Fauset portrays with her satiric eye is that of the bohemian artist and intellectual of Greenwich Village. This type is associated with the New Woman of the Jazz Age and the possibilities of free love, radical politics, and artistic and professional freedom. Although Angela aspires to pass among the Greenwich Village bohemian set, she is separated by the realities of racial, class, and gender difference. After a brief stint at the Union Square Hotel, Angela significantly chooses to live on Jayne Street in Greenwich Village and not among her African American peers in Harlem. To Angela, the Village represents a kind of Eden of freedom and golden opportunity: in springtime, "Washington Square was a riot of greens that showed up bravely against the great red brick houses on its north side. The Arch viewed from Fifth Avenue seemed a gateway to Paradise. The long deep streets running the length of the city invited an exploration to the ends where pots of gold doubtless gleamed. On the short crosswise streets the April sun streamed in splendid banners of deep golden light" (138). But the reality of a segregated and stratified New York soon becomes apparent.

Fauset satirizes the figure of the bohemian New Woman through the figures of Angela's classmates and fellow Village residents Paulette Lister and Martha Burden, with their exaggerated sexual promiscuity and specious progressive values. Paulette is described in androgynous terms as a modern woman who smokes, drinks, and takes lovers with abandon. A highly independent career woman, she has worked as a press agent for a New York daily newspaper and is currently an illustrator for a fashion magazine. Paulette is a woman of the world; her apartment on Bank Street is decorated with art and books from her travels abroad, and she is planning a trip to Italy and Russia with her current love interest. But Angela is struck most by the presence of "a man's shaving mug and brush and a case of razors" (104) in open view in the bathroom, which she learns belong to one of Paulette's various lovers. The thought of love for personal gratification and as a form of play or gamesmanship without the goal of marriage is alien to Angela, who sustains a sense of traditional morality and a practical awareness of her sexuality as a prized possession saved to secure marriage. Angela was raised with the stringent "sex morality" of her "housekeeper, companion, and chaperone" from Philadelphia, Hetty Daniels, who proudly declares, "I kept my pearl of great price untarnished. I aimed then and I'm continual to aim to be a verjous woman" (66). This difference in approach to female sexuality reinforces the stark contrast for educated white women and uneducated Black women, or even aspiring New Negro Women, when it comes to sexual freedom.

Fauset portrays Paulette as an exaggerated form of the modern woman, whose androgynous appearance and sexual promiscuity become a kind of performance of independence from which the biracial Angela is removed. "There is a great deal of the man about me," boasts Paulette. "I've learned that a woman is a fool who lets her femininity stand in the way of what she wants. I've made a philosophy of it. I see what I want; I use my wiles as a woman to get it, and I employ the qualities of men, tenacity and ruthlessness, to keep it. And when I'm through with it, I throw it away just as they do. Consequently I have no regrets and no encumbrances" (105). Her invocation of the terms "masculine" and "feminine" and her self-conscious performance of gender roles betray an awareness of the perceived difference and power imbalance between men and women. Paulette reveals her own gender and racial bias when she seeks to gain the attention of the distinguished African American intellectual and activist Van Meier, modeled on Du Bois, after attending one of his lectures on "racial sacrifice" and "racial pride" in Harlem (218). While she considers herself to be highly progressive, she is incredulous at Van Meier's indifference toward her advances, dismissing it in jest: "I played the biggest joke on myself" (220). Paulette here shows a sense of social superiority, assuming that even the most distinguished African American male would be interested in a white woman's advances, a racial bias that belies her seemingly progressive values.

If Paulette represents the fiercely independent "New Woman"—"'I don't care what people think,' was her slogan" (112)—Martha Burden is a subtler and more sophisticated model of the progressive individualist. She is, nonetheless, the object of satire, as Fauset exposes the pretensions and self-indulgence of the Greenwich Village bohemian intellectual of the 1920s. Martha and her husband, Ladislas Starr (she has kept her own name), live in an elegant yet understated house in the Village. Their bookcases are lined with progressive magazines—"the *Nation*, the *Mercury*, the *Crisis, a magazine of the darker races*" (113)—and they host mixed-race parties with leftist intellectuals, artists, writers, actors, and professionals where men and women debate radical politics. For these predominantly white guests, discussions of social justice remain theoretical ideals. The other African American woman in attendance, a teacher of the disabled, recognizes the distance of this privileged crowd from realities of racial and class oppression. Angela recalls the earnest and urgent debates she used to have among her Black peers back on Opal Street—"the men talking painfully of rents, of lynchings, of building and loan associations; the women of childbearing and the sacrifices which must be made" (116)—and she concludes that Martha's cohort "represented an almost alarmingly unnecessary class" (118). Despite Angela's attempt to pass among the bohemian leftist Village artists and intellectuals, her racial and class consciousness provides a sobering reality and awareness that separates her.

The ironic laughter directed against the predominantly white, bohemian smart set of Greenwich Village is contrasted with the joyful laughter and sense of community among the residents of Harlem. Angela's view of this thriving Black metropolis reflects a change in the perception of her own racial identity and sense of belonging. When she first arrives in New York, she is enthralled by the liveliness and diversity of Harlem, but she views it with a kind of distance and condescension of a passing, white outsider. "She was amazed and impressed at this bustling, frolicking, busy, laughing great city within a greater one. She had never seen coloured life so thick, so varied, so complete" (96). Yet she is skeptical about finding successful professionals and stylish citizens among them, and she ultimately finds Harlem to be lacking: "In all material, even in all practical things these two worlds were alike, but in the production, the fostering, of those ultimate manifestations, this world was lacking, for its people were without the means or the leisure to support them and enjoy" (97). She ascribes a coarse vitality to Black life in Harlem and chooses instead to live in Greenwich Village: "Just as these people could suffer more than others, just so they could enjoy themselves more. She watched the moiling groups on Lenox Avenue; the amazingly well-dressed and good-looking throngs of young men on Seventh Avenue at One Hundred and Thirty-seventh and Thirty-fifth Streets. They were gossiping, laughing, dickering, chaffing, combing the customs of the small town with the astonishing cosmopolitanism of their clothes and manners. Nowhere downtown did she see life like this. Oh, all this was fuller, richer, not finer, but richer with the difference in quality that there is between velvet and silk" (98). Angela associates the vitality of Harlem life with a joyful laughter, though she still sees it as lacking in a certain refinement.

We see a different Harlem through the eyes of Angela's sister, Virginia, who comes to New York to take her teaching exam. Unlike Angela, Virginia heads directly for Harlem, where she is greeted by a sense of community as well as the cosmopolitan sophistication of the New Negro. In a dramatic scene reminiscent of Angela and her mother's refusal to acknowledge Angela's darker-skinned sister and father in front of the Hotel Walton in Philadelphia, Angela rebuffs her sister upon her arrival at the train station in Harlem. Her sister, familiarly described as Jinny, approaches Angela with a "gay, childish voice saying laughingly, assuredly: 'I beg your pardon, but isn't this Mrs. Henrietta Jones?'" (159), invoking the name of their beloved childhood caretaker. Jinny's innocent laughter as she attempts an inside joke with her sister stands in contrast to Angela's frigidity and fear of having her racial identity exposed in front of her wealthy, white suitor.

Virginia's Harlem is associated with the gaiety of Black laughter and community, though it also exposes the stereotype of racial uplift and bourgeois respectability of the New Negro. "Virginia spent a good deal of time with a happy, intelligent, rather independent group of young coloured men and women; there was talk occasionally of the theatre, of a dance, of small clubs, of hikes, of classes at Columbia or at New York City College" (209). Virginia's elite status in Harlem is reinforced by her association with Van Meier, "a great coloured American, a littérateur, a fearless and dauntless apostle of the rights of man" (209), modeled on Du Bois. Angela covets the sense of camaraderie and contentment among Virginia and her coterie and in the larger Harlem community. Virginia is part of "a gay, *laughing* party. . . . The girls were bright birds of paradise, the men, her artist's eye noted, were gay, vital fauns" (209; emphasis added). Angela's idealized vision of Virginia's happy laughter in Harlem reflects her own growing sense of alienation among white, bourgeois society.

While Angela comes to New York City in hopes of finding freedom from racial restrictions by passing for white, she discovers the value of community and belonging through affirmation of her Black roots. Angela arrives with a measured sense of possibility: "'free, white and twenty-one,'— this was what it meant then, this sense of owning the world, this realization that other things being equal, all things were possible" (88). She recognizes, however, that all things are not equal, and even with the prospect of racial equality, she still faces gender inequality. "'If I were a man,' she said, 'I could be president,' and laughed at herself for the 'if' itself proclaimed a limitation" (88). This is the self-conscious laughter of the realization of her illusion of equality. Angela is aware of the racial and gender hierarchy that puts Black women at the bottom, and she is prepared to use her light complexion and her sexuality as means to pursuing what she sees as a better future. "She knew that men had a better time of it than women, and coloured men than coloured women, white men than white women. Not that she envied them. Only it would be fun, great fun to capture power and protection in addition to the freedom and independence which she had so long coveted and which now lay in her hand" (88–89).

Fauset exposes the failure of the passing plot and the bourgeois marriage plot with Angela's misguided attempt to find happiness by marrying a wealthy, white man. "Marriage is the easiest way for a woman to get those [power and money]," thinks the naïve Angela, "and white men have them" (112). In this game of love, Angela is reduced to using her virginity as a commodity to be negotiated, with the ultimate prize of marriage to Roger Fielding. But her lack of experience and naïve belief in his good intentions are no match for Fielding's cunning indifference, and Angela risks losing herself in adopting the passing persona of Angèle.

Angela's conflicted sexual identity as both an independent New Woman and modest New Negro Woman is expressed in a near rape scene with

Roger Fielding. While she preserves her virginity, as instructed by her Black nanny, she feels a certain sexual attraction. "There was one enemy with whom she had never thought to reckon, she had never counted on the treachery of the forces of nature; she had never dreamed of the unaccountable weakening of those forces within. Her weapons were those furnished by the conventions but her fight was against conditions; impulses, yearnings which antedated both those weapons and the conventions which furnished them" (198). This aggressive language of battle and betrayal signals the conflict within Angela between her higher morals and her baser instincts. Angela begins to develop an emotional attachment and a physical desire for Roger that make her question the conventions of propriety, which now seemed to her "prudish and unnecessary. . . . In the last analysis her purity was a matter not of morals, not of religion, not of racial pride; it was a matter of fastidiousness" (199). Although some critics see Angela's sexual desire as an expression of the racial stereotype of the lascivious Black woman, it can also be seen as an expression of the New Woman's sense of sexual independence and pleasure. Angela ultimately succumbs to Roger's advances and false promises in a near rape scene that mocks the style of the conventional sentimental novel.

Angela's encounter with Roger precipitates her disillusionment with the false ideals of the passing myth and the illusion of bourgeois marriage. Once Angela has lost her virginity or "plum bun," her value on the marriage market precipitously declines, and Roger quickly loses interest. After he refuses to take her phone calls, she responds incredulously, "But you call me whenever you feel like it," to which he responds, "Of course I do, that's different. I'm a man" (228). This scene recalls Dorothy Parker's "A Telephone Call," in which the abandoned female lover waits in vain for her suitor to call, powerless to make the first move. Angela comes to the belated realization of her subordinate status: the telephone call "represented for her the apparently unbridgeable difference between the sexes; everything was for men, but even the slightest privilege was to be denied to a woman unless the man chose to grant it" (229). Angela, however, still holds out some hope in the institution of marriage, with the right man. She turns to the somber and tormented artist Anthony Cruz from Brazil, who she later discovers is of mixed race and shows empathy for the socially disadvantaged.

In addition to Anthony providing a romantic and racial connection for Angela, his heritage exposes the sordid history of racial violence. His Black father had suffered lynching and castration after his light-skinned mother refused the advances of a white man. This trauma leaves Anthony with the burden of a dark secret as he seeks to pass in New York City and ultimately leads to a genuine connection when Angela and Anthony openly accept their true racial identities. That Fauset shows the intergenerational effects of racial trauma as well as the ongoing racism in the US speaks against those critics who see her as an apologist for the New Negro narrative of racial uplift. However, the persistence of the heterosexual marriage plot, albeit in modified form, does show a certain conformity to narrative conventions of the Victorian novel.

Plum Bun highlights the reality of racial inequality through its ironic treatment of the passing myth. Ironically, Angela's failure to lose her racial identity by passing allows her to find her authentic self as a Black woman artist. Fauset expresses a tension between racial pride and the universalism that Angela and her mother aspire to by passing. "Life, life was what she was struggling for, the right to live and be happy. And once more her mother's dictum flashed into her mind. 'Life is more important than colour'" (266). Fauset herself is inclined toward a universalist perspective, arguing that African American literature need not be focused exclusively on the "race problem." In the foreword to *The Chinaberry Tree* (1931), she claims that the African American "is not so vastly different from any other American, just distinctive." He is "a dark American who wears his joy and rue very much as does the white American. He may wear it with some differences, but it is the same joy and the same rue."[32]

Despite Fauset's aspirations to universalism, *Plum Bun* reveals the harsh realities of racial discrimination. After Roger Fielding abandons Angela, exposing his racist, sexist, and class prejudice, she is forced to make it on her own and seek a genuine sense of belonging in the impersonal city. To her surprise, she becomes more earnestly engaged as an artist and an independent woman: "It both amused and saddened her to realize that her talent which she had once used as a blind to shield her real motives for breaking loose and coming to New York had now become the greatest, most real force in her life" (332). Angela finds a job drawing designs for a reputable fashion journal and has aspirations of studying abroad. She prepares her "Fourteenth Street types" for entry in an international competition to study art at the Fontainebleau School of Fine Arts in Paris. Meanwhile, her fellow Black art student Miss Powell submits a portrait of "A Street in Harlem" to the same competition. Angela recognizes in Miss Powell's choice of subject "the self-consciousness of colour" and sense of "racial responsibility" (334) that she was hitherto lacking. Where she once felt a distance from the down-and-out Fourteenth Street types, in her isolation and desolation, she can now relate to the downtrodden masses.

Angela's ultimate crisis of conscience occurs when Miss Powell is asked to rescind her scholarship to study in Paris on the basis of her race. Since she would be required to travel overseas by ship, the committee determines, it would be impossible for her to segregate, and her racial presence might make the other award recipients uncomfortable. Outraged by the injustice and the taunting of Miss Powell by reporters, Angela outs herself as biracial and stands in solidarity by refusing her own scholarship award to study abroad. This act of racial identification is ironically liberating for Angela, who is free to pursue her painting on her own terms and without the fear of her true identity being exposed by another. Angela is struck by the irony of racial bias—that as a person and an artist, she is valued differently based on the perception of racial difference rather than any change in her identity or ability. She observes, "Looking just the same as I've ever looked I let the fact of my Negro ancestry be known. Mind, I haven't changed the least bit, but immediately there's all this holding up of hands and the cry of deceit is raised. Some logic, that! It really would be awfully funny . . . if it couldn't be fraught with such disastrous consequences for people like, say, Miss Powell" (353). Although Angela can see the ironic humor of the situation, she recognizes that the implicit bias of racism has devastating consequences for those who are less fortunate like Miss Powell, who do not have the means or the will to fight or get ahead. Angela is described as "bubbling over with mirth at the silliness of it all" (359). Here we see laughter as a kind of release, but it is a short-lived happiness, for it carries the serious awareness of the consequences of such injustice.

Angela also comes to a renewed understanding of the value of home and family, as she sees her sister, Virginia, living a life of contentment and belonging with another African American teacher on the top floor of a gracious house in the elite Striver's Row on 139th Street in Harlem (242). Angela tries in vain to return "Home Again," as the nursery rhyme suggests, and when she returns to Opal Street in Philadelphia to visit her old home, she is met by the angry refusal of the current occupant, who shunts her off as "poor white trash" (363). By contrast, the steadfast local young man Matthew Henson, who had once pursued Angela and now confesses his love for the more domestic Virginia, shows Angela some hospitality, but Angela realizes that she is estranged from both her local roots and her new, urban identity.

While the prospect of passing through marriage to a wealthy, white husband is disrupted, the possibility of a different type of marriage persists. Fauset's message of social justice is thus tempered by the more conventional, romantic ending of the novel. Perhaps with an awareness of the expectations of publishers and audiences alike, Fauset cannot present the triumph of two independent African American career women in the 1920s. As Angela is discovering her artistic independence and rediscovering her racial identity, she also acknowledges her love for the sullen biracial artist Anthony Cruz. Despite Angela's progress as an artist and a woman, her love for Anthony is expressed in exaggeratedly conventional terms: "At the cost of every ambition which she had ever known she would make him happy. After the manner of most men his work would probably be the greatest thing in the world to him. And he should be the greatest thing in the world to her. He should be her task, her 'job,' the fulfilment of her ambition" (293). This can be seen as a satiric reference to the New Negro Woman's project of racial uplift, subordinating herself in the interest of supporting the Black man's progress. Fauset goes even further to describe Angela in terms of the New Negro Woman's ideal of femininity and bourgeois domesticity: "She wanted to be a beloved woman, dependent, fragile, sought for, feminine; after this last ordeal she would be 'womanly' to the point of ineptitude" (296–97). The exaggerated tone and language of fragility and femininity suggest a satiric critique of the domestic ideals that she purportedly seeks to uphold.

In a complication of the sentimental romance plot, Angela discovers that Anthony is engaged to her sister, Virginia. She is struck by the irony that she is in love with Anthony, who is engaged to Virginia, while Virginia has feelings for Matthew, Matthew loves Virginia, and Anthony loves Angela. "The irony of it was so palpable, so ridiculously palpable that it put her in a better mood; life was bitter but it was amusingly bitter; if she could laugh at it she might be able to outwit it yet. The thought brought Anthony to mind: 'If I could only get a laugh on life, Angèle!'" (316). Laughter is seen as a form of empowerment, a means of coping and overcoming adverse circumstances—laughing to keep from crying/dying. Fauset further uses laughter as a form of self-assertion as Angela ultimately rejects the belated offer of marriage made by a contrite Roger Fielding: "Not unsympathetically she laughed up into his doleful face, actually touched his cheek. 'If you only knew how much you look like a cross baby!'" (322). Through laughter, Angela is able to reverse the racial/gender/class hierarchy, as Roger is infantilized and she stands in a position of power over him.

While laughter can be a means of asserting individual control against unjust conditions, laughter can also be seen as the sinister force shaping the lives of individuals. Since coming to New York, Angela is haunted by a vision that she has put onto canvas of life as a "tall, cloaked form of a woman, thin to emaciation, her hands on her bony hips, slightly bent forward, laughing uproariously yet with a certain chilling malevolence" (280). Far from the empowering laughter that Angela feels when asserting her sexual or racial independence, this is a menacing vision of a force beyond our control who "laughs at the poor people who fall into the traps which she sets for us" (280). The figure is significantly female, like Hélène Cixous's laughing Medusa, who can be seen as at once terrifying and beautiful depending on one's point of view, and the painting remains unfinished, an ambivalent figure perhaps, in Angela's as-yet-unfinished journey through life.

There is further irony in that, by seeking to pass for white, both Angela and Anthony obstruct rather than facilitate the relationship between them. Angela is able to laugh with the joke that life has played on the lovers, as she states to Anthony, "You in your foolishness, I in my carelessness, 'passing, passing,' and life splitting her sides at the joke of it" (298). But not all jokes are as harmless or as easily overcome when confronting the serious obstacles of a racist society. While Angela has not given up on the prospect of remaking herself in a new city, that place of self-discovery is significantly abroad in Europe. Anthony encourages her to pursue her artistic dream of study abroad and joins her in Paris in what can be seen as a future "companionate" form of marriage, whereby a woman need not abandon her professional aspirations for domestic life.[33] In the chapter "Market Is Done," Angela no longer seeks marriage as a means to an end but finds love as an end in itself. Virginia is reunited with Matthew, presumably to pursue her career as an educator as well as her role as a wife in Harlem. Despite the progress and opportunity that the Harlem Renaissance offers to African American women, Fauset's *Plum Bun* uses irony and satire to reveal at once the possibilities and the limitations of the New Negro Woman in the US. "So," as Fauset concludes in the foreword to another fictional work, "in spite of other intentions I seem to have pointed a moral."[34]

Critical discussions about Jessie Fauset's work revolve around her historical association with the bourgeois, sentimental tradition versus a more ironic reading of her work as subverting conventional racial and gender norms. Contemporary critics like Hazel Carby continue to see Fauset in the conservative, Victorian tradition, while critics like Joseph J. Feeney,

Carolyn Wedin Sylvander, Cheryl A. Wall, and Ann duCille acknowledge the traditional context and style of her writing while recognizing a more subversive social critique through her engagement with themes of racial, class, and gender inequality.[35] As early as 1979, Joseph J. Feeney emphasized a sardonic ambiguity in Fauset's writing: "Her books have a double structure: On the surface they read as conventional middle-class love stories with happy endings; underneath these developing romances, though, lies a counter structure which expresses either the souring of childhood hopes, or a near-tragedy, or sardonic comedy." Feeney acknowledges some "conventionality and sentimentality in her books. Her style was formal and she wrote novels about the Negro middle class." However, he contends, "She displaced a sensibility which comprehended tragedy, sardonic comedy, disillusioned hopes, slavery, prejudice, confusion, and bitterness against America."[36] Thus, it is not merely *what* she writes about but *how* she writes about it that matters.

In Carolyn Wedin Sylvander's pioneering study *Jessie Redmon Fauset, Black American Writer*, she recognizes *Plum Bun* as the "intentional satire of romantic racial themes." "While she uses the plot freedom of the romance," argues Sylvander, "she satirizes traditionally romantic assumptions in American literature, particularly in regard to race and sex."[37] Fauset thereby complicates the sentimental tradition of the romance novel and the racial underpinnings of social protest fiction of the time. "Contrary to the repeated claim that Fauset wrote to promote respectable middle-class Black life," disputes Sylvander, "she in fact emphasizes individual morality which is at variance with society's codes."[38] This emphasis on the representation of individual experience over a universal, racialized typing of the Black experience is essential to an understanding of the meaning and value of Fauset's writing. Ann duCille's analysis focuses on the complexity of Black female subjectivity and the ways in which Fauset and Larsen "comment on and critique the bohemian as well as the bourgeois, and implicitly challenge the hegemony of primitivism and exoticism that critics have long read as the real stuff of the Harlem Renaissance to the extent that they critique both the conservative middle class and the primal peasantry," thereby arriving at a more complex and authentic expression of Black female subjectivity.[39]

Debates continue over the subversive versus the conservative nature of Fauset's work, much of which depend on the ironic and satiric interpretation of her writing. Susan Tomlinson characterizes *Plum Bun* as "a feminist, anti-racist project [that] explores the intersection of race and gender constructions of black and white American women."[40] Catherine Rottenberg takes issue with Elizabeth Wilson's notion, in *The Sphinx in the City*, of the emancipatory city, which offers women an increased possibility of sexual and professional freedom and opportunity during the modern era. Rottenberg instead notes the racial and class limitations of such tropes for the New Negro Woman: "The city as a space of emancipation often assumes a *white* subject."[41] Catherine Keyser examines Fauset in the context of modern magazine culture, noting that "Fauset revises the model of wit embodied by the white smart magazine writer in order to support the model of irony and activism."[42] Most recently, Lisa Mendelman challenges what she considers the false dichotomy between irony and sentimentality by arguing for Fauset's use of "ironic sentimentalism" in subverting the Victorian sentimental conventions of the novel in a modern, interwar context.[43]

I would argue that through the use of irony and satire, Fauset launches an indirect form of social critique against the racial, gender, and class stereotypes of the New Woman and the New Negro Woman. Rather than imitating the conventions of domestic fiction, *Plum Bun* is a subtle satire that critiques the conventions of the marriage and passing plots. Fauset neither reinscribes sentimental, bourgeois conventions of domestic fiction, as argued by early critics, nor radically challenges racial and social hierarchies. Instead, using humor to mock social norms, *Plum Bun* projects a complex and individual expression of racial and gender identity that anticipates what Danielle Fuentes Morgan terms "kaleidoscopic Blackness."[44] Fauset can thus be seen as engaging in the ethical project of satire by raising awareness of the racial and gender injustices of postwar American society as a step toward social change.

Dawn Powell and the Lafayette Circle
Satirist of Greenwich Village Bohemia and Modern, Midtown Publishing Culture

5.

"[I] cannot exist without the oxygen of laughter."[1] So wrote Dawn Powell, a self-described "permanent visitor" to New York, who uses satire to chronicle Greenwich Village bohemian life from the 1930s through the 1950s. Born in Mount Gilead, Ohio, Powell was reborn as a satirist of the New York literary and cultural scene and modern, Midtown publishing culture. Her 1936 novel *Turn, Magic Wheel* satirizes New York Greenwich Village café culture, while her later novel *The Wicked Pavilion* (1954) looks back at the dying bohemian culture surrounding the fictional Café Julien, based on the demise of Powell's local Lafayette café. Her final, highly acclaimed novel, *The Golden Spur* (1962), chronicles the displacement of 1920s bohemian café society by the pseudobohemian beatniks of the 1950s surrounding the Golden Spur, a Greenwich Village bar based loosely on the historic Cedar Tavern. Despite the admiration of reputed literary figures and personal friends—including Edmund Wilson, John Dos Passos, Ernest Hemingway, and Genevieve Taggard—and her attempted revival by Gore Vidal and Tim Page, Dawn Powell's literary reputation remains somewhat obscure. We will look at ways in which her sharp wit, often aimed at the very middle-class readership she sought, as well as her refusal to conform to female stereotypes, has affected her reception as a New York woman of wit.

Powell's expansive career can be divided roughly between her early Ohio novels, *She Walks in Beauty* (1928), *The Bride's House* (1929), *Dance Night* (1930), *Come Back to Sorrento* (1932), and *The Story of a Country Boy* (1934), which are considered in the more sentimental tradition, and her later, satiric New York novels, *Turn, Magic Wheel* (1936), *The Happy Island* (1938), *Angels on Toast* (1940), *A Time to Be Born* (1942), *The Locusts Have No King* (1948), *The Wicked Pavilion* (1954), and *The Golden Spur* (1962), with her autobiographical Ohio novel, *My Home Is Far Away* (1944), spanning in between. In addition, she wrote several plays; contributed over one hundred stories to such magazines as the *New Yorker, Mademoiselle, Story*, and the *Saturday Evening Post*, as well as more obscure publications like *Munsey's* and *Snappy Stories*; and published numerous book reviews.

Often compared with Dorothy Parker, who shared the same initials and was considered a rival New York wit (as if there were room for only one woman of wit at a time), Powell considered Parker more of a self-promoter with limited literary output. The writers of the Algonquin Round Table, whom she loosely satirized in her novel *The Locusts Have No King* (originally titled *The Destroyers*) were seen as smug, self-indulgent, and juvenile (*Diaries of Dawn Powell* 209). Others agree that Parker's relative fame is attributable in part to her public bon mots being recorded by her entourage of journalists and publicists, while Powell's wit was more of a private affair.[2] The cultural critic Diana Trilling, a sometime admirer of Powell's, went even further to say, "Miss Powell, one of the wittiest women around, suggests the answer to the age-old question, 'Who really makes up the jokes that Dorothy Parker gets the credit for?"[3] In contrast to Parker, Powell would forgo publicity events and eschew the cult of celebrity, which was a factor in her relative obscurity.[4]

For Powell, the function of the writer was as a chronicler of civilization, what starts as the record of a particular time and place and ultimately stands as a timeless testament to common humanity. Such a record of civilization, in Powell's view, could be best expressed through satire. "The only record of civilization is satire—Petronius, Aristophanes, Flaubert" (*D*, 215). Among Powell's favorite literary works and strongest influences is Petronius's *Satyricon*, an ancient Roman Menippean satire (*D*, 323). Satire for Powell is a record of truth in all its beauty and ugliness; it captures a certain authenticity that goes beyond that of the so-called realist novel. In her diaries, which read at times like literary commentary, Powell takes a somewhat cynical view of satire: "Satire is people as they are; romanticism, people as they would like to be; realism, people as they seem with their insides left out" (*D*, 119). Despite what Powell sees as the truth telling of satire, satirists are often falsely accused of malice and moralizing. "In my satire," says Powell, "I merely add a dimension to a character, a dimension which gives the person substance and life but which readers often mistake for malice" (*D*, 118). "In giving this picture," observes Powell, "with no malice in mind, no desire to show the grievers up as villains, no wish more than to give people their full statures, one would be accused of 'satire,' of 'cynicism,' instead of looking without blinders, blocks, ear mufflers, gags, at life" (*D*, 119). Her often-cutting portraits of New York types reveal a darker side to her satire than she declares.

Powell has been criticized for a lack of character development and somewhat amorphous plots without closure or clear endings. This tendency toward caricature and minimal plot is a common technique among satirists and may be a self-conscious approach on the part of the author. Dustin Griffin, among others, notes that in satire, there tends to be "a certain flattening of character toward caricature, a stylizing of action toward the emblematic, a reductive sharpening of narrative tone toward ridicule, and what Mikhail Bakhtin would call 'monological' discourse." Alvin Kernan elaborates that in the disorderly nature of satire, "the plot always takes on the matter of purpose followed by passion, but fails to develop beyond this point."[5] Powell is more interested in constructing a social reality than in individual character development, linear plot, or moral purpose. "My characters are not slaves to an author's propaganda," says Powell, with a dig against social protest fiction writers of the time. "I give them their heads. They furnish their own nooses," she notes, with characteristic wit and flippancy.[6] While Powell may have no malicious or moralizing intent, her jabs are often targeted to expose the foibles of a particular individual or group of people, if not for social reform, then as a masked form of social critique.

Powell offers a kind of democratic satire, whose object spans across class lines to include the rich, the middle class, and the poor. In trying to create a comedy of manners that crosses social strata, she has been criticized by more highbrow reviewers for the levity of her subject matter. In an oft-cited review of *The Locusts Have No King*—which satirizes the literary, publishing, and advertising world in Midtown Manhattan in the 1940s—Diana Trilling calls Powell out for her "choice of characters, or—more accurately— in the discrepancy between the power of mind revealed on virtually every page of her novel and the insignificance of the human beings upon whom she directs her excellent intelligence." Powell focuses on contemporary New Yorkers who live "by association with the arts—playwrights, publishers, press agents, culture-promoters, painters. A shabbier crowd of hangers-on and barflies would be hard to find," in Trilling's assessment. Trilling here reveals an elitist bias that the subject of satire should be a person or group of high stature: "The size of a satire necessarily derives from the size of the object being satirized. . . . We are always, after all, only as big as the thing we laugh at." Trilling's criteria for satire would negate a whole category of satirists of bohemian and bourgeois life, including Sinclair Lewis, George S. Kaufman, and others. Trilling significantly attributes this perceived disparity between the seriousness of Powell's mind and the superficiality of her subject matter to her gender. "Perhaps the imbalance springs from the anomalous role an intelligent woman still plays in our culture—the myriad subtle pressures exerted on her to prove her 'womanliness' by disproving her seriousness, to disarm male hostility by asserting a basic frivolity," speculates Trilling. "Certainly no man of Miss Powell's intellectual endowment would fritter away his powers on the small-time creatures to whom Miss Powell devotes herself, or be guilty of the sentimental gestures that so markedly diminish the values of her keen social perception."[7] Trilling here points to a gender bias in society that associates and limits women writers to more "feminine," less serious subject matter and style in the sentimental tradition. Ironically, Trilling reinforces the very gender bias to which she objects in her gendered and class critique of Powell's work.

Powell responded to Trilling and other critics who perceived her subject matter as too parochial in a 1948 diary entry: "Gist of criticisms (Diana Trilling, etc.) of my novel is if they had my automobile they wouldn't visit my folks, they'd visit *theirs*. . . . Again there is the shaking of heads over not writing about 'nice people—people one likes.' *Who* likes? *I'm* doing the work. I write about people *I* find interesting, largely because they are often representative. My readers and critics never recognize themselves" (*D*, 271). Implicit in Powell's response is a belief that the purpose of satire is truth telling, and the scope of satire is a broad spectrum of society. Powell's outside status as a midwestern settler to the city at once offered a valuable perspective but also separated her from the cultural elite of New York society. Gore Vidal similarly defended Powell against accusations by Trilling and others of not being serious enough. "Apparently, a novel to be serious must be about very serious even solemn people rendered in a very solemn even serious manner. *Wit?* What is that?"[8]

In a 1940 diary entry, Powell defensively responds to reviewers who brand her a bitter satirist for targeting the middle class. "There are, I have learned, rigorous rules for wit," says Powell ironically. "Wit is not wit unless directed above or below. There is nothing funny in a property holder. The middle class is wit-proofed" (*D*, 180). And she later writes, "It is considered jolly and good humored to point out the oddities of the poor or of the rich. . . . I go outside and can't help believing that the middle class is funny, too."[9] Powell here accuses not only the reviewers but by extension the publishers and patrons of the arts, whose primary motivation is profit and popularity. The publishing industry and arts patrons themselves become objects of Powell's satire, which did not do much to boost her own sales and reputation.

For Powell, satire is rooted not in profit but in pain, as a means of releasing anger and coping with personal suffering and social injustice. Like her fellow female satirists Mary McCarthy and Dorothy Parker, who suffered parental loss and mistreatment at a young age, Powell's sense of ironic detachment can be seen as a means of coping with pain. Powell lost her mother at the age of six due to a botched abortion, her father was often absent as a traveling salesman, and her stepmother notoriously burned her journals as a child, prompting her to seek refuge with a free-spirited aunt.[10] Further burdened with an alcoholic husband with whom she stayed married until his death and a mentally disabled son who was in and out of institutions, Powell turned to writing and satire in particular as a means of financial and personal freedom. She subscribes to the Juvenalian view of satire as an expression of anger or suffering: "Wit is the cry of pain, the true world that pierces the heart. . . . If it does not pierce then it is not true wit. True wit should break a good man's heart."[11] Powell describes humor as the unconscious release of rage in the form of fancy: "Humor. Wit. In my case a form of panic or rage, essentially—or fatigue. Like poetry which occurs when the brain is asleep and the hidden treasury of memory, imaginings, undeveloped pictures is freed" (*D*, 446).

Laughter, according to Powell, is a great equalizer, to be enjoyed by the haves and the have-nots alike and can thus elicit resentment on the part of the privileged, who wish to reserve it for themselves: "It is the great pleasure of the poor, the crippled, the doomed—laughter when they can—and the Haves are furious because their laughter-means are so limited. Look, they say, what are you laughing at? . . . What are you people in wheelchairs, in hovels, in institutions, in debt, in a beat-up old car or shack, how can you laugh? . . . Even if you aren't rich, maybe you love your tiny security of laughter so much you are smugger than the rich" (*D*, 422–23). Humor could thus be used by marginalized populations not only as a mode of coping and an expression of pleasure but as means of exposing the failings and misgivings of people in positions of power.

Powell has been accused of being both too aggressive and too gentle in her use of satire, a double bind particularly common among female satirists. She tends to write a more sympathetic form of satire, mixing pathos with anger, especially in her portrayal of the bohemian, Greenwich Village set, in a self-deprecatory humor often found among women writers. In a belated tribute to Powell, Edmund Wilson attributes Powell's relative obscurity in part to her role as a female satirist and her unwillingness to subscribe to the cult of female celebrity as did her better-known counterparts like Edna St. Vincent Millay, Dorothy Parker, and Mary McCarthy. According to Wilson, Powell showed a "complete indifference to publicity. She rarely goes to publishers' lunches or has publishers' parties given to her; she does not encourage interviews or the appearance of her photograph on book jackets. No effort has been made to glamorize her, and it would be hopeless to try to glamorize her novels." He goes on to make a sexist claim that Powell's serious subject matter does not appeal to female readers: "She does nothing to situate feminine dreams. The woman reader can find no comfort in identifying herself with Miss Powell's heroine. The women who appear in her stories are as likely to be as sordid and absurd as the men. There are no love scenes that will rouse you or melt you." As a midwesterner and New York transplant, says Wilson, Powell is aware of the comic possibilities in this newfound freedom and exploits them "with a wit, a gift of comic invention, and an individual accent that makes her books unlike any others." She has, in Wilson's assessment, a unique mix of urban sophistication and "Middle Western common sense, capable of toughness and brusqueness; yet a fairyland strain of Welsh fantasy."[12]

Like Edmund Wilson, Gore Vidal asks why Dawn Powell, "our best comic novelist," did "not get her due?"[13] In two influential essays for the *New York Review of Books*, "Dawn Powell, the American Writer" (1987) and "Dawn Powell: Queen of the Golden Age" (1996), Vidal spurred a Dawn Powell revival with his assessment of her as one of the United States' greatest and most neglected novelists. The music critic Tim Page, prompted by Vidal's piece, along with his own admiration for the writer, picked up the mantle with his influential biography of Powell, his edited collection of her diaries and letters, and his instigation of the reprinting of much of her fiction by Steerforth Press. Vidal attributes Powell's neglect largely to her gender and choice of genre: "Powell was that unthinkable monster, a witty woman who felt no obligation to make a single, much less final, down payment on Love of the Family; she saw life with a bright Petronian neutrality, and every host at life's feast was a potential Trimalchio to be sent up." The reference to a female wit as a "monster" recalls Hélène Cixous's "Laugh of the Medusa," in which female laughter is seen as monstrous from a conventional male perspective, which fails to recognize its beauty and power. "Wit, deployed by a woman with surgical calm, is a brutal assault upon nature—that is, Man," observes Vidal. "Attis, take arms!"[14] In "Queen of the Golden Age," Vidal elaborates on Powell's outsider status as a female wit with a modern outlook: "She was a wit, a satirist, and a woman, a combination that did not enchant the book chatterers of that era. Most of all she did not affirm warm mature family values."[15]

By contrast, as Powell observes in a 1934 diary entry, women writers of the day—Nancy Hale, Louise Bogan, Kay Boyle—"made their art serve their female purpose whereas once it warred with their femininity. Each page is squirming with sensitivity, every line—no matter how well disguised the heroine is—coyly reveals her exquisite taste, her delicate calm, her never-at-a-disadvantaged body" (D, 92). Conversely, Powell disparages what she terms "he-man writers—Hemingway, Burnett, Cain—imitation he-manners whose words tersely proclaim their masculinity, every tight-lipped phrase shows the author's guts, his decency, his ability to handle any situation" (D, 93). Despite Hemingway's reported admiration for Powell—in a reputed letter to Powell, he called her his "favorite American writer" (D, 226)—and their shared social circles, Powell satirizes the egotistical, celebrity "he-man" writer modeled on Hemingway in her portrayal of Andrew Callingham in *Turn, Magic Wheel*, among others.[16]

Like Powell's fellow wits Dorothy Parker and Mary McCarthy, Powell resisted the label of woman writer. She did, however, acknowledge the limitations placed on female professionals who often served as primary caretakers. In a 1957 diary entry, Powell reflects on the cost of being a primary caretaker on her career: "One reason women (and some men) writers are kept back is that they spend their brains and heart on writing but their fighting ability they must use for others—to protect, advance, heal, feed, support. Whereas the complete egotist not only writes but fights every minute for his writing and his own professional advancement, losing no tears or blood on family or friends or even difficult lover" (D, 373). In reflecting on George Bernard Shaw's relationship to his wife, she observes, "In order for a genius to be a genius, he must have a selfless slave between him and the world so that he may select what tidbits he chooses from it and not have his brains swallowed up in a chaff. For women this protection is impossible" (D, 306). Powell managed to balance the demands of an alcoholic husband who eventually lost his job and a mentally disabled son with a prolific career as a writer. Her satiric writing is distinguished by a sense of pathos and common humanity, even for those whom she targets.

Powell's most lasting contribution is as a satirist of the New York literary and artistic worlds of Midtown Manhattan and Greenwich Village bohemia from the 1930s through the 1950s. As a midwesterner coming to New York City, Powell brought at once the admiration and critical perspective of the outsider operating from within. Like the "seeker" in E. B. White's *Here Is New York* (1949), who comes to the city in pursuit of a dream, the protagonists in Powell's New York novels are often outsiders from the Midwest in search of themselves and of the freedom of becoming that New York promises. In Ann Douglas's literary and cultural history of Black and white New York in the 1920s, *Terrible Honesty: Mongrel Manhattan in the 1920s*, she similarly identifies the mythical import of New York City as a city of dreams, a liminal place of possibility that is a product of the imagination more than a reality.

In *Republic of Dreams: Greenwich Village: The American Bohemia, 1910–1960*, the former *Village Voice* cultural critic Ross Wetzsteon identifies the physical location of Greenwich Village as "more or less four square miles, roughly bounded on the north by Fourteenth Street, on the West by the Hudson River, on the South by Houston Street, and on the East by Third Avenue," but the Village is less a geographical location than "a state of mind." Greenwich Village in the 1920s and '30s was a "mythic place" in the American imagination and a "revolution of consciousness" associated with romantic rebellion, sexual emancipation, nonconformity, and an anti-bourgeois bohemianism of the marginalized outsider.[17] Though it is also associated with a sense of loss or the fleeting nature of youth and adolescent rebellion.

Powell's dream of leaving rural Ohio for the big city began in childhood, when she fled the oppressive home of her cruel stepmother in Mount Gilead, Ohio, at the age of thirteen to live with her permissive and supportive Aunt Orpha May, a divorcee who ran a boarding house over a train station in Shelby, Ohio.[18] Powell literarily lived at the crossroads of several major cities that were only a train ride away. After winning a scholarship to Lake Erie College, where she wrote for the newspaper as well as an underground satiric paper, Powell relocated to New York City at the age of twenty-one in 1918, at the end of World War I. Powell worked as a writer and editor, and she met and married her lifelong partner, Joseph Gousha, who worked as an advertising executive. They lived in an apartment at 35 East Ninth Street off University Place near the famed Washington Square, where Henry James and Edith Wharton, among other New York literary icons, once resided. Greenwich Village life was formative to Powell's identity, and the café culture surrounding the Lafayette Hotel (at University Place and Ninth Street) and the Brevoort Hotel (on Fifth Avenue and Eighth Street) served as an informal salon for Powell and her coterie and provided the subject matter for much of her fiction.

"I *am* New York—this minute—now," wrote Powell in a 1949 diary entry. "I know more about it than anyone—not historically, but momentarily" (*D*, 285). But Powell's dedication to New York went beyond the moment to show a historical appreciation for the city. "There is really one city for everyone just as there is one major love," wrote Powell in 1953. "New York is my city because I have an investment I can always draw on—a bottomless investment of twenty-one years (I count the day I was born) of building up an *idea* of New York—so no matter what happens here I have the rock of my dreams of it that nothing can destroy" (*D*, 326). So wrote Powell when her beloved Lafayette café was soon to be demolished to make way for high-rise apartments, part of a larger urban-renewal project led by Robert Moses in the 1950s that transformed New York and threatened the existing Greenwich Village bohemian life. In Powell's New York, the writer John Updike recognizes an appreciation for the diversity, inclusivity, and vitality of American, urban life: "Give us your lonely, your misunderstood, your sexually malcontent, your stubborn provincial dreams: responding to this siren call, Dawn Powell stayed loyal to New York with an ardor beside which that of celebrities like Scott Fitzgerald and E. B. White appear fickle. Such loyalty was in effect a loyalty to the human voice, which she saw with an unhappy child's uniform skepticism and macabre imitations."[19]

Powell's New York centered around Greenwich Village and the so-called Lafayette circle, a literary and artistic social circle over which she presided, surrounding the Lafayette Hotel café. Edmund Wilson, Gore Vidal, and Matthew Josephson recall wild Greenwich Village house parties at Powell's residence, particularly during Prohibition; Powell reportedly kept an aquarium filled with gin to prepare the drink of the day, a martini.[20] Her list of guests reads like a who's who of the New York literary scene, including Edmund Wilson, Djuna Barnes, Van Wyck Brooks, Malcolm Cowley, John Dos Passos, Matthew Josephson, Gore Vidal, J. B. Priestley, and on occasion Ernest Hemingway.[21] She maintained a thirty-five-year friendship with Wilson and was close friends with Dos Passos, as documented by her diaries and their correspondence. Powell embraced the sexual freedom of the modern woman, living in an open marriage with her husband, Joseph

Gousha, and her longtime lover, the journalist Coburn (Coby) Gilman.[22] She is also reputed to have had an ongoing affair with the playwright and critic John Howard Lawson.[23] For Powell, says Updike, "the city is more than its geography and buildings; it is the secret eroticism that a place so purely human concentrates, like a perfume pressed from a thousand flowers."[24] Her raunchy humor and sharp tongue led to comparisons with Mae West, whose "earthy and hospitable manner" she was known to mimic.[25]

Powell's coterie centered around the Lafayette Hotel café, which was located across the street from her apartment. Powell reportedly quipped to Malcolm Cowley, "For years I lived so close to the Lafayette that I could look down from my apartment window and see my own checks bouncing there."[26] Powell's remark captures part of the appeal of café culture in the '30s and '40s: a familiar café offered a place to meet and converse with fellow writers, artists, and intellectuals; regular waiters; a telephone message taker; and an owner who provided meals on credit. It was also a place to observe people from all walks of life, and "out of the talk and gossip the intrigues of everyday, the couplings and uncouplings, [Powell] shaped her novels."[27] The Lafayette was an elegant, French-style hotel, which Matthew Josephson recalls as having "a wide, high-ceilinged room with tall windows giving on the street; it had mirrored walls, green shaded lamps, and marble-topped tables, some of them reserved for players at dominos or chess; in a corner there used to be a rack filled with French newspapers and magazines"; it had a "sumptuous restaurant," and during Prohibition "they served wine in coffee mugs to known clients."[28] Powell famously presided over a corner table, where she could see patrons enter the café and selectively call them over, or she could summon the telephone person over if she wished to be called away. The Lafayette was a place where writers could work on their manuscripts (there was even a place to leave your manuscript until the next day) and was frequented by a diverse mix of writers, publishers, artists, art patrons, advertising executives, theater people, and "hangers on."

Unlike the Algonquin Hotel—with its exclusive, regular "Round Table" of wits presided over by Dorothy Parker and revolving around the Midtown magazine writers, journalists, publishers, and theater crowd—the Lafayette Hotel café had a less clearly defined, more inclusive crowd. Among the Lafayette circle were "people associated with the avant-garde theatre, such as Paul Peters, the playwright, the directors Murdock Pemberton and Leon Throckmorton, and the . . . literary agent, Ivan von Auw, Jr." After World War II, Powell's coterie included the *New Yorker* writers John and Mary Cheever, A. J. Liebling, and Joseph Mitchell, as well as the artists Stuart

Davis, Niles Spencer, and Reginald Marsh (who illustrated the original cover of *The Wicked Pavilion* at Powell's suggestion).[29]

Like the Lafayette Hotel, the nearby Brevoort Hotel and café, founded in 1854, was owned by the French hotelier Raymond Orteig and was "designed to have the look and feel of an old Parisian café, with a room for dominoes, the magazine rack, a flavor of Flaubert," a reflection of a bygone era.[30] In Ann M. Peters's PhD dissertation, "Travelers in Residency: Women Writing New York at Mid-Century," she documents the importance of New York City hotels particularly for women in the early and mid-twentieth century, both as places of residency and public gathering places. While there were the more upscale, Uptown or Midtown hotels like the Plaza or the Hotel Astor, more modest hotels like the Vanderbilt and the Murray Hill offered single working women, career women, widows, and divorcees the safety and respectability to live on their own. (When Powell herself could no longer afford to live in her duplex apartment on Ninth Street and University Place, she relocated to the Madison Square Hotel, among others.) And it was in fact female activists, led by Jane Jacobs, who mounted the opposition to Robert Moses's plans to build the lower Manhattan Expressway through the West Village, threatening to destroy local neighborhoods and playgrounds along with local Village culture. Hotels and cafés were "small, neighborhood centers," where "middle-class business could mingle with aspiring painters and artists."[31] They offered more intimate public spaces, what Powell termed "privacy in the midst of sociability," where women and bohemian outsiders could find a place of belonging, "a temporary home for the homeless to hang their hats."[32] The decline of hotel and café life in the late 1950s and early '60s to make room for office buildings and apartment buildings coincided with the movement to the suburbs and emphasis on domestic life for women after World War II. The Brevoort Hotel closed in 1949, and its dining room and sidewalk café were demolished along with the Lafayette Hotel and café in 1953, displacing bohemian writers and artists to bars like the San Remo and the Cedar Tavern, on which Powell's novel *The Golden Spur* is based.[33]

This shift in the landscape of New York bohemian life from the 1930s through the 1950s and Greenwich Village café culture in particular is the subject of much of Powell's New York fiction. "Dawn's novels remain the best record of the Village landscape of the thirties, forties, and fifties," according to the Village historian Ross Wetzsteon. "The most convincing character [in her fiction] is the city itself, for Dawn reveals how its moods and rhythms insidiously invade the psyche, color perception, motivate behavior. The Village—a kind of contemporary Vanity Fair—can be gay, openhearted, overflowing with opportunities but it can also be dissipated, thoughtless, destructive of dreams."[34] The critic Edmund Wilson shares Powell's nostalgia for the "Golden Age" of Greenwich Village, "the days of such old-fashioned resorts as the Brevoort and the Lafayette, with their elegant and well-served French restaurants and domino-playing café, . . . the days of those small cheap and decent hotels, . . . now almost entirely destroyed to make way for huge apartment buildings, to the era of those noisy abysmal bars," with "bearded beatniks and abstract painters [who] have seeped in among the Guggenheim fellows, the raffish NYU professors and adult education students," all of whom are the object of Powell's satire and Wilson's disdain.[35] Despite the decline of bohemian café culture, Powell's New York novels maintain a sense of possibility and longing for the dream of New York.

Dawn Powell's New York novels can be loosely divided among her early (1930s), middle (1940s), and late novels (1950s and '60s), as well as between her "Uptown" and "Midtown" novels and her "Downtown" or "Greenwich Village" novels. Her New York fiction is largely satiric in tone, as distinguished from her earlier Ohio novels and autobiographical writing, which can be more sentimental. *Turn, Magic Wheel* (1936) satirizes the literary and publishing world surrounding Midtown Manhattan in the 1930s. *The Happy Island* (1938) focuses on gay and bohemian life surrounding the theater world in the 1930s, based in part on her friendship with Dwight Fiske. *Angels on Toast* (1940) satirizes the bourgeois life of the traveling businessman. *A Time to Be Born* (1942) is a satire of the publishing world of Midtown Manhattan and the aspirations of the professional woman, based loosely on the lives of Clare Boothe Luce and the publishing magnate Henry Luce. *The Locusts Have No King* (1948) is a satire of the literary and publishing world of Midtown Manhattan, inspired by members of the Algonquin Round Table. *The Wicked Pavilion* (1954) and *The Golden Spur* (1962) are later novels that satirize the decline of Greenwich Village bohemian café culture in the 1940s and '50s. My analysis focuses on Powell's satire of the literary and publishing world in *Turn, Magic Wheel* as well as her satire of the bohemian café culture and art world of post–World War II New York as portrayed in two of Powell's latest and best novels, *The Wicked Pavilion* (1954) and *The Golden Spur* (1962).

In addition to documenting the themes of love and art, as Edmund Wilson observed, "the real theme [of Powell's novels] is the provincial in New York who has come on from the Middle West and acclimated himself (or herself) to the city and made himself a permanent place there, without, however, losing his fascinated sense of an alien and anarchic society."[36] This bohemian seeker often takes the form of a writer and can be seen as a stand-in for Powell herself. Such characters recur in Powell's fiction, and the character of Dennis Orphen in particular is introduced in *Turn, Magic Wheel* and returns more peripherally in *The Wicked Pavilion*. Powell describes the novel as "a thoroughly New York book with the beauty and sheer thrill of New York running through it, in contrast to the imprisoned life it is possible to live here and which Lila [renamed Effie] does. A novel of no plot but of mood, feeling, atmosphere, even glamour, seen but never attained. This should be one in shaded fleeting photographic shots with the basic reality of the book her heartache—not a neurotic ache but a real one" (*D*, 80). Powell here discusses subordination of character and plot to the primary focus on New York, where the female protagonist's personal suffering is told through the fabric of city life and becomes emblematic of the frustrated dreams of city dwellers.

By December 1934, Powell shifts the focus of the novel to a male protagonist and writer, Dennis Orphen, whom she significantly sees as having greater freedom and being closer to herself (*D*, 96). Powell thus chooses to express her unconventional ideas through the voice of a male protagonist. The name Orphen may be linked to her own orphaned identity and the protective care of her Aunt Orpha May. Dennis Orphen wrote a novel, *The Hunter's Wife*, based on Effie's abandonment by a famed author and ladies' man, Andrew Callingham, modeled on Ernest Hemingway. He is further trapped in a three-way relationship with Effie, the subject of his novel with whom he is having an emotional relationship, and Corinne, an attractive but vacuous married woman with whom he is having a physical affair. Through the lens of the writer Dennis Orphen, Powell satirizes the writing and publishing world as well as the bourgeois world of marriage and money, the wealthy world of patrons of the arts, and the dream of love and self-discovery in New York City.

Powell's New York City not only is the setting of the novel but in many ways shapes the lives of its characters. In *Turn, Magic Wheel*, writes Powell, "I believe firmly that I have the perfect New York story, one woman's tragedy viewed through the chinks of a writer's book about her, newspaper clippings, café conversations, restaurant brawls, New York night life, so that the story is tangled in the fritter of New York—it could not happen anyplace else" (*D*, 106). That individual suffering is subordinated to the distractions and action of the city may seem callous or inhumane, observes Powell, but "the truth is that in New York, a city of perpetual distractions—where superficial senses are perpetually forced to react to superficial impressions—the inner tragedies, no matter how intense, are viewed through the tawdry lace of New York life" (*D*, 106). The "tawdry" life of the city is paradoxically sustaining in that it helps to minimize one's personal suffering and to make us feel that, in our isolation, we are not alone. In the novel, Powell balances individual narratives with the overarching sights and sounds of the city to create a portrait of urban life that is at once cacophonous and comforting.

Powell is both enthralled with and alienated by the modern, urban landscape. Several of the signature descriptions of New York are based on Powell's personal observations and taken almost wholesale from her diaries. The post–World War I New York landscape, with its skyscrapers and art deco style, is epitomized in the figure of the Empire State Building, at once a testament to progress and a symbol of the depersonalization of the New York skyline. Powell captures this ambiguity in *Turn, Magic Wheel* on a romantic outing between Dennis and his mistress, Corinne, looking down from the newly built Empire State Building: "Clouds as white as the sky was baby-blue instead of black swam softly about them, stars were below and above, glittering through the plumes of the moon, listening for compliments from the Tower visitors."[37] This passage is based on Powell's July 1931 diary entry of her first excursion to the newly built Empire State Building, "the huge tomb in steel and glass," and the surreal experience of seeing "a thousand feet below, New York—a garden of golden lights winking on and off, automobiles, trucks winding in and out, and not a sound. All as silent as a dead city—it looks *adagio* down there" (*D*, 32).

In an oft-cited passage from the novel taken almost verbatim from her 1932 diary entry (*D*, 54), Powell uses irony to convey the ambivalent message of the modern urban landscape: "New York twinkled far off into Van Cortland Park, spangled skyscrapers piled up softly against the darkness, tinseled parks were neatly boxed and ribboned with gold like Christmas presents waiting to be opened. Sounds of traffic dissolved in the distance, all clangor sifted through space into a whispering silence, it held a secret, and when letters flamed triumphantly in the sky you felt, ah, that was the secret, this at last was it, the special telegram to God—Sunshine Biscuits. On and off it went, Eat Sunshine Biscuits, the message of the city" (*TMW*, 156). There is no mistaking the ironic message of the city, breaking its holy silence with the incessant, capitalist message of modern advertising and worship of the new materialism in a scene reminiscent of the

ubiquitous eyes of Dr. T. J. Eckleberg in *The Great Gatsby*. Powell is captivated by the push and pull of the city in what seems like a never-ending
dance, in which the tempo and the steps may change but the movement is
constant.

The title of the novel, *Turn, Magic Wheel*, speaks to the magical possibilities of the New York dream of love and success as well as the power
of fate or forces beyond our control in determining the lives of individuals. The characters find themselves in situations of their own making that
also reflect larger societal forces. The epigraph from the ancient Greek
poet Theocritus—"Turn, magic wheel, / Bring homeward him I love"—
is invoked ironically, for the novel is a story of the failure of modern love.
The female protagonist, Effie Thorne, becomes the emblem of the self-sacrificing, self-doubting woman who, despite her style and sophistication,
finds herself waiting in vain for the return of her unfaithful husband. The
writer Dennis Orphen creates a satiric portrait of Effie as the woman in
waiting for the macho man in his novel, *The Hunter's Wife*.

Like Powell, Dennis is a writer from the Midwest (South Bend, Indiana)
of modest origins (his father was a traveling salesman like Powell's own father)
who comes to New York City in pursuit of his dreams. He forgoes a career
in his uncle's shoe factory and rejects the bourgeois life of marrying a local
girl and having a family in favor of the bohemian artist world of New York.
There is something lacking, however, in Dennis, and his failure to commit
in love and in life contributes to Powell's satire of the passivity and narcis-
sism of the writer/observer. Despite his quirky charm, Dennis can be seen
as a kind of parasite, living off others' experiences rather than creating his
own. He uses Effie not only as the subject of his book but also as a kind of
buffer against what he sees as the trap of romantic attachment. His triangu-
lated relationship with Effie and Corinne becomes a trope for the freedom
as well as the alienation and ultimate loneliness of modern love.

In *Turn, Magic Wheel*, Powell's female characters lack the independence and wit of Prudence Bly in *The Happy Island* or Amanda Keeler in
A Time to Be Born and are portrayed more as victims of their place in society. Effie tries to show a modern tolerance of her husband's infidelity and
his desire not to have children, but she masks her true desire for a more
traditional marriage and motherhood. She blames herself for his trans-
gressions and only realizes after he cheats on his jealous mistress that he
would have been unfaithful regardless of her actions. After her husband's
fifteen-year absence, Effie still keeps her married name on her mailbox, and
in a mock bridal chapter ironically titled "the Trousseau," the aging Effie

refashions herself and her apartment in bright, youthful colors in anticipation of her husband's return. It is not until Dennis callously tells her, "Why everyone's always known that he walked out on you" (*TMW*, 23), that she begins to face the truth. Effie fears that she will be publicly ridiculed by the publication of Dennis's book and avoids being seen with him in public: "Everyone would know then that it really was about me—everyone would laugh" (*TMW*, 15). Laughter can be empowering for the joke teller—"any minute with your shiny little pen you can make everybody laugh and laugh" (*TMW*, 17)—while it victimizes the object of laughter. Effie momentarily reverses the power of laughter by mocking herself—she forgives Dennis and laughs out loud at the satiric portrayal of herself—but the damage to herself and their relationship is done. Dennis tries to justify his actions as intending to free the captive princess from the dragon, but in his scathing portrayal of Effie and her exploitative relationship, he has damaged that which he sought to liberate.

Through the character of Dennis's lover, Corinne, Powell satirizes bourgeois marriage and the figure of the conniving and seemingly conventional, docile woman. She seems to love wearing an apron and cleaning up, responds to diminutives like "my pet," and seems on the verge of tears, such that "strangers felt impelled to offer a shoulder with a 'There, there, little girl, cry it out'" (*TMW*, 58). Powell adds with exaggeration that "a shoulder would not really be enough, one felt, she would burrow in the neck, in the armpits, under the skin like a cunning little beast" (*TMW*, 59). While Corinne and her husband, Phil Barrow, address each other with sweet platitudes like "my little Honey Bear" and "baby," the harsh reality of her infidelity threatens to sour the relationship. Corinne shows the characteristic bourgeois indifference to the suffering of the poor and empathy for the plight of the rich: "She could see plays or read books on revolution, poverty, and starvation with a detached 'tough luck' as if among the oppressed further misfortune were the rule and left her unmoved. But when she saw hearts really break, as only hearts under ermine can break, then tears by the gallon did she shed, did Mrs. Baby Barrow, her whole exquisite nervous system bathed and sublimated in sympathetic anguish over Harlow's diamond-studded woe" (*TMW*, 125).

Dawn Powell's sharpest satire is directed against the wealthy Belle and Tony Glaenzer, who are sequestered from the din of Depression-era New York in their palatial Fifth Avenue apartment. The cacophony of New York streets was "only a dim noise outside the Glaenzer coffin doors, a cry, a wish, a dream [from] the rich fat enemy world of the Glaenzers ... peering out at New York through Fifth Avenue lace curtains, listening to the Help! Help! of the city through symphonic arrangements of Stokowski, . . . swimming in their goldfish bowl, observed rather than observing, swimming in and out of their skeleton castle, pressing their little blind noses to the glass, blinking, aware of only light or dark" (*TMW*, 9). Powell contrasts the gritty vitality of the New York streets with the sterile indifference of the Glaenzers, absorbed in their self-indulgent pursuit of culture and materialism to the neglect of the people in need around them.

Belle Glaenzer in particular is a grotesque parody of the excess and indulgence of the wealthy, Jewish elite. She is described as "a vast dough-faced shapeless Buddha in black velvet that flowed out of the chair and spilled its inky folds into the du Barry roses of the thick carpet" and a "monument to Hollandaise in the black velvet chair" (*TMW*, 75). Her home, like her person, is decorated in opulent vulgarity in an attempt to approximate European aristocracy that only emphasizes its lack of taste. "The ceilings were so high that the rococo splendors of the cornice, dividing as it did green tapestried walls from a ceiling pool of cupids, was lost in shadows" (*TMW*, 75–76). A lion skin (a gift from Andrew Callingham) was draped across the floor with closed mouth "because stuffing the tongue cost fifteen dollars extra at the taxidermist" (*TMW*, 76). This mix of indulgence and cheapness characterizes the Glaenzers' approach to spending, and the visiting Dr. MacGregor brands Belle "the meanest, stingiest old woman of all the mean stingy old women in New York" for her refusal to help fund a children's hospital while she sits in her $500 chair. The Glaenzers nonetheless are protective of Effie, and they view the aspiring writer Dennis with suspicion: "Union Square never recommended any visitor yet, young lady. Is he one of those radicals?" (*TMW*, 78). Powell here emphasizes the great divide between the wealthy and bourgeois worlds of Uptown New York and the radical, bohemian world of Downtown Greenwich Village, Chelsea, and Union Square.

Powell also satirizes the bourgeois publishing world of Midtown Manhattan in its conformity, unreliability, and profit motive, a risky move for an author dependent on publishing houses and the press for promotion of her own work. As the biographer Tim Page, among others, has documented, Powell had a conflicted relationship with the publishing industry and changed publishers repeatedly over the course of her career, despite being with some of the best-known editors in the industry. She worked with Max Perkins at Scribner's, the same editor and publisher as Hemingway and Fitzgerald, and after disagreements with Perkins's successor John

Wheelock, she turned to Rosalind Wilson, daughter of Edmund Wilson, at Houghton Mifflin.[38] She nonetheless expressed frustration at the some-time misrepresentation and lack of promotion of her work.

Powell's hostility toward the publishing industry comes out in her satiric portrayal of Dennis Orphen's publisher, MacTweed and Company. MacTweed tries to rationalize abandoning Dennis, whose negative portrayal of the famed author Andrew Callingham threatens to jeopardize the publisher's prospects of keeping him as a client. MacTweed falsely claims that Dennis's book is potentially libelous, a claim with which Powell as a satirist was all too familiar. In reality, Dennis's writing does not conform to current trends in publishing: "It was an age of the present tense, the Stevedor style. . . . The older writers who had taken twenty years to learn their craft were in a bewildering predicament, learning alas, too late, that Pater, Proust, and Flaubert had betrayed them, they would have learned better modern prose by economizing on Western Union messages" (*TMW*, 102–3). Powell here mocks literary fads that devalue the complexity of the great masters in favor of a more accessible, business style. The oversimplified style of journalists and reviewers is also parodied in a chapter titled "*announcements in* Publishers Weekly" followed by a series of one-word reviews of Dennis's novel: "'Fine . . .' Louis Bromfeld; 'Significant . . .' Hugh Walpole; 'Timely . . .' J. B. Priestely," as well as the required disclaimer, "All the characters in this novel are highly fictitious" (*TMW*, 107). The publishing industry seems more concerned with avoiding a lawsuit and making sales than in promoting the aesthetic value of art.

Powell's harshest satire of the business and publishing world is reserved for the conformity of the company men. "These And Companys, many in publishing, some in their uncles' devious businesses, were all men of good taste, and if Semitic were decent enough to be blond and even a little dumb just to be more palatable socially. But they all looked and talked alike" (*TMW*, 108). Powell here takes a dig at the WASP conformity of the old boys' network that has infiltrated the New York corporate scene. There is a conformity of ideas, and Johnson, an up-and-coming editor, prides himself on landing the greatest number of "proletarian writers," ironically a profitable trend in the 1930s. "He was so brilliant he could tell in advance that in the years 1934–35 and –36 a book would be hailed as exquisitely written if it began: 'The boxcar swung out of the yards. Pip rolled over in the straw. He scratched himself where the straw itched him'" (*TMW*, 98). Powell mocks not only the false valuation of the pared-down language of social realism but the herd instinct and profit motive of critics and publishers. Dennis

Orphen is destined to stagnate amid the rush to follow the current trends in publishing and to land the biggest authors.

Powell's sardonic portrayal of love and literature in the interwar US coalesces in the figure of Andy Callingham, the best-selling author and unfaithful husband of Effie Thorne, whose transformation by fame makes him unrecognizable to his forlorn wife. While Powell is careful to disclaim any direct connection, the character of Andy Callingham is by all accounts inspired by Ernest Hemingway. Despite knowing Hemingway socially and professionally and his being an admirer of her work, Powell parodies him as a "he-man" writer and seems to view with disdain the cult of celebrity surrounding him and other celebrated writers. Powell satirically portrays Andy as "a big hairy roaring sort of guy—he-man. Loved trying out every woman he met, especially the difficult virginal type" (*TMW*, 34). Andy is seen as a philanderer, cheating on his first wife, Effie, with Marian, a Kansas City girl, whom he cheats on with his latest love interest, a chorus girl. Effie ironically identifies with the jilted Marian, and when Marian falls terminally ill and is hospitalized, Effie contacts Andy to return to the US and pay his last respects. Effie's illusion that Andy's return might be an opportunity to rekindle their long-lost relationship is foiled when she has to wait with other journalists and admirers for an audience with him.

Andy Callingham is a caricature of the egotistical male rotter, who boasts, "I'm the best goddam writer this country ever turned out, yes, or France or England too for that matter" (*TMW*, 210). When Effie does finally meet with him, he is barely recognizable through his "Andy-façade" of celebrity and self-promotion. "There was no Andy left," muses Effie. "He had been wiped out by Callingham the Success as men before him had been wiped out by the thing they represented" (*TMW*, 212). This realization is ironically liberating for Effie, who no longer seeks to recapture their lost romance and introduces Dennis as her new love interest (perhaps replacing one romantic illusion with another). Andy is so caught up in promoting his public image that he ironically has no time or creative energy to generate the very literature for which he became famous. Thus, Powell makes a negative comment on the cult of success among writers/artists that is often the enemy of creativity and authenticity.

The novel ends in Powell's characteristic ambiguous style, with both of Dennis's love interests, Effie and Corinne expressing interest in a future with him and his noncommittal ongoing pursuit of them. The ups and downs of Powell's narrative mirror the vicissitudes of New York itself, which offers the promise, the frustrated hopes, and the renewed possibilities of dreams of love and self-discovery.

In Powell's last two novels, *The Wicked Pavilion* (1954) and *The Golden Spur* (1962), she chronicles the decline of Greenwich Village bohemian life after World War II. Her focus shifts from the literary world to the art world and from the bohemianism of the '30s and early '40s to what can be seen as the pseudobohemianism of the beatniks and poseurs surrounding Greenwich Village bars like the Cedar Tavern in the postwar era. Powell's satire is directed at the self-manufactured industry surrounding the art world—from the dealers and promoters to the critics and academics to the patrons and ultimately to the artists themselves—who are caught in the ethical dilemma of whether to compromise their artistic integrity for the sake of profit and recognition. Powell's subject is thus an extension of her earlier satire, which was largely directed at the publishers, patrons, critics, and writers who lose themselves in pursuit of success. For Powell, the subject was highly personal and founded in part on her own frustration at not being sufficiently acknowledged as a female satirist in the reduction of the artist to a marketable commodity. As always, the individual characters and plots are subordinated to the larger setting, and New York, the city of hopes and at times frustrated dreams, takes center stage.

The title of Powell's novel *The Wicked Pavilion* is inspired by the *Creevey Papers*, the correspondence and diaries of the eighteenth-century British member of Parliament Thomas Creevey, which Powell read while visiting Gerald and Sara Murphy in the winter of 1950 (*D*, 289). The epigraph is taken from a letter that Mrs. Creevey wrote to her husband: "Oh this wicked Pavilion! We were kept there till half-past one this morning waiting for the Prince, and it has kept me in bed with the head-ache till twelve to-day."[39] The Wicked Pavilion comes to represent "the place everyone enjoys till after midnight, drinking so they cannot get up till noon, and then with heads" (*D*, 289). For Powell, such a place is the fictional Café Julien, a composite of her beloved Lafayette Hotel café and Brevoort café and a place at once of belonging and escape, where the writer and artist can go to hold court or to get lost in the lives of others. In the novel, Powell was particularly interested in trying to convey the gossip and innuendo of journal and letter writing or café conversation in re-creating New York in the style that Balzac and Flaubert chronicled Paris. "I wish to convey the complete vivid details of New York life and varied characters not in conventional fiction guise but with the *complete* reality of the eighteenth- and nineteenth-century letter writers who told all the inside scandals chattily, informatively, real paces, real names, etc.—and a kind of special woman of the last two decades, as peculiar to this age as certain Balzac types" (*D*, 292). Powell's novel chronicles the artistic world of Downtown and Midtown Manhattan at midcentury. She further takes on the figure of the modern American woman, who is at once liberated and confined by her newfound freedom in the modern urban setting.

The novel is framed by the narrative of Dennis Orphen, the writer and stand-in for Powell, and covers the period from 1948 to 1953. Dennis expresses nostalgia for a bygone era and a sense of foreboding in the post-atomic age. From his perch at his regular corner table of the Café Julien, located around the corner from Washington Square in Greenwich Village, Dennis observes the plight of New York: "There was nothing unusual about the New York winter of 1948 for the unusual was now the usual. Elderly ladies died of starvation in shabby hotels leaving boxes full of rags and hundred-dollar bills, bands of children robbed and raped through the city streets, lovers could find no beds, hamburgers were forty cents at lunch counters. . . . Citizens harassed by Internal Revenue hounds jumped out of windows for want of forty dollars, families on relief bought bigger television sets to match the new time-bought furniture" (*WP*, 4). The paradox of the pursuit of material acquisitions in an era of scarcity and the suppression of free speech during the age of conformity in the McCarthy era defined the US at midcentury. "In the city the elements themselves were money: air was money, fire was money, water was money, the need of, the quest for, the greed for. Love was money. There was only money or death" (*WP*, 5). In this race toward "progress" and material success on the "cosmic Ferris wheel" of life, Dennis asks the artist's question: "What became of Beauty, where went Love?" (*WP*, 5). For Dennis, like Powell, the Greenwich Village café serves as a stay against the confusion and rapid change of modern life and a potential haven for art and love. "I want the cafe to be a place where people come to remind themselves that once one could dream of doing something for oneself, for the world" (*D*, 302), writes Powell. This possibility is connected for Powell and her characters to New York City.

The narrative of *The Wicked Pavilion* is framed by the love story and quest of Rick Prescott and Ellenora Carsdale. Rick is one of Powell's typical seekers from the Midwest, a transplant from Michigan to New York. Powell creates a romantic illusion of New York on the brink of war that stands in contrast to Dennis's somber postwar portrait and one that cannot withstand the realities of modern life. Rick recalls the first time he came to New York seven years earlier as a young officer about to embark for World War II:

It was the first time he'd ever been in New York, the city of his dreams. . . . New York loved him as it loved no other young man, and he embraced the city, impulsively discarding everything he had hitherto cherished of his Michigan boyhood loyalties. In Radio City Gardens he looked up at the colossal Prometheus commanding the city's very heart and thought, Me! He wandered up and down in a kind of smiling daze, . . . strolled happily down Fifth Avenue, finding all faces beautiful and wondrously kind, the lacy fragility of the city trees incomparably superior to his huge native forests. Under the giant diesel hum of street and harbor traffic he caught the sweet music of danger, the voices of deathless love and magic adventures. (*WP*, 11)

This enchanted view of New York, like a personal calling to the provincial outsider, is classic Powell, and though the illusion is fleeting, it is irresistible nonetheless. Rick could not believe "his day's adventure had been with a city and not a girl" (*WP*, 12). The Café Julien, a meeting place for artists and lovers, becomes a destination for Rick and his love interest, the young and beguiling photographer Ellenora, who "represented New York or his idea of New York" (*WP*, 25). Throughout the novel, they continue to search for each other by leaving messages and stopping by the Café Julien, a place of constancy amid the chaos of the city.

The primary focus of Powell's satire is on the art world of Downtown and Midtown Manhattan, from the artists to the critics and patrons, whose integrity is compromised in the search for profit and success. The plot centers around the mystery of the famed artist Marius's apparent death and the frenzied industry surrounding his reputation that follows. Marius is one of a group of struggling artists in New York at midcentury, including his contemporaries Dalzell Sloane and Ben Forrester. Both Marius and Ben are seen as typical chauvinists who disparage their wives and mistresses as "clinging vines," yet they need them to hold their "rotting branches together" (*WP*, 246). Dalzell is captivated by the notorious art patron and seductress Cynthia Earle. After false reports of Marius's death in Mexico following his arrest for wrecking a stolen car, he decides to take advantage of the situation to escape "creditors, fights, dames" (*WP*, 247).

Marius's reported death ironically elevates his reputation in the art world, creating increased demand and valuation of his work by patrons, critics, and dealers, who all seek to profit from his loss. "The greatest favor Marius, the man, had ever done for Marius, the artist, was to die at exactly the right moment" (*WP*, 171), the narrator ironically notes. Dalzell self-ironically envies his fellow artist's newfound celebrity: "How well he knew that hurt flash of jealousy on learning that Marius had been the one to win the Grand Immortal Prize of death which opened the gates closed in life to all of them!" (WP, 48). He mockingly resents Marius for "'selling out,' . . . dropping his old friends merely for the publicity and success of death" (WP, 48). There is a double irony in that Dalzell does not realize at this point that Marius has, to a degree, sold out his life for the fame and unaccountability of death.

Frustrated at the injustice and difficulty of making it in the art world, Dalzell and Ben discover that they have the same idea to complete and sell some of Marius's unfinished works themselves. This mutual understanding of artist outsiders seeking revenge on the establishment is precipitated by the release of laughter: "They began to laugh again, tried to talk but couldn't stop laughing. It was wonderful to have fear and loneliness transformed at last into a great joke between friends" (WP, 158). They rationalize this moral transgression by imagining that Marius would support them in their joke against the system: "The affair became a wonderful joke, something Marius himself would have loved" (WP, 48). Powell here satirizes the injustice and corruption of the putative art world, which reduces talented artists to manipulating the system through forgery and death in order to get the attention they deserve. That Marius would purportedly laugh with his fellow artists at the absurdity of the situation shows the power of laughter among outsiders to create community and subvert existing power structures. When Dalzell and Ben do ultimately find the hidden Marius, laughter releases the tension between them. Dalzell and Ben imagine the empowering laughter of Marius, who has orchestrated his death and is watching the ensuing chaos of the art world to lay claim to his legacy. "That *would* be his idea of a fine practical joke, letting us go out on a limb for him, making fools of ourselves, while he has a good time laughing at us!" (WP, 255). While Marius's fellow artists feign resentment at the joke, they are unified in laughter at their fight against the art world that they paradoxically loath and depend on.

Powell also directs her satiric eye at the art critics and academics who make a living profiting off the creativity of others and who undermine genuine talent and originality by conforming to aesthetic trends and reinforcing the cult of celebrity of a select few. Powell mocks scholars and academics, that "ravening horde of cultural necrophiles" (WP, 172) who feed off dead and dying writers and artists and perpetuate an industry from which they stand to benefit. "They rushed to stake claims on the great names of the past, boasted with a genuine sense of a deed accomplished that they were about to write a book on Dostoyevsky, Tolstoy, El Greco, or Bach, and dined out with dignity on nifties panned from the richly plumed legends. Some, who had the chance, stalked aging celebrities who might do them the favor of dropping dead and providing juicy material for future memoirs" (*WP*, 172). Sometimes, these aging legends have the indecency to live on or degenerate to a point where they lose value, observes Powell ironically.

The character of Okie, the publisher who was introduced in *Turn, Magic Wheel* as the editor of the middlebrow magazine the *Town*, returns as the publisher of *Hemisphere*, who seeks to profit off writing the definitive biography of Marius. An ironic contrast with Okie is Alfred Briggs, a young journalist for *City Life*, an aspiring sports reporter, who was hired as an art critic precisely for his ignorance of the subject to provide a sort of "man on the street" view of the New York art scene. Powell mocks the superficiality of modern magazine culture in its cultivation of mediocrity for the common reader, particularly when it comes to the arts, "a department where inexperience and ignorance would not be noticed" (*WP*, 174). In writing a piece on Marius for the paper, Briggs goes for his first time to an art museum and hangs out at Marius's old haunt, the Café Julien, to try to cultivate "the right Marius atmosphere" (*WP*, 182–83). Briggs personifies the next-generation poseur who has displaced the genuine bohemians and artists of Greenwich Village in the 1930s and early '40s. His philosophy of life—that you can judge people based on their financial worth—represents what is wrong with the new materialism of modern life. Briggs ironically loses his job at the magazine for writing too smart a piece on Marius and betraying the "average citizen approach" (*WP*, 265).

Powell's sharpest satire is directed at the wealthy art patron Cynthia Earle, another figure modeled on Peggy Guggenheim, a New York art collector and socialite known as much for bedding as for supporting struggling artists. She is described as an aging nymphomaniac, who seduces promising young artists in exchange for her patronage. Powell captures Cynthia's mix of coquettish girlishness and brazen sexuality: "She was not ugly as they said, but handsome in a swarthy, gamy, medieval way. She was overtall but had a coy way of ducking her head to look up at you with a bashful little-girl smile, hands clasped behind her, all but twisting her apron strings, and she spoke in a tiny tinkling Betty Boop voice" (*WP*, 166). Dalzell seeks artistic validation through Cynthia's sexual advances and is crushed when she loses interest at his easy conquest. Cynthia's patronage of the arts is revealed to be an extension of her lust for power and sexual satisfaction rather than having any basis in aesthetic value, another strike against the art industry.

Powell parodies the failed attempt by Cynthia to throw a tribute party for Marius in the masterful chapter "The Playback." In a gathering of artists, publishers, promoters, academics, media personalities, and even an ex-wife, Cynthia seeks to record personal tributes to Marius. Instead, the microphone picks up the gossip, insults, and innuendo of private conversations that make a mockery of the hypocrisy of the art world and the superficiality of its members.

An equal-opportunity satirist, Powell also exposes the bourgeois superiority and self-interest of the wealthy Hookley family. In a subplot to the bohemian artist scene, Powell follows the lives of Wharton Hookley, who lives in a duplex apartment on Gracie Square on the Upper East Side of Manhattan, and his sister, Eleanor, a divorced Baroness who lives in an apartment in Greenwich Village. The Hookleys are descended from an elite Boston family, and they fight over their family inheritance, with Wharton threatening to disinherit his sister. Eleanor, who is in her fifties, takes a vicarious interest in her younger neighbor Jerry, an aspiring model and party girl who plays on her girl-next-door looks and chance opportunity to make her way up the social ladder. Powell here makes a negative comment on the limited opportunities for modern women, both young and old, who are trapped in the double bind of free love in a society where a woman's financial stability still depends on her marriageability.

The unifying hub of the novel is the Café Julien, a geographic location and symbolic place of possibility around which the various stories revolve. The Julien was a common meeting place where artists like Marius, Dalzell, and Ben crossed paths with publishers like Okie, patrons like Cynthia, and young lovers like Rick and Ellenora. While the newcomer Briggs sees the Julien as "a bleak old dump" (*WP*, 183), Ellenora recalls the essence of café culture, which has not faded: "You find yourself coming back again and again not quite knowing why. The tables look bare, the lights cold and bright, so the people and the talk become the only furnishings, and you come back to find just that" and "that ever present atmosphere of something delightful about to happen" (*WP*, 183, 190). Powell parodies the café patrons, who represent all walks of life: "The Van-Dyked old gourmet with the velvet-draped Brunhilde wife laying into an angry-looking lobster about to be drowned in Piper-Heidsieck, . . . the Wall Street Sunday painter who came to the Julien to watch the professional artists, and . . . the pompous painter and his sculptor wife who were Sunday brokers, keeping themselves artistically fit by playing the stock market. There was the savage drama critic, . . . the voracious columnist, . . . the unsuspecting university professor who leered wolfishly across the table at his latest pet pupil" (*WP*, 191). Powell's satiric vision, at once affectionate and cutting, reveals her ambivalent relation to the Greenwich Village café culture, past and present.

In the late 1940s, this Greenwich Village bohemian world was under assault, and by 1953, at the novel's end, the symbolic world of the Café Julien comes to a literal end. Like the Lafayette and Brevoort on which it was modeled, the Julien is owned by the "last of a formidable dynasty of French chefs" (*WP*, 269), a New York branch of a Parisian café founded early in the century. It endured the crash of 1929 and was saved by the "Friends of Julien," a group of lawyers, bankers, jurists, and "men of affairs" who took on the moniker to avoid the appearance of "Depression opportunism" (*WP*, 270). This mix of elite and bohemian clientele characterized the elegant hotel cafés of old and made them the more susceptible to decline in the era of high-rise apartments and dive bars. Rumor had it that the Julien was being destroyed to make way for new apartment buildings, and Rick wistfully witnesses the wreckage of the building, while "the handsome Victorian Gothic façade with the imposing marble steps" still stood and the fallen laurel vines were "still breathing and quivering with life" (*WP*, 277).

The destruction of the structure signals the end of an era, displacing the literal and figurative "old birds" that resided inside. A "rouged and dyed old lady elaborately dressed in the fashion of pre–World War One" comes running from the building, crying out for her "poor birds," whose nest has been disrupted (*WP*, 277). One of the workmen matter-of-factly comments on "a lot of queer old birds flushed out of their nests" who lived over the Julien and are left to wander around Washington Square park (*WP*, 278). Powell here addresses the more serious issue of housing scarcity among low-income and marginalized urban populations, which was exacerbated by Robert Moses's urban development plan in the 1950s and '60s. While we are told that the aging single woman Jerry Dulaine moved to the Hotel Delorne on Park Avenue to write a book on the problems of career women, the hotels that were once a haven for single women, divorcees, and career women are also being replaced by high-rise apartments and office buildings.

For Dalzell Sloane, "the Café had been gone from him long, long before the building came down" (*WP*, 279). He had sold out his artistic integrity by becoming a portrait artist for Hastings Hardy, an advertising executive, and was in danger of losing his identity as "Mr. Earle," the husband of the famed art patron Cynthia Earle. Dalzell accepts the change: "No good looking around the old neighborhood for souvenirs of the vanished past" (*WP*, 280). Others are left with a loss of purpose and sense of belonging. The novel ends as it began, with the outside observations of the writer, Dennis Orphen: "It must be that the Julien was all that these people really liked about each other for now when they chance across each other in the street they look through each other, unrecognizing" (*WP*, 280). The café provided a connection, a bridge among New Yorkers from different worlds, and without it, they fade and are diminished in the fabric of the city streets. "The Café Julien was gone and a reign was over. Those who had been bound by it fell apart like straws when the bailing cord is cut and remembered each other's name and face as part of a dream that would never come back" (*WP*, 281). Powell offers a typical ambiguous ending, whereby the geographic location of the Julien is lost but the memory of what it represented lives on.

In Powell's final novel, *The Golden Spur*, the dream of Greenwich Village bohemia changes form but takes on new life at the Golden Spur. When Powell is asked about her motivation for writing, she says, "[The query is] almost always answered in my case by a sense of historical duty to get a picture of a fleeting way of life. . . . Usually the urge comes when the special scene is fading—the new one hasn't been formed yet but is waiting in the wings. Swan Songs are my specialty" (*D*, 452). Powell's final novel, *The Golden Spur* (1962), is her swan song to the bohemian Greenwich Village life of the 1920s and '30s from the perspective of the 1950s bourgeois and new bohemian art scene. Powell's novel revolves around place and the characters who pass through the Golden Spur, a onetime speakeasy and gathering place for writers and artists in the 1920s that has become a dive bar for poseurs in the 1950s. This locale provides the backdrop for Powell's satire of the naïve, midwestern seeker; the bohemian writers and artists who have been corrupted by success; the narcissistic academic; the repressed, bourgeois professional; and the self-interested, wealthy art promoter. As with other Powell novels, her nostalgia for the lost city of the past takes center stage.

Powell's last novel is carefully crafted around the quest of Jonathan Jaimison, a young transplant from Silver City, Ohio, who searches for his identity by seeking to uncover his mysterious paternity in New York City. Upon the death of his mother, Connie Birch, Jonathan learns that he is not the natural-born son of Jonathan Jaimison Sr., a prominent businessman who abandoned the family when Jonathan Jr. was a young child. According to his mother's diary, his father could be one of several men who were part of the bohemian arts scene that revolved around the Golden Spur in the 1920s. Thus, Jonathan sets up a dichotomy between the bourgeois respectability and impersonality of his legal father and the imagined artistic talent and vitality of his biological father. What follows is an ironic twist on the quest myth, whereby a series of dissipated New York has-beens seek to claim paternity over the promising, young midwesterner in an attempt to find relevance and escape a captive present.

Jonathan arrives in New York in 1956 with his mother's journal and a postcard of the Hotel DeLong in hand, in search of his mother's 1927 New York experience. The reality of the run-down hotel lobby, with "only a few old crones and decrepit gentlemen hobbling or wheeling through the modest hall," is the first of numerous disappointments for the naïve midwesterner.[40] Powell re-creates an idealized vision of Greenwich Village bohemia through Connie's memory: "She was awed by everybody she had ever encountered in New York, just as she found all places incredibly charming, such as the Horatio Street rooming house, the Hotel Brevoort, . . . the Black Knight, Chumley's (where all the great writers and artists congregated in better style than at The Golden Spur), the Washington Square Bookstore, . . . Romany Marie's, the Café Royale, and other romantic names that he could not find in the directory" (GS, 3). With a notable realism, Powell here recalls a fading Greenwich Village with names of actual cafés, hotels, bars, and bookstores that were under assault at the time of her writing.

One of the opening scenes of the novel is the site of demolition of one of New York's first and most historic department stores, Wannamaker's. The department store and hotels, which were ironically themselves a sign of progress at the turn of the twentieth century, were being displaced by high-rise apartment and office buildings by midcentury. The demolition operation draws a crowd, with the giant crane as "the star performer" and a "doomed monster clock" on the façade of the building playing resistance (GS, 8). The audience seems ambivalent about its destruction: "'They can't get the clock,' someone exulted. 'Not today!' 'Hooray for the clock!' The spectators smiled and nodded to one another. Good show. Well done, team!" (GS, 8). In this battle of building versus machine, one senses that humanity is the loser. "Destruction is what pays today," comments a cynical academic onlooker. "Wreckers, bomb-builders, poison-makers. Who buys creative brains today?" (GS, 9). Nonetheless, even the professor is fascinated by the destruction of the old order by the new: "This was a splendid old landmark and people like to see the old order blown up. Then there is the glorious dirt and uproar which are the vitamins of New York, and of course the secret hope that the street will cave in and swallow us all up" (*GS*, 10). New York is by definition about change and spectacle, and such demolition scenes become a part of the life of the city. The professor's sense of guilt in not helping to sustain the department store ultimately gives way to acceptance and resignation: "If I had paid their nasty little bill, perhaps they would never have come to this. Well, mustn't get sentimental," he says. Powell here mocks the false sense of liberal guilt of the bohemian New Yorker, whose loyalty to the local merchant is replaced by the appeal of what is shiny and new, as signaled literally by the "great glass and chromium supermarket advertising its opening" across the street (*GS*, 10).

Despite the signs of decay and destruction, for Jonathan, like Powell, New York continues to be animated with energy and possibility: "There rose the contented purr of the city, a blend of bells, whirring motors, whistles, buildings rising, and buildings falling. The stage was set, the orchestra tuning up, and in a moment he would be on, Jonathan thought" (*GS*, 2). He returns to the Golden Spur, the Village bar that has taken on mythic proportions through his mother's tales of romantic encounters with writers and artists, in search of his lost father. The grand stage turns out to be more of a run-down bar in the form of a stable: "Not the grand Piranesi palace he had vaguely imagined, with marble stairs leading forever upward to love and fame, but a dingy little dark hole he must have passed before without noticing" (*GS*, 11). The legacy of the Golden Spur is shrouded in infamy; it was won by a retired cowboy to settle a gambling debt, and he outfitted the place with an equestrian theme, complete with "dark stalls with dim stable lanterns perched on their newel posts. Framed photographs of the great horses of old covered the wainscoted walls, horse-shoes and golden spurs hung above the bar itself, and photographed clippings of old racing forms" (*GS*, 14). There is something ironic about this western-themed bar in the heart of the city and an even greater irony in the midwesterner's search for his roots in this imitation-rural, urban landscape. Back in the day, the Golden Spur was a haven for jazz musicians, then actors and artists, but when Jonathan arrives, its old charm and cachet have been displaced by ragtag advertisements and job listings. Hardly the site of aspiring artists or celebrities, the old bar is a haven for the downtrodden and becomes a symbol of a bohemian Greenwich Village in decline.

Jonathan discovers three contenders for his possible paternity, all of whom spent time at the Golden Spur and were romantically involved with his mother. The first is Dr. Walter Kellsey, whom Powell satirizes as the unscrupulous, self-absorbed academic. One of Powell's typical womaniz-ers, he has a wife, Deborah, a former student of his at UCLA who tricked him into marrying her under the pretense of being pregnant, as well as a mistress, Anita Barlowe, a fellow professor in his department who is pres-suring him to leave his wife to marry her. Jonathan's mother, Connie, was a former student of Dr. Kellsey's, and the professor recollects meeting with her at the Golden Spur. Kellsey is eager to claim Jonathan's parentage, going so far as to find an apartment where the two of them can live, as an act of revenge against the conniving women in his life. He could get back at his wife for lying about her pregnancy and dispel his mistress's accusations of sterility as grounds for not committing to a "normal" relationship. Jonathan dissociates himself from such exploitation and nefarious origins: "Might as well be a Jaimison, Jonathan brooded, as to find his veins coursing with academic ink" (*GS*, 124)—a dig by Powell at academics, whom she consid-ered to be parasites of creative artists.

Powell satirizes bourgeois privilege and liberal guilt in her portrait of Jonathan's second prospective father, George Terrence. A successful attor-ney and family man living in the wealthy suburb of Stamford, Connecticut, George came from an elite and cultured family and attended Yale. Having used his family name to obtain a job at a distinguished law firm, George compensates by allowing others to take advantage of him and take credit for his work. Like Wharton Hookley in *The Wicked Pavilion*, George seems to be stuck in a loveless marriage and is a repressed homosexual. In a jab at psychoanalysis, George is told by his therapist to try to overcome his repressed sexuality by sleeping with someone of his own sex, and he is now being blackmailed by his lover from the past. Powell satirizes the pretense and repressed emotion of bourgeois marriage in the Terrences' relation-ship, as they communicate indirectly through their daughter, using her as a human intercom.

The Terrences' daughter, Amy, is the product of the hypocrisy of middle-class social expectations. She is living a double life, as Amy, the Vassar girl, taking secretarial courses and art and cooking classes to improve her chances in "the race for husbands" (*GS*, 158), and under her assumed identity as Iris Angel, an aspiring actress living in Greenwich Village and having an affair with the famed painter Hugow. Her roommate in New York City, who also seeks to escape her confining family life, is having an affair with a married university professor and "had the usual agonies of an abortion" (*GS*, 158). Powell thus exposes the limitations of bourgeois social expectations for women while also revealing the false illusion of free love and self-creation of modern bohemia. George offers to set up Jonathan with a job at a New York City law firm and is eager to have a protégé in the profession and to counter any doubts about his own sexuality. In a contrived plot twist, Jonathan has fallen in love with George's daughter under her assumed name of Iris Angel, and he dispels the possibility of George being his father, which would make Iris his sister.

Through Jonathan's third prospective father, Alvine Harshawe, Powell satirizes the bohemian writer/artist turned celebrity and the corruption of success on the creative mind. This macho, larger-than-life novelist, based loosely on the figure of Ernest Hemingway, has appeared previously in Powell's fiction, most notably with the character of Andrew Callingham in *Turn, Magic Wheel*. Like Andy, Alvine is stuck in "his own prison of fame" (*GS*, 182), consumed by promoting his work and receiving awards, and has not written anything new in eight years, since his marriage to his fourth wife, Peg. He ironically proclaims, "Damn it, you didn't have time to write if you wanted to keep your fame in good condition" (*GS*, 185). Alvine sees in Jonathan the prospect of rejuvenating his career by seeing the world from the perspective of "an ordinary man in an ordinary situation with ordinary everyday people" (*GS*, 182), something he has become estranged from in his fame. Fathering an illegitimate child would further free him from a loveless marriage and the accusations of sterility by his wife, who is engaged in an affair with a foreign Lord who offers her the prospect of a title and release from her present marriage. By coming to New York to find his imagined illustrious parentage, Jonathan instead encounters a number of egotistical, declining male figures who seem to need him more than he needs them. Powell here makes a negative comment on the inner self-doubt and fragility of the outwardly successful male professional and the corrosive effect of the new commercialism and materialism on artistic integrity.

Powell's greatest satire in *The Golden Spur* is directed against the vacuousness of what has become the New York art industry, from artists to promoters to patrons and even consumers or connoisseurs. In this sense, *The Golden Spur* is an extension of *The Wicked Pavilion* and its satiric indictment of the end of bohemia. If Alvine Harshawe represents the writer turned celebrity, then Hugow is his artistic equivalent. A celebrated abstract expressionist painter and one of "the Spur's leading attractions," Hugow leaves his bohemian Village roots on East Tenth Street to summer in Cape Cod under the patronage of the notorious vamp and art patron Cassie Bender. Hugow longs for the grit of the city and a return to the struggles of authentic, artistic life: "He had wanted to throw up the fine Cape Cod air, the beach, the crystalline sunshine, Cassie's smothering love, and the rooms full of intelligent appreciators, and get back to a slum full of over-turned ash-cans, Bowery bums and sprawling over the doorstep, lousy barflies, who insulted him, jerks, Eagle jerks, Cub jerks, people who hated him for himself alone and not just because he was doing alright" (GS, 72). Burdened with the glut of comfort and complacency, "he wanted to *want*" (GS, 72), that physical and personal striving necessary for artistic creation. Powell parodies not only the excess of the world of artistic celebrity but also the idealized vision of the struggling artist.

The harsh reality of those who want is ironically exposed by the women in Hugow's life, who are forced in effect to sell themselves in order to secure some kind of financial stability and whom Hugow casually disposes of when they wear out their usefulness. The paradox of modern love and the false freedom of the New Woman are revealed through the characters of Lize Britten and Darcy Trent. Working women and former lovers of Hugow, they are forced to share an apartment abandoned by Hugow in order to make ends meet. While they enjoy the sexual freedom and professional opportunities of the modern woman, they are still trapped in the reality of depending on marriage to secure their future, a prospect that is becoming increasingly distant as they age and lose value on the marriage market. Even the young Iris Angel is exploited by Hugow; captivated by his charm and success, she passes up the earnest interest of the naïve midwesterner Jonathan Jaimison in favor of the occasional dalliance with the famed painter.

Powell satirizes the "insatiable lady art dealer," modeled on the real-life Peggy Guggenheim, through the character of Cassie Bender. Like the figure of Cynthia Earle in *The Wicked Pavilion*, Cassie is a parody of the aging seductress and art patron, known as much for her taste for men as her taste in art. Powell, with her typical use of irony, describes Cassie as a woman of "forty-three—well, all right, forty-eight, if you're going to count every lost weekend" (GS, 200). No longer coquettish, she is described as "a hundred and sixty pounds of solid female" (GS, 201), whose embrace was "more a bruising hug from a statue, for Cassie's flesh had no nonsense about it, a nose could be broken on those marble breasts" (GS, 202). Powell self-ironically describes Cassie as an aging seductress; she was want to say, "This darling man must see me home, . . . and sometimes, it was said, he was never seen again, and only Cassie could tell whether he had escaped or been broken on the wheel" (GS, 201–3). When Cassie learns that Jonathan has inherited a fortune from his purported father—the recently deceased

Major Wederburn, with whom his mother, Connie, among others, had an affair—she convinces him to invest his newfound fortune in her art gallery.

With this plot twist, Powell resolves the two threads of her New York chronicle: Jonathan's quest for his parentage and the satire of the New York art scene. In seeking to carry on Major Wederburn's patronage of Cassie's art gallery, Jonathan ironically finds himself part of the corrupt artistic establishment that stands in opposition to the more authentic Greenwich Village bohemian art scene. Jonathan, now "the promising art dealer," is relegated to the role of "Cassie Bender's bouncer" as he ousts unruly artists and art lovers from Hugow's gallery opening (GS, 258). Much like the celebrated artist Hugow, Jonathan finds himself longing for an idealized past among the aspiring artists and ordinary folk around the Golden Spur. He "thought wistfully of the pack of gallery flies prowling through the night, . . . brawling and bustling down to the Golden Spur, and he thought those were the real backers of art, those were the providers, the blood-donors, and Cassie's salon of critics, guides, and millionaires, were the free-loaders, free-loading on other people's genius" (GS, 261). Powell romanticizes the gritty, aspiring artists of the Village bar scene. Meanwhile, the successful artist, Hugow, has lost faith in the future of art and cynically and somewhat ironically says that the future is in demolition: "The iron ball, that's our god" (GS, 263).

Powell ends her novel on a characteristically ambivalent note, with Hugow, Iris, and Jonathan heading in a cab Uptown and then turning back Downtown, "perhaps to the Spur, where they could begin all over" (GS, 264). As in Fitzgerald's modernist novel of failed dreams, The Great Gatsby, there is an awareness in Powell's novel that you can't repeat the past. Like Fitzgerald, Powell maintains an ambiguous sense of possibility. As Claire Van Orphen, the aging writer who somewhat resembles Powell, says, "You went on running because in the end that was the only place there was—to be alive, to be in the race" (GS, 244). For Powell, The Golden Spur was her final and one of her most acclaimed novels before her death. Powell speculates on the positive reception of the novel as a change in the public perception of satire at midcentury. The audience, says Powell, seemed "parched for fun and irreverence and a mood to praise humor as a virtue instead of a forgivable vice" (D, 445). Finally, one hopes, we are ready to embrace Powell's brand of feisty, female wit.

Mary McCarthy and the
Partisan Review Crowd
Satire and the Modern Bitch Intellectual

6.

"Satire is usually written by powerless people; it is an act of revenge."[1] So wrote Mary McCarthy, a woman intellectual and satirist associated with the anti-Stalinist liberal magazine *Partisan Review*, in the 1930s and '40s. Subscribing to the Juvenalian view of satire as an expression of malice or anger intended to expose human vice and folly, McCarthy here makes an assumption about the role of the satirist as an outsider, who is necessitated by their marginalized identity to mask their anger and social protest through the indirect form of humor.[2] "The best satire seems to spring from hatred and repugnance: Swift, Juvenal, Martial, Pope," says McCarthy. "I resist the notion that there can be such a thing as 'gentle satire'—Addison and Steele, Horace." Paraphrasing Juvenal and looking at the hypocrisy of the modern condition, she says, "It is difficult not to write satire."[3] In *Modern Satire*, Alvin Kernan similarly notes that the folly of the modern world—that is, the belief in progress, optimistic assumptions about human nature, faith in machines versus the hypocrisy of nuclear war, mechanized war, the Holocaust, and the fallacy of advertising—necessitates the writing of satire and the exposure of hypocrisy.[4] McCarthy turns her satiric eye on the false ideals of progress among the leftist intellectuals and the "liberated" women of the interwar period, thereby voicing her social critique through the guise of laughter.

McCarthy bridges the false dichotomy between male and female, sexuality and purity, intellect and emotion, and aggression and subordination, for which she received praise and blame. Fellow writer Alison Lurie lauds McCarthy for offering new possibilities for the smart, passionate woman:

> Before McCarthy, if [she] did not become a "happy housewife," the intelligent woman had two roles: the Wise Virgin and the Romantic Victim, Athena or Psyche. . . . Most of us couldn't imagine any alternative until Mary McCarthy appeared on the scene. Her achievement was to invent herself as a totally new type of woman who stood for both sense and sensibility; who was both coolly and professionally intellectual, and frankly passionate. When we learned that she had also managed to combine a lively and varied erotic life with marriage and motherhood, we were amazed. Maybe, as the editor of *Cosmo* was to put it much later, we could have it all.[5]

Mostly male reviewers were less sympathetic, labeling her as "our leading bitch-intellectual" and the "dark lady of American letters," while at the same time dismissing her as a "trivial lady's book writer."[6] Having a keen wit and a sharp tongue to match was perceived as a threat to male writers and to the very foundation of female identity. McCarthy was further criticized by some feminists for her equivocal stance on women's issues and her identification with the traditionally "feminine" domestic arts of cooking, gardening, and fashion.[7]

How, then, does the smart, sexy woman of wit find a voice in a largely male-dominated, intellectual landscape? She had to conceal her aggressive and critical nature through female self-fashioning and through the indirection of irony and satire. Like Dorothy Parker, who assumed a ladylike guise with hats and suits and by insisting on being addressed as "Mrs. Parker" long after her divorce, McCarthy was known for her fashion flare, her collection of Chanel suits, and she even admitted to taking several suitcases of clothing on her trip to cover the Vietnam War for the *New York Review of Books*. In a 1970s interview, she states, "I like the so-called domestic arts, cooking and gardening. I like clothes very, very much. . . . I am interested in beauty, let's say. . . . I also like the social gifts that women develop, . . . gifts of observation and analysis."[8] But such attention to appearance, while rendering her less threatening and even seductive, may have undermined her perceived intellectual seriousness. She describes her first meeting with the reputed literary and cultural critic Edmund Wilson, where she was wearing a black silk dress with a silver fox fur hanging from her neck, "more suited to a wedding reception than to a business meeting in the offices of a radical magazine"—she was soon after courted by Wilson and later married him. McCarthy notes that, while she was accepted into New York intellectual circles, it was in part through her male relationships, and she maintained a kind of peripheral status: "I was a source of uneasiness and potential embarrassment to the magazine, which had accepted me, unwillingly, as an editor because I had a minute 'name' and was the girlfriend of one of the boys, who had issued a ukase on my behalf," recalls McCarthy.[9] She is here referring to the *Partisan Review* editor Philip Rahv, with whom she had a relationship, until she moved on to Edmund Wilson. "They let me write about theatre because they thought the theatre was of absolutely no consequence," says McCarthy. The *PR* boys considered her to be "absolutely bourgeois throughout": "They always said to me very sternly, 'You're really a throwback. You're really a twenties figure.' . . . I was a sort of gay, good-time girl, from their point of view. And they were men of the thirties. Very serious."[10] McCarthy here highlights the gendered dichotomy that existed between the serious man of intellect and the frivolous and flirtatious woman, a gap she bridged through her sharp intellect and feminine appeal.

The juxtaposition of sharp wit and feminine charm has led male critics in particular to characterize McCarthy as a kind of femme fatale, at once threatening and beguiling. In an essay aptly titled "The Dark Lady of American Letters," the New York intellectual Norman Podhoretz describes Susan Sontag as carrying the sexual/intellectual mantle from Mary McCarthy: "The next Dark Lady would have to be, like her [McCarthy], clever, learned, good-looking, capable of writing . . . criticism with a strong trace of naughtiness."[11] He then goes on to describe the physical resemblance between McCarthy and Sontag, as temptresses, with their attractive figures and black hair. Would any male intellectual be characterized as "naughty" and described or judged in terms of physical appearance? Other male reviewers describe McCarthy in similarly beguiling and menacing terms. Norman Mailer brands McCarthy "a modern American bitch," while Brock Brower says she has "one of the most knife-like female intelligences" and a "devastating female scorn."[12] McCarthy's fellow *Partisan Review* editor Dwight Macdonald, who was satirized in her depiction of Macdougal Macdermott in *The Oasis*, describes her as "having a rather sharkish smile. When most pretty girls smiled at you, you felt great. When Mary smiled at you, you checked to see if your fly was undone."[13] Many of these images revolve around violence and aggression and serve as threats of emasculation.

For a woman, assuming an aggressive and intellectually/sexually dominant position is seen not as a sign of strength but as a form of transgression deserving of negative judgment, hence the label "bitch." In Beverly Gross's essay "Our Leading Bitch Intellectual," a phrase appropriated by Gross from a review by Hilton Kramer, she explores the misogynistic implications of the word "bitch," traditionally used by men to describe "a lewd woman, an unfaithful woman, a frigid woman, a malicious woman, a powerful woman," to which one might add a smart, funny, and outspoken woman. About McCarthy, she states, "Above all, she was a woman who had a mind and spoke it. In a man, power, assertiveness, and contentiousness are laudable. A woman with the same traits is domineering, threatening, castrating—in a word, a bitch."[14] For McCarthy and other female wits, there was a necessity to mask their social critique through humor and feminine charm. As McCarthy's fellow female intellectual Elizabeth Hardwick observed, "A career of candor and dissent is not an easy one for a woman."[15]

Despite McCarthy's outspoken and sexually liberated stance, she maintained an ambivalent relationship to feminism. She resists classification of herself as a "woman writer," taking a more universal perspective, and she is wary of what she considers the shrillness and defensiveness of certain feminists: "I don't have much suffragette side. I think of myself as a person, not as a woman; belonging, you know, to the world, not to a lot of other women. I can't stand people who hold themselves together, in pressure groups and interest groups, and are motivated usually by envy of other people. . . . I'm sure envy and self-pity are the great sins of our particular period, and are companion sins to each other," says McCarthy in a 1963 interview.[16] She clarifies her stand on feminism in later interviews, explaining that she supports legal rights for equality—"I believe in equal pay and equality before the law and so on"—but that she does not see it as a gendered issue: "As for public issues, like the right to legal abortion? I'm for that. But that has nothing to do with feminism. . . . To me it's just a question of freedom. If men could have abortions I'd be for that."[17] What McCarthy objects to is the tone of some feminists, which she considers to be "the self-pity, the shrillness, and the greed" or "covetousness" of what men have.[18] Particularly in the domestic sphere of marriage, McCarthy sees equality not as a question of gender but as a matter of practicality: "In marriage, or for that matter between a woman and her lover or between two lesbians or any other couple, an equal division of tasks is impossible—it's a judgment of Solomon. You really would have to slice the baby down the middle."[19] While this may be a theoretical argument, subordination based on gender and class proves to be a different reality.

Although McCarthy resists the category of "woman writer," she says that she identifies more with the "women writers of sense" than the "women writers of sensibility." The "sense women [Jane Austen, George Eliot, Edith Wharton] are strong with a kind of robust mind, with common sense, a certain knowledge of the world and the way things work, and with humour." McCarthy here significantly associates intellect with humor. Women sense writers, says McCarthy, are not very good at creating male heroes; their men tend to be "cads" or "rotters," "charming, weak men." And the heroines tend to be highly self-conscious and self-doubting. "She's always thinking about herself, and doubting herself, she's partly observing and partly doubting herself, and this is rather the conventional heroine of the woman novelist." As with the comedic turn in her writing, which seems to take over her writing unintentionally, the portrayal of the self-doubting, hyperconscious heroine seems to come naturally to McCarthy. "I always try to make [the heroine] different from myself, . . . but as soon as she begins questioning her motives and representing, let's say, the conscience, at that moment she's too close to me and I don't like her."[20] Like Tess Slesinger, McCarthy finds the personal in the political in her notable satire of New York intellectuals and leftist politics. These include *The Oasis* (1949), a *conte philosophe*, or philosophical tale, satirizing attempts by intellectuals in the 1940s to form libertarian social utopias after World War II, and *The Groves of Academe* (1952), a satire on fellow-traveling liberal faculty at a small, liberal arts college (read: Bard) during the 1950s McCarthy era. Her most powerful writing, however, addresses the gender politics of humor and the conflicted role of the woman intellectual in more autobiographical works like *The Company She Keeps* (1942) and in her best-selling novel about the Vassar class of 1933, *The Group* (1963).

The Company She Keeps satirizes the hypocrisy of leftist intellectuals and the conflicted role of the woman intellectual in the late 1930s and early 1940s. Her autobiographical heroine, Margaret Sargeant, is a Trotskyist and writer for the leftist magazine *The Liberal* (read: *Partisan Review*) who is engaged in a string of unsatisfying sexual relationships with men in a quest to find her "self" or true identity. This combination of moral and intellectual superiority and feminine self-doubt typifies the McCarthy heroine and is exacerbated by her relationship with men. As a kind of truth seer and bringer of knowledge who is valued for her insight and resented for critical judgment, Margaret finds herself at once in a position of intellectual superiority and physical subordination to the men around her. This seeming physical and intellectual assertiveness belies a vulnerability and insecurity of McCarthy's self-doubting heroines. Through her use of satire and comic exaggeration, McCarthy exposes the pretense of leftist intellectuals and the failure of progressive ideals to which she and her heroines aspire.

In the opening story, aptly named "Cruel and Barbarous Treatment," Margaret gets a kind of sadomasochistic pleasure in playing her soon-to-be-estranged husband against her soon-to-be-rejected lover. The operative word is "play," since Margaret describes her actions in the language of performance, separating her mind from her body, with a third-person power of observation over her own actions. The extramarital affair is viewed by Margaret as "a momentous game whose rules and whose risks only she herself knew."[21] She sees herself as a "stage manager" and the affair as an occasion "for exercising superiority over others" (9–10); that is, she plays the devoted wife to make her lover jealous, she discloses details about her affair to evoke reactions from her female friends, and she orchestrates the "reveal" about the affair to her husband to maximize the emotional impact in a sadomasochistic emotional tour de force. "This was, she knew, the most profound, the most subtle, the most idyllic experience of her life. All the strings of her nature were, at last, vibrant. She was both doer and sufferer— she inflicted pain and participated in it" (15). Though Margaret indulges in the pathos of the moment, she is left feeling empty when her husband does not fight for the marriage and leaves her to confront the prospect of marriage to "the Young Man," a vapid ingénue. Margaret goes on to have a string of unsatisfying affairs with a bourgeois businessman in "Man in the Brooks Brothers Shirt" and a liberal intellectual in "Portrait of the Intellectual as a Yale Man," in a vain quest for self-validation and self-knowledge through sexual and intellectual conquests. McCarthy thereby exposes the hypocrisy of the liberated woman's assertion of free love, which leaves her feeling trapped and unsatisfied.

McCarthy's heroine here resembles herself, and in her autobiography, *Intellectual Memoirs: New York, 1936–1938*, McCarthy describes her sexual promiscuity and separation of thought and feeling as a not-so-gay divorcee living on the ironically named Gay Street in New York's Greenwich Village, after her divorce from first husband, the actor Harold Johnsrud: "It was getting rather alarming," confesses McCarthy. "I realized one day that in twenty-four hours I had slept with three different men. And one morning

I was in bed with somebody while over his head I talked on the telephone with somebody else. Though slightly scared by what things were coming to, I did not *feel* promiscuous. Maybe no one does."[22] But, as the cultural critic Diana Trilling observed, there was something desperate and even pathological in McCarthy's promiscuity and emotional disengagement, a sense of compensating for some perceived lack or form of self-punishment, perhaps.[23] Her protagonist, Margaret Sargeant, couches her actions in terms of social and intellectual, if not moral, superiority:

> The men she had known during these last four years had been, when you faced it, too easily pleased—her success had been gratifying but hollow. It was not difficult, after all, to be the prettiest girl at a party for the sharecroppers. . . . And if she had felt safe with the different men who had been in love with her it was because—she saw it now— in one way or another they were all of them lame ducks. . . . Somehow each of them was handicapped for American life and therefore humble in love. And was she, too, disqualified; did she really belong to this fraternity of cripples, or was she not a sound and normal woman who had been spending her life in self-imposed exile, a princess among the trolls? (*CSK*, 86)

These sharp verbal put-downs—"prettiest girl at a party for the sharecroppers," "princess among the trolls"—and the characterization of her leftist lovers as "lame ducks" and "fraternity of cripples" earned McCarthy the reputation for being cruel and condescending, a Vassar girl condescending to what were largely her immigrant, Marxist intellectual counterparts.

McCarthy's fellow *Partisan Review* editor Dwight Macdonald complained, "Why does she have to be so goddamned snooty, is she god or something? You begin to feel sorry for her poor characters, who are always so absurd or rascally or just inferior and damned—she's always telling them their slip's showing. . . . The trouble is she is so damned SUPERIOR to her characters, sneers at most of them and patronizes the rest."[24] But if McCarthy casts a cold eye on her male characters, she is similarly critical of female characters (note her satire of the educated, elite Vassar grads of *The Group*) and in particular of her autobiographical heroines like Margaret Sargeant. She is further indicted by male critics for her critical outlook and seeming lack of empathy in her depiction of character. William Barrett says McCarthy's work lacks "the simple virtue of feeling."[25] In a more recent review of McCarthy's work, Morris Dickstein says, "She has the essayist's gift for describing a world but not the novelist's power to make it move, or make it moving."[26] But why is this superior and critical stance, which is at the heart of the satirist's project, considered inappropriate for a woman, as if being female and being superior or intellectual were incompatible? In McCarthy's 1987 autobiography, *How I Grew*, she reflects on the power of laughter as a coping mechanism and the resulting desensitization. Recalling her traumatic childhood being raised in the abusive household of her Aunt Margaret and Uncle Myers in Minneapolis after the death of her parents from influenza, McCarthy notes, "over the years I have found a means—laughter—of turning pain into pleasure." She continues,

> My laughter is a victory over circumstances, and insofar as it betokens a disinterested enjoyment I imagine it to be a kind of pardon. I had the choice of forgiving those incredible relatives of mine or pitying myself on their account. Laughter is the great antidote for self-pity, maybe a specific for the malady. Yet it does tend to dry one's feelings out a little, as if by exposing them to a vigorous wind. So that something must be subtracted from the compensation I seem to have received for injuries sustained. There is no dampness in my emotions, and some moisture, I think, is needed to produce the deeper, the tragic notes.[27]

McCarthy uses humor and satire in particular as a means of asserting control over adverse circumstances, though at a self-admitted cost of a lack of feeling. It is in part this defensive and defiant stance not typically associated with women writers that merits her distinction and also elicits her detractors.

Behind McCarthy's intellectually superior and sexually liberated posture is an underlying sense of self-doubt, as expressed by the conflicted role of heroines such as Margaret Sargeant. In "The Man in the Brooks Brothers Shirt," Margaret plays the bohemian intellectual to Mr. Breen's bourgeois businessman. On a train trip to Reno to get a divorce before her marriage to her fiancé, the "Young Lover," Margaret indulges in a one-night stand with this conventional business type, but it is not without moral or physical consequence. While she helps the businessman gain a degree of self-awareness regarding his life and marriage, her physical encounter is described in masochistic terms as a kind of self-sacrifice, using Christian imagery of martyrdom: "This, she thought decidedly, is going to be the only real act of charity I have ever performed in my life; it will be the only time I have ever given anything when it honestly hurt me to do so" (*CSK*, 88). McCarthy uses italics to separate her inner thoughts from her physical actions. She extends the Christian metaphor, describing the sexual act as "the mortification of the flesh achieved through the performance of the act of pleasure." She "stretched herself out on the berth like a slab of white lamb on an altar. While she waited with some impatience for the man to exhaust himself, for the indignity to be over, she contemplated with burning nostalgia the image of herself, fully dressed with the novel, in her Pullman seat, and knew with the firmest conviction, that for once she was really and truly good, not hard or heartless at all" (*CSK*, 88). Her sexual encounter is at once an act of self-abnegation and moral ascendency, with Margaret achieving a kind of spiritual goodness in helping others while being a "bad" girl in the eyes of society.

Like McCarthy, Margaret is conflicted by a Christian sense of morality, in which extramarital sexuality is associated with sin and punishment, a feeling that is exacerbated by her ambivalent relation to paternal authority, in the form of the austere patrician morality of her father (read: McCarthy's grandfather), the denial and deprivation associated with her Catholic aunt, and the loss of her mother. McCarthy, who was orphaned at the age of six when both her parents died in the flu epidemic of 1918, had a romantic, idealized image of her rebellious Irish Catholic father and was raised in part by her Protestant grandfather, an established attorney in the West, and for a period by her austere Catholic aunt and uncle in Minnesota. Margaret further sheds light on Mr. Breen's life at her own expense: "At the sign of his life, waiting to be understood, she had rolled up her sleeves with all the vigor of a first-class cook confronting a brand-new kitchen" (*CSK*, 97), an oddly domestic metaphor for this worldly woman. By making light of Margaret's encounter with the bourgeois businessman, McCarthy uses humor as a means of coping with the more serious issue of gender subordination and sexual violation.

McCarthy further satirizes the hypocrisy of the leftist intellectual and the breakdown of progressive values in "Portrait of the Intellectual as a Yale Man." Jim Barnett, based loosely on the critic John Chamberlain, with resemblances to Dwight Macdonald, is a Yale graduate and assumes the role of "the average thinking man" (*CSK*, 126), who remains cautiously committed in all aspects of his life, from his relationships to his political affiliation.[28] His wife, Nancy, is "the Average Intelligent Woman, the Mate" (*CSK*, 126). He is well liked and appropriately noncommittal in his job at *The Liberal*, and he takes a moderate stand during the Trotsky hearings, a touchstone for liberal and radical intellectuals. By contrast, Margaret Sargeant is passionate and enjoys the public display in both her personal and political life. When she joins the staff of *The Liberal*, she is outspoken and contentious in speech and provocative and beguiling in her actions. Margaret again assumes the role of the temptress or femme fatale, who brings knowledge, both sexual and intellectual, to this average Adam and is similarly cast out for her sacrifice. Jim is attracted to her and has a brief affair with her while his wife is pregnant in the hospital, but he continues to be haunted (and tempted) by her presence. Even when they are no longer sleeping together, Jim internalizes her sense of moral judgment: "Only she had the power to make him feel honestly, unsentimentally, that his life was a failure. . . . Through her he had lost his primeval innocence, and he would hate her forever as Adam hates Eve" (*CSK*, 181). So Margaret, the temptress and bringer of knowledge, continues to bear the burden of womanhood. While Jim moves on (or sells out) to a secure job at a commercial magazine appropriately titled *Destiny* (as Dwight Macdonald went on to *Fortune* magazine), Margaret loses her job at *The Liberal* for her outspoken support of Leon Trotsky and is prevented by Jim from getting a job at *Destiny* (as retribution for her ultimate rejection of him and final refusal to sleep with him). When he thanks her some years later for helping him find himself, she sarcastically replies, "I'll have a brass plaque made to hang around my neck saying, 'Jim Barnett slept here'" (*CSK*, 153). Sex has been a stepping stone for Jim to better things, while it only leaves Margaret as the one who was stepped on. This witty, self-deprecatory remark typifies the McCarthy heroine, who has the knowledge but is unable to realize the power of her own potential. McCarthy exposes the limitations of the bourgeois, pseudointellectual Yale man while showing a certain pathos for the earnest, self-destructive autobiographical heroine, Margaret Sargeant.

In the final story of *The Company She Keeps*, "Ghostly Father, I Confess," McCarthy satirizes the limitations of what she considered the pseudoscience of psychoanalysis while exploring her heroine's search for self. As the title implies, this vignette explores Margaret's ambivalent relation to paternal authority and how it affects her ability to find self-fulfillment and satisfaction in her relations with others. The father of the title refers at once to the Catholic Church father, her fictional Protestant father, and the secular authority of the psychologist. When Margaret's second husband, an architect (part artist / part businessman), expresses discontent with the marriage, he urges her to see a psychologist to "cure" her of her brooding introspection and self-doubt, or, as Margaret sees it, to obliterate her conscience and her personality. (McCarthy expressed similar aversion to psychology and its normalizing tendency when her husband Edmund Wilson had her temporarily institutionalized for her unstable behavior.) Her analyst, himself a representative of bourgeois mediocrity, claims that her marriage to Frederick, the architect, is more daring than her string of escapist affairs, for in returning to the confinement and protection of her household, she is replicating the conditions of her childhood, and in confronting the past, she might overcome it. But Margaret realizes that the analyst is just another male authority figure from whom she seeks validation and that true self-knowledge lies in self-acceptance: "Now for the first time she saw her own extremity, saw that it was some failure in self-love that obliged her to snatch blindly at the love of others, hoping to love herself through them, borrowing their feelings, as the moon borrowed the light, she herself was a dead planet" (*CSK*, 222).

In this, the most serious of McCarthy's vignettes, Margaret has an epiphany in turning inward for self-knowledge and self-acceptance rather than seeking validation from others. She realizes that she is not a dead planet, that "her inner eye had remained alert" (*CSK*, 222), and this self-conscious, critical inner eye, this insight, is the key to self-acceptance and happiness. Rather than seeking to let others define her or to find some external definition of her being, she comes to accept her own conflicted self: "Oh my God, do not take this away from me. If the flesh must be blind, let the spirit see. Preserve me in disunity" (*CSK*, 222). Margaret paradoxically looks to God, the holy father, in her declaration of selfhood. She further continues to separate mind and body, with the mind in control and the body in submission. But for Margaret, and for McCarthy, this valuation of individual insight is a step toward self-knowledge and female self-assertion. While McCarthy's acerbic wit and sexual freedom may be seen in part as a defense, a sublimation, and even, at times, a form of self-punishment, it is also a positive assertion of female identity in a male-dominated society.

In one of McCarthy's best-known novels, *The Group* (1963), she turns her satiric gaze on herself and fellow graduates of the Vassar class of 1933 to expose the failure of progressive ideals and the conflicted role of the modern, liberated woman in the Depression-era US. McCarthy describes *The Group* as a "mock-chronicle novel" about "the idea of progress" as "seen in the female sphere" of "home economics, architecture, domestic technology, contraception, childbearing; the study of technology in the home, in the play-pen, in the bed. It's supposed to be the history of the loss of faith in progress."[29] The novel is set in the seven-year period between the inauguration of Franklin Delano Roosevelt in 1933 and the start of World War II, and the individual lives of the group members are placed against the backdrop of the larger historical and sociological events of the Great Depression, the New Deal, Stalinism versus Trotskyism, Freudianism versus behaviorism, the rise of fascism, and the outbreak of World War II. The novel is perhaps most notable for its frank treatment of such taboo subjects as birth control, premarital sex, rape, infidelity, lesbianism, and divorce, which is made permissible in part through the use of satire, irony, and humor. Despite the popularity of the novel, *The Group* was predictably criticized both for its controversial subject matter (most notably by some of the Vassar graduates themselves) and for what some critics deemed its "trivial" subject matter. Nonetheless, *The Group* continues to have a lasting impact for its bold and satiric treatment of female sexuality and traditional gender roles.

The Group is not merely a study in "sociology" or "social reporting of a decade," for McCarthy uses the social context to expose a more general failure of values.[30] She critiques the "group" mentality, the mass marketing of products and *idées reçus* that had become the hallmark of "progress" of the age. For the Group, "clichés precede experience. Experience is turned into manufactured clichés before it happens. This is a consumer society and the girls in 'the Group' are trainees for this society. They think of everything in terms of social formulas: eating is turned into recipes, sex into contraceptives, and child-bearing becomes the question of nursing or bottle feeding," observed McCarthy in an address before the Women's National Press Club.[31] McCarthy's satire is thus aimed at a particular class of women for whom the idea of progress was a form of social currency or "keeping up." McCarthy further defends her use of social description and realistic detail as "both factual and—and a kind of comic epic," whereby progress is reduced to a grotesque form of material acquisition.[32] In a 1966 interview, McCarthy defends her use of realistic detail against accusations by Norman Mailer and others of writing a failed realist novel or merely a "fact novel": "These lists of what they wore and the grotesque things they ate and so on in this period—these catalogues of mine—were not at all close to, say, the documentation of Balzac or Defoe which I admire. But they were almost fantasy. That is, it's true people did dress this way and eat this way. But the very fact of the lapse of time turns these things into grotesque catalogues. Just as if you see a movie in period costume. . . . There's always sort of the bloomer joke in it."[33] At least one reviewer was not convinced. John Aldridge says her method of documenting and cataloguing undermines her satirical intent: "Its obsessive concern with material externals gives rise after a while to the suspicion that she is herself more attracted to those values than she knows, that her choice of method may perhaps be a better indication of just where her true sympathies lie than are the overt assumptions of her conscious satirical intent."[34] One has to wonder if the same criticism would be launched at a male, realist writer like Balzac or Tolstoy.

The Group, with its emphasis on things, has been cited for insufficient characterization. As with McCarthy's other social satires, *The Group* subordinates matters of plot and characterization to a moral purpose, namely, exposing the fallacy of progressive ideology as manifest in the female sphere of the educated elite. The voices of the Group constitute the content as well as the form of the novel. "It is all talk," says McCarthy about *The Group* in her letter to a translator. "As if everything that occurred had instantly to be converted into a kind of specie or currency that could be spent or hoarded (usually spent)." "The event, whatever it is—losing your virginity, having your husband lose his job, breast-feeding your baby—is a rather shaky small bridge between past and future gossip, speculation, boasting, moralizing, debate." It is this discussion, and what it reveals about the popular opinions and values of the time, rather than the action itself, that interests McCarthy. The lack of a central intelligence or, for that matter, of a narrative point of view is deliberate. "*The Group*, unlike my other books," says McCarthy, "has no heroine and no one to act as the author's stand-in, telling the reader what to think and feel."[35] Instead, the novel has a collective heroine—the Vassar girl as represented by the eight Group members plus Norine—and through a shifting narrative point of view, McCarthy parodies the received ideas of the day.

In most comic novels, the characters show little progress or change; *The Group*, however, tells a clear story of descent. The Vassar girl's faith in progress and belief that "the wide, wide world was our oyster" are thwarted by the realities of marriage, divorce, infidelity, child care, social hardship, and lack of career opportunity.[36] In "The Vassar Girl" (1951), McCarthy observes that the average Vassar girl had "two plus children and was married to a Republican lawyer." The discrepancy between the possibility of "making a difference" and "finding oneself" and the reality of becoming a suburban housewife like one's mother creates a deep dissatisfaction in the Vassar grad. "The Vassar alumna," says McCarthy, "uniquely among American college women is two persons—the housewife or matron, and the yearner or regretter."[37] The greatest fear among the Group members is "to become like Mother and Dad, stuffy and frightened," and to "marry a broker or banker or cold-fish corporate lawyer."[38] Ironically it is the older generation of mothers—who were suffragettes and fought for women's rights—who are seen as more progressive than their imitative daughters. In a 1963 interview, McCarthy elaborated on her preference for the mothers' generation: "Well, I'm afraid I do think the mothers are better than the daughters. The mothers sort of belong to the full suffragette period with its great amplitude—you know, women smoking cigarettes in holders and dancing the cha-cha—and the girls are rather tinny in comparison with their mothers, I'm afraid."[39] By the end of the novel, most of the girls abandon their ambitions of serving the community or of becoming career women to the social (and biological) pressure to marry and have children. The Vassar girl's conformity seems inevitable, as if she were a victim of paradoxically progressive social ideas within the traditional domestic realm. "In a certain sense," noted McCarthy, "the ideas are the villains and the people their hapless victims."[40]

The most autobiographical of McCarthy's heroines in *The Group* and the structural center of the novel is Kay Strong. The novel opens with the sense of possibility of Kay's wedding and ends with the sobering reality of Kay's funeral. Like Kay, McCarthy was somewhat of an outsider among the New York society girls of Vassar. Kay is the daughter of a prominent orthopedist from Utah and comes to represent the modern consumer, appropriately becoming a buyer for Macy's after graduation. Kay's failed relationship with her husband, Harald, an aspiring playwright, resembles that of McCarthy with her first husband, Harald Johnsrud. Harald is what McCarthy would term a "rotter," or egotistical male lout, whose mistreatment of Kay has serious consequences. In a scene reminiscent of McCarthy's own hospitalization by Edmund Wilson, Harald commits Kay to the Payne Whitney Clinic after beating her during a drunken argument. In 1938, after a dispute in which McCarthy attested that Wilson was drunk and abusive and he accused her of emotional instability, Wilson had McCarthy committed to the Payne Whitney Clinic for three weeks. Their conflicting testimony can be found in their respective divorce depositions in 1945.[41] That none of the doctors believes Kay shows the limited options for the female victim of abuse. The first of the Group to marry, Kay is also the first to divorce, leading to the loss of her job at Macy's, the loss of a place to live, and her accidental death when she falls from an open window at the Vassar club while spotting for war planes. There is something comical and absurd in the way Kay dies, though it can also be seen in political terms, as Kay was showing support for the war effort in opposition to Harald, an outspoken America Firster.

As one of the mothers ironically puts it at the funeral, "You might say . . . that Kay was the first American war casualty" (*TG*, 379).

McCarthy takes on some of the most controversial issues surrounding the modern, sexually liberated woman through her comic portrayal of Dottie Renfrew. Dottie, the oldest member of the Group at twenty-three and from a wealthy family in Boston (a "Boston Brahmin"), is conflicted between her newfound sexual freedom and the traditional expectations of female propriety. In a scene noted as much for its exacting detail as its salacious content, Dottie the virgin is instructed by the married player, appropriately named Dick, on how to achieve an orgasm. McCarthy uses humor to confront the controversial subject of premarital sex and contraception in some of the most notorious scenes of the novel. Dottie tries to display a modern woman's detachment between love and sex, which plays into Dick's sadistic treatment of her and refusal to show intimacy by kissing her on the lips. After he clinically instructs her in bed, she is embarrassed when she achieves orgasm "in a series of long, uncontrollable contractions . . . like the hiccups" and is afraid that she has made a "faux pas" and spoiled things by screaming out (*TG*, 39). She further blames herself when he falls asleep on top of her "like a ton of bricks" and is mortified that the "sticky liquid had dried and was crusting on her stomach" (*TG*, 40). The vivid description and comic physicality of this supposed love scene are offset by the self-doubt and humiliation of the young woman. She feels further demeaned when Dick commands her, "Get yourself a pessary," which she interprets as a rebuke, recalling the lines of Hamlet to Ophelia, "Get thee to a nunnery. I love you not" (*TG*, 52). McCarthy here defuses some of the tension of the situation with a comic allusion to confront the controversial subject of birth control and premarital sex. The more experienced Kay (though she admits to not having achieved the elusive orgasm) explains that it is a sign of commitment if a man invests in your birth control—they would be "wedded, as it were, by proxy, with the 'ring' or diaphragm pessary" (*TG*, 56), and "he was bonded . . . like a bank employee" (*TG*, 60) not to bring another woman to his house. The ironic use of the language of business and hardware is hardly the endorsement of romantic love that Dottie is searching for. While birth control can be liberating in enabling sexual pleasure outside of marriage and pregnancy, Kay's socialist husband points out that it can also be seen as a form of class exploitation, intended to limit reproduction among poorer populations.

McCarthy diffuses the emotionally charged situation of an unmarried woman going to the doctor for contraception with slapstick humor. In a memorable (and scandalous) scene at a birth-control clinic, the doctor instructs Dottie on how to insert the diaphragm: "As she was trying to fold the pessary, the slippery thing, all covered with jelly, jumped out of her grasp and shot across the room and hit the sterilizer. Dottie could have died" (*TG*, 73). The ultimate humiliation, however, occurs after the doctor's visit, when Dottie is waiting for Dick in Washington Square Park with her "equipment" in a brown paper bag. After waiting for several hours and counting to a hundred five times, she looks around, "hoping that she was unobserved," and "slipped the contraceptive equipment under the bench she was sitting on and began to walk swiftly as she could, without attracting attention, to Fifth Avenue" (*TG*, 77). Women's liberation exacts its toll on the uninitiated, and McCarthy uses comic pathos to diffuse the tension. In typical Vassar fashion, Dottie ends up in a "suitable" marriage to a wealthy Arizona widower, a poke at the failed progressive beliefs of the educated elite.

McCarthy further uses humor to explore the conflicted role of the liberated, progressive woman of the 1930s through the figure of Libby MacAusland. Libby becomes the type of the single, career woman with a successful job in publishing against the odds. McCarthy discusses the taboo subject of masturbation in describing how Libby sometimes takes herself "Over the Top" on the bathmat (*TG*, 235). McCarthy uses comic relief to confront the more serious subject of rape. Libby becomes a near victim of rape by another male "rotter," the Nordic ski jumper Nils Aslund. In the moment, she seems more concerned for her dress than her reputation: "She heard a fearful sound of ripping material—her brand-new dress bought at Bendel's spring sale!" (*TG*, 234). When Nils discovers that she is a virgin, he insults her by saying, "Oh what a bore! . . . It would not even be amusing to rape you" (*TG*, 235), leaving one of the most sexually progressive Group members conflicted and demeaned. Libby seems strangely insulted that Nils has lost interest and almost regrets that the act was not consummated. "He wanted to rape her and go berserk like the old Vikings," she consoles herself, but was stopped by his aristocratic code. "At least that would have been something dramatic and conclusive" (*TG*, 235), she thinks. Libby is so embarrassed by what happened (and what did not happen) that she pretends that Nils tried to rape her. Libby's ambivalence at her near rape speaks to the conflicted feelings of the sexually liberated woman.

The remaining Group members for the most part find themselves in unfulfilling traditional gender roles as wives and mothers or in compromised public service and professional roles. The most earnest of the Group members, Polly Andrews, gives up her dream of becoming a doctor after her family loses their money in the stock market crash, and instead she becomes a medical technician and marries a doctor. Through the character of Polly, McCarthy satirizes the then-new field of psychoanalysis as well as the misguided materialism of her fellow Vassar classmates. The most self-sacrificing in her relationship with men, Polly is involved in an extramarital affair with the weak-willed publishing mogul Gus Trenor. Though Polly tries to help Gus leave his wife, in a parody of psychoanalysis, Gus is instructed not to make any change while undergoing treatment. In a kind of deus ex machina, Polly ends up marrying a psychiatrist who takes care of her and her mentally unstable father. The Group warn Polly against allowing her father to live with the newlyweds. In an ironic assertion of selfhood, they contend, "It was very important, they thought, for a woman to preserve her individuality; otherwise she might not hold her husband" (*TG*, 321), and preserving one's marriage is the ultimate end for many of the Vassar elite. Though the Group members pity Polly, McCarthy shows her to be less status conscious and more of a genuine do-gooder. Yet even she offers a limited alternative for the educated woman of the 1930s.

Through the character of Helena Davison, McCarthy satirizes the asexual, socially conscious Vassar girl and exposes the hypocrisy of her more conventional classmates and the privilege of her elite upbringing. Unlike the arriviste Kay, Helena Davison is among the old money at Vassar (her father was the first vice president of Oneida Steel), whose parents "lived 'on the income of their income'—i.e., plainly" (*TG*, 107). Helena "had been registered for Vassar at birth" (*TG*, 108) and enjoyed every privilege growing up. She had been tutored since childhood in music (she could play the violin, the piano, and the flute and sang in the choir), art, and dance (ballroom, classical, and tap), as well as in every branch of athletics (tennis, golf, skiing, figure skating, and even horseback riding). Helena mystifies her parents after graduation by choosing not to marry and to pursue a career at a nonprofit. She teaches Dalcroze (a progressive approach to music through movement known as eurythmics) and finger painting at an experimental school in her home town of Cleveland to what her father deems "a darned lot of kikes' children" (*TG*, 114). This is one of several anti-Semitic references in the novel, pointing to the racial/ethnic prejudice among the Vassar-educated elite and their families. Helena's entry into public service is seen by her classmates as somewhat of a necessity. According to Kay, Helena "was a neuter, like a little mule," and therefore "it was up to her to realize her potentialities" (*TG*, 115). This sexist mentality—that a woman would only realize her professional aspirations as a default to marriage—further exposes the hypocrisy of the progressive ideals of these educated women.

Through the characters of Priss Hartshorne and Norine Schmittlapp, McCarthy satirizes the institution of marriage and progressive ideals of child rearing. Priss embodies the social idealism of the Vassar graduate and gets a job working for the National Recovery Administration (NRA) after graduation. She gives up her aspirations of making a difference in public policy upon marrying Sloan Crockett, a staunch Republican and aspiring pediatrician. Priss is a consumer of ideas: she refers to a Department of Labor pamphlet and *Parents' Magazine* for current trends in child rearing. Her social policy is at odds with that of her husband, who uses her as an advertisement for his natural approach to medicine. Sloan pressures his wife to breast-feed rather than to bottle-feed, touting her as the "flat-chested wonder" until her infant demands the dreaded "supplementary bottle" (*TG*, 252). In a final insult, we learn that Priss is partially motivated to nurse her baby "so that she could give Sloan, who was entitled to it, more fun in bed" (*TG*, 243). The masochistic Priss manages to be both a self-sacrificing wife and mother. Having come to measure herself by the current standards of good mothering, Priss considers herself to be a failure.

By contrast, Norine defies traditional practices of marriage and child rearing. Through Norine and her Communist activist husband, Putnam Blake, McCarthy satirizes the hypocrisy of the socially conscious elite. A Marxist in principle, Norine was seen at a sympathy strike wearing a full-length evening gown, jeweled tiara, and long white gloves, "as though she were in a box at the opera" (*TG*, 155). Norine ultimately insists on her own sexual pleasure by straying from her impotent husband. After having an affair with Kay's husband, Harald, and divorcing Putnam, Norine ends up remarrying a "Jew," much to the dismay of her elitist classmates.

Through the characters of Norine and Priss, McCarthy satirizes progressive theories of child rearing. Norine sees Priss as following an outmoded behaviorist model: in Priss's son's day (three years ago), Norine tells Priss, "you were still hipped on scales and clocks and thermometers. The age of measurement. . . . Your tribal totem is the yardstick" (*TG*, 360). According to Norine, ideas of progress in child care had been replaced by a return to primitivism, the influence of Margaret Mead and the cultural anthropologists. Priss takes an interventionist approach to child rearing: her son is on a regimented diet, sleep schedule, and toilet-training program (Priss sees his refusal to be toilet trained as a form of rebellion), and hygiene is paramount (rattles and pacifiers are out).

Through exaggeration and parody, McCarthy shows how Norine takes the laissez-faire approach to an extreme: her son "needed the fun of playing with his own excrement, just as he needed sucking" (*TG*, 258), advocates Norine. Once he enters nursery school, "the pressure of the group will encourage him to give up his anal pleasures" (*TG*, 259), she claims. In the interest of "keeping up" with the latest in medical and social science, both mothers defy nature and common sense and even jeopardize the well-being of their children to satisfy their own egos. For all of their current ideas in child care and despite their elite education, few of the Group make any real progress. While seemingly focusing on the "trivial" subject of trends in parenting, McCarthy satirically lampoons the emerging field of psychology as applied to child rearing while showing the misguided application of the progressive ideals of the Vassar girl in the conventional realm of marriage and motherhood.

McCarthy further exposes the failure of the Group's modern thinking through the character of Eleanor Eastlake, or Lakey, a lesbian who stands outside both the narrative structure and social structure of the Group. Lakey is distinguished from the other Group members by her exoticism and sophistication (her green eyes with dark-blue rims are taken as "a sign of her Indian blood"; *TG*, 20). While the other Group members are busily securing husbands and potential careers, Lakey goes abroad to pursue a doctorate in art history at the Sorbonne. The Group members are shocked to make the "terrible discovery" that Lakey has taken a lesbian lover, the German-born French Baroness Maria d'Estienne (*TG*, 390). Though the Group come to accept Lakey and the Baroness at social occasions like any "normal couple," they harbor a feeling that what "happened" to Lakey was a "tragedy" and in some way "perverted" (*TG*, 391). Helena and Polly see Lakey as "an exquisite captive of a fierce robber woman, locked up in a Castle perilous" (*TG*, 392). (It is rumored that Maria has a revolver and a set of brass knuckles and keeps a pair of vicious watchdogs.) For McCarthy, who characterizes Lakey as the most compelling member of the Group, her reception is more a reflection of the limitation of the Group members than a judgment of her character.

At the end of the novel, a fragmented Group reassembles, not for the celebration of Kay's marriage, a new beginning, but in commemoration of her death. The tone, however, gives the event a mock-epic quality. Like Kay's wedding, the funeral is treated as a social occasion that requires much planning and preparation: the ceremony (cremation or burial?), the casket (plain pine box, open or closed?), the refreshments (sandwiches, open or closed?), the flowers, the dress (Lakey bought Kay an off-white silk pleated gown from Fortuny's, not quite the pure white of a bride's gown), even the guest list (they did not want Harald "taking the joy out of Kay's funeral"; *TG*, 377). Though the funeral is considered a "success"—"It was quite a society funeral, which would have delighted Kay" (*TG*, 381)—a remaining controversy surrounds her death. McCarthy satirically lampoons these society women, who even reduce the seriousness of a funeral into a cataloguing of fashion, brands, and consumption measured for its style over its significance.

While *The Group* was a commercial success, there was a backlash against Mary McCarthy for its sexually explicit subject matter and brazen, satiric tone. McCarthy's novel was deemed at once too sentimental and superficial and too serious and aggressive in its scathing satire of a class of educated women. The greatest offense, perhaps, was taken by graduates of Vassar, who considered her work to be a roman à clef, impugning both the character of individuals and a whole class of educated elite. *The Group* goes beyond a mere satire of the idea of progress in the domestic sphere. The inability of the Group members to realize their intellectual and personal potential signals a more serious social message behind the comic surface, namely, the inequality of the sexes in US society in the interwar period. What may appear to be a "trivial lady's book" thus contains elements of a protofeminist chronicle masked through the guise of satire and style.

Epilogue
Fighting Funny: Postfeminism, Postracialism, and the Fumorist of the Future

A "fumorist," said the comedian Kate Clinton, is a "feminist humorist," with its implications of celebrating female difference while expressing underlying feelings of rage or fuming mad.[1] Once considered the "F" word, feminist humorists and female humorists in general have been viewed with trepidation. Seen as too bold, too brainy, too bawdy, and too bitchy, female humorists have been resisted and overlooked by predominantly male critics, with their preconceptions of what is worthy of laughter. The foremothers of women's humor, like Dorothy Parker, Mary McCarthy, and Dawn Powell—who bore the burden of being perceived as sharp, sassy, saucy, or worse, not funny—have forged the path for more overtly feminist comedians of today, like Amy Schumer, Wanda Sykes, Ali Wong, Hannah Gadsby, and Samantha Bee.

While the New York women of wit of the interwar period may have paved the way for future generations of feminist humorists, they had a complex relationship to feminism. Though many of them embodied the "feminist" qualities of being outspoken, even aggressive, and sexually independent, writers like Mary McCarthy and Dorothy Parker were wary of the category of "woman writer." McCarthy famously criticized what she considered the shrillness of second-wave feminism and the women's movement while upholding the "feminine" arts of fashion, cooking, and gardening. This wariness of identity politics—of categories of gender, race, religion, class, or national standing—is seen by some critics as an essentialist, elitist assumption of a kind of universal humanism, though it can also be viewed as anticipating an intersectional, inclusive understanding of the category of woman. As Bonnie Honig observes in her discussion of Hannah Arendt, the philosopher and friend of Mary McCarthy who resisted classifications of identity like "woman" and "Jewish" and "German,"

> It is this care for difference and plurality as conditions of politics and action that accounts for her hostility to the nation-state. . . . And it might also account for her silence on the subject of feminist politics: Arendt would have been quite wary of any proclamation of homogeneity in "women's experience," or in "women's ways of knowing." She would have been critical of any feminist politics that relies on a category of woman that aspires to or implies a universality that belies (or prohibits, or silences) significant differences and pluralities within—and even resistances to—the bounds of the category itself.[2]

The same might be said of many female humorists of the interwar period.

Defining women's humor is further complicated in what some scholars consider to be the postfeminist and post-soul or postracial era. "Postfeminism," like "postmodernism" and "postracialism," is a contested term that is self-ironic and self-reflexive in that it contains that which it disavows. The British feminist Angela McRobbie defines "postfeminism" as a kind of "*faux* feminism," "marked by a new kind of anti-feminist sentiment" that appropriates words like "empowerment" and "choice" in the service of a "more individualistic discourse" deployed by media and popular culture "as a kind of substitute for feminism."[3] It simultaneously invokes the feminist premise of gender equality as having already been achieved while eschewing what is perceived as the shrillness, lack of joy or humor, and denial of pleasure associated by some people with second-wave feminism. Instead, it posits a new form of feminism, what has been termed "consumer feminism," "feel-good feminism," or "marketplace feminism," which has been incorporated into media and popular culture and reclaims the pleasure and aesthetics associated with female sexuality and "feminine" appearance. The danger of postfeminism, argue Yvonne Tasker and Diane Negra, is that by commodifying female sexuality and empowerment as forms of individual self-expression and denying the need for collective social/political action to advance gender equality, it reinforces sexist gender stereotypes and silences "the necessity of feminist critique, at a time when women face significant challenges to their economic well-being, hard-won reproductive rights, and even authority to speak, while popular culture blithely assumes that gender equality is a given."[4]

Susan J. Douglas warns against the dangers of what she terms "enlightened sexism" in using an ironic superiority as a way of distancing oneself from the reinforcement of gendered and sexist stereotypes in the media under the guise of irony. Such "group ridicule" allows an audience to view sexist stereotypes under the disclaimer that "it's just for fun," a variation on the all-too-familiar "it's just a joke."[5] In defining postfeminist humor, Limor Shifman and Dafna Lemish identify an intertwining of feminist and antifeminist ideas: while there is an emphasis on choice and empowerment rather than oppression, postfeminism tends to focus on consumerism (purchasing beauty products) and ideal feminine bodies rather than political activism and work. There is a further focus on gender differences and male/female behavior, which are seen as natural rather than a result of social injustice. "In this fun(ny)mist world, 'old' debates about gender inequalities are superseded by fun(ny), celebratory texts about differences between men and women, depicted as essentialist: natural, unavoidable, universal, and therefore assumedly eternal. So while on the face of it such humour may seem to have a liberating effect, . . . it may in fact be a new way to maintain a conservative view of what is framed as the irresolvable 'battle of the sexes.'"[6] This "*Men are from Mars, Women are from Venus* principle that women are fundamentally different from men and can never be equal to them" thus serves to reinforce gender differences without acknowledging gender hierarchies or gender-nonconforming behavior.[7]

The impact of postfeminism on women's humor has until recently been a dissociation of female humorists (as well as audiences and critics) from what is seen by some opponents as the sharp, aggressive, and "unfunny" tone associated with feminism. This association of feminism with aggressive, outspoken, sexually explicit "unfeminine" behavior of the "unruly woman" is at the root of much of the resistance to women's humor, as previously noted. But we seem to be on the cusp of a new age of feminism, not the postfeminist backlash against "angry" second-wave feminism or the "marketplace" commodification of feminist values of female empowerment and sexuality but a new, socially conscious feminism that is part of a larger, intergenerational social justice awakening as evidenced by the #MeToo, Time's Up, Black Lives Matter, and #SayHerName movements, demanding political and social change for racial and gender equity. Comedians like Amy Schumer, Samantha Bee, Wanda Sykes, Ali Wong, and

Hannah Gadsby, among others, have taken up the mantle of feminism in an unprecedented proliferation of female and feminist humor in multiple media, from stand-up to sketch comedy to late-night satire to digital media.

The rise of female comedians is focused on urban centers like New York, Chicago, and Los Angeles, where there are greater opportunities for stand-up and media outlets and more openness to racial and gender diversity. Despite the show's reputation for being mostly a boys' club, *Saturday Night Live* in New York has fostered the careers of prominent female writers and performers like Tina Fey, Amy Poehler, Kate McKinnon, and Leslie Jones, among many others. In Fey's autobiography, she nonetheless assumes a self-deprecatory tone, following in a long line of female comedians like Phyllis Diller and Joan Rivers, known for poking fun at their own expense. For comedians like Amy Schumer and Sarah Silverman, their explicit humor can be seen at once as a positive expression of female sexuality and a negative objectification of women, whose use of profanity is considered titillating for its incongruity. But Schumer's self-consciously feminist humor deliberately explodes gender stereotypes with sketches like "Last Fuckable Day," which subverts the stereotype of the unappealing aging woman, and "Compliments," which parodies the tendency of women to belittle themselves. In revealing and laughing about their own struggles with mental health, disability, discrimination, and illness, comedians like Silverman, Schumer, Sykes, and Gadsby reinforce the view of women's humor not only as a means of social change but as a source of coping and community building.

For many contemporary female comedians, the embrace of their sexuality and no-nonsense attitude has continued to generate backlash and reinforce sexist stereotypes. In a noted response to Christopher Hitchens's *Vanity Fair* article "Why Women Aren't Funny" (2008), Alessandra Stanley's "Who Says Women Aren't Funny?" (2008) refutes the false dichotomy of pretty/funny that is often used to deny women's humor, by featuring a host of popular female comedians including Sarah Silverman, Tina Fey, Amy Poehler, Kristen Wiig, Maya Rudolph, Chelsea Handler, Sandra Bernhard, Wanda Sykes, and Amy Sedaris, complete with a pictorial by the famed photographer Annie Leibovitz. The cover features Silverman, Fey, and Poehler in long, flowy, Grecian white gowns with golden garlands in their hair, suggesting a variation on the ancient Muses, with Poehler suggestively touching Fey's breast while Fey delivers a knowing glance— these are not your Muses of antiquity. While most of the comedians are in provocative poses dressed in lingerie and evening wear, Sedaris challenges gender stereotypes with a grotesquely exaggerated pregnant belly, smoking what appears to be a cigar, and grabbing the crotch of a smiling, male police officer. Though Stanley seeks to subvert the pretty/funny dichotomy in a postfeminist embrace of wit mixed with female sexuality and feminine appearance, by choosing to emphasize their seductive appearance and by featuring predominantly white, heterosexual, conventionally attractive comedians, Stanley perhaps does more to reinforce traditional racial and gender stereotypes than to challenge them. Not to be outdone, Hitchens retrenched with the rejoinder, "Why Women Still Don't Get It," claiming that Stanley's defense of attractive, female comedians only confirms his purported point that "there are a lots of sexy and aggressive chicks on the comedy circuit but . . . they are in a male game run by male rules."[8] While Hitchens's original essay points to some "exceptions," he held fast to his overall claim that "women aren't funny." The stridency of his chauvinist response against the mounting evidence of successful women in comedy reveals a certain desperation of one who senses that his reign over the kingdom is coming to an end.

Both postfeminism and what has been termed "postracialism" or the "post-soul" myth further complicate the production and reception of minority women's humor and Black women's humor in particular. The term "post-soul" was coined by Nelson George to refer to the post-1960s, post-civil-rights-era aesthetic that can be seen both as an expression of a new Black aesthetic and as the appropriation and consumption of Black culture and identity through popular culture and media (mis)representation.[9] By reinforcing racial and gender stereotypes in popular culture and the media, postfeminism and postracialism arguably promote certain racist and sexist behavior and beliefs that they purport to oppose. In Kimberly Springer's essay "Divas, Evil Black Bitches, and Bitter Black Women: African American Women in Postfeminist and Post-Civil Rights Popular Culture," she argues that "postfeminism seeks to erase any progress toward racial inclusion that feminism has made since the 1980s. It does so by making racial difference, like feminism itself, merely another commodity for consumption." Springer contends that "seemingly harmless cultural representations of black women are incorporated into institutional enactments of discrimination, including racist, sexist, classist, and hetero-sexist social policies." From the antebellum period through the 1980s, argues Springer, Black women were represented in popular culture and even in public policy through the iconography of the mammy, the jezebel, the sapphire, the matriarch, the welfare queen, and the crack-addicted mother (254). Add to that more recent depictions of the modern mammy, the Black lady, the diva, and the "angry Black woman," heightened by the proliferation of media and digital representations that perpetuate the stereotypes that are supposedly ironically invoked. What these racial and gender stereotypes fail to ask is, What are the underlying social conditions of oppression that create and perpetuate these stereotypes, and how can these injustices be addressed? "The question very rarely asked, though," Springer contends, "is *why* these black women are so angry. The answer lies where postfeminism meets post-civil rights: both discourses erase history and claim equality as today's norm for women and people of color," a fallacy that perpetuates rather than confronting racial and gender inequality.[10]

Jessyka Finley argues that contemporary Black women's satire, like the "metarepresentations" of stereotypes by Leslie Jones on *Saturday Night Live*, invokes the postmodern aesthetic using techniques like "antinarrative, parody, citation, and intertextual bricolage permeated with disgust" to undermine stereotypical tropes of Black women as "unruly, incompetent, irresponsible, and interchangeable—tropes so deeply embedded (such as the Angry Black Woman, the Welfare Queen, and a Bad Black Mother) that they often prevent black women from speaking and being heard."[11] There is a danger in invoking such racial and gender stereotypes to a mixed audience that may lack a sense of shared "cultural citizenship" and mistake the object of satire as the stereotypes themselves rather than the injustices of society that creates them. As Finley notes, "Satirical citation of racial stereotypes is prone to misrepresentation by audiences not attuned to its critique, and then it fails to be satire at all, failing to shift from comic to political discourse when interpreted as the unproblematic reinforcement of the very stereotypes the satire intends to undermine."[12]

Lisa Guerrero applies Du Bois's concept of "double consciousness" to the postmodern, "postracial" condition, arguing that the postracial myth, "the desire to erase race in American discourse in America—even as race remains a powerful ideological sign that operates in real, material ways to affect black life"—creates a new form of invisibility whereby Black people are denied a sense of racial difference/identity in theory while they continue to be subject to racist stereotypes and discrimination in practice. Guerrero claims that Black satire in the postracial age—as exemplified in sketch comedy by Key and Peele and Dave Chappelle, among others—"gives voice and legitimacy to *black rage*—not the black rage that post-racial white America has imagined to justify racial violence and injustice against black people, but rather the black rage that gives form to the *black subject* in a time and place that have rendered all aspects of black life to be invisible, unimaginable, or wholly impossible."[13] The expressions of Black rage and humor as *disgust* build on Bambi Haggins's earlier concept of "laughing *mad*" and Glenda Carpio's idea of "laughing fit to kill," transforming what is seen as the unfit unruliness displayed by marginalized populations like minorities and women into a potential site of empowerment, transgression, and identity. As noted by Jessyka Finley and Rebecca Krefting, for women and Black women in particular, who have traditionally been barred from expressions of political speech and social critique—even through the more traditional, predominantly white, male form of satire—postmodern satire offers a potential outlet for social criticism, a first step toward social change.

These issues—of the moral purpose as well as the efficacy of humor to translate social critique into political action—continue to be the focus of more recent discussions of humor in general and women's humor in particular.[14] Comics like Hannah Gadsby argue that comedy by definition limits the expression of serious content and the ability to instigate social change in the name of the disenfranchised. In her stand-up comedy special *Nanette*, Gadsby points to the limitations of joke-telling, with its build-up of tension and release through laughter, thereby undermining the narrative power of sharing the serious subject matter of her experience as a victim of gender violence and sexual assault. Using the example of Gadsby, Rebecca Krefting identifies the limitations of satire in using a play frame to expose social injustice, which undermines the gravity of the situation and serves to diffuse anger rather than channel it into social and political action. This division of comedy in two modes of discourse, "serious (angry) or humorous (funny)," is itself reductive and undermines the power of comedy to sustain the moment of tension and ambiguity rather than resolve it through humor.[15]

While debates over the efficacy and purpose of humor and marginalized humor in particular are ongoing, we owe much to the pioneering women of wit of the interwar period for giving voice to the underlying issues of gender, race, and class oppression through the subversive and salient form of laughter.

Notes

INTRODUCTION

1. Qtd. in Grumbach, *The Company She Kept*, 147.

2. Highet, *Anatomy of Satire*, 240.

3. See Sochen, introduction to *Women's Comic Visions*, 11–12; Finney, introduction to *Look Who's Laughing*, 2.

4. Norman Mailer branded McCarthy a "modern American bitch" in his 1963 review of *The Group*, and Hilton Kramer called her "our leading bitch intellectual. Mailer, "Mary McCarthy Case"; Kramer, "Mary McCarthy's Valentine to Fanny Farmer"; Gross, "Our Leading Bitch Intellectual."

5. Douglas, *Terrible Honesty*, 8, 15.

6. White, *Here Is New York*, 26.

7. Meade, *Dorothy Parker*, 117.

8. Douglas, *Terrible Honesty*, 17.

9. Wetzsteon, *Republic of Dreams*, 11.

10. Qtd. in ibid., 9.

11. Wilson, "Dawn Powell," 531–32.

12. Wetzsteon, *Republic of Dreams*, 572.

13. Bender, *Unfinished City*, xi.

14. Williams, *Country and the City*, 1.

15. Elizabeth Wilson, *Sphinx in the City*, 7–10.

16. See Rottenberg, "New Woman Ideal"; Goldsmith, "Strangers in the Village."

17. Qtd. in Patterson, *Beyond the Gibson Girl*, 2.

18. See Rudnick, "New Woman," 71.

19. Felski, *Gender of Modernity*, 19.

20. Wetzsteon, *Republic of Dreams*.

21. Rudnick, "New Woman," 73.

22. "Editorial Statement," qtd. in Miller, *Making Love Modern*, 262.

23. "Harold Ross' Vision for *The New Yorker*."

24. Yaross Lee, *Defining New Yorker Humor*, 28.

25. Patterson, *Beyond the Gibson Girl*, 26.

26. Kessler-Harris and Lauter, introduction to *The Unpossessed*.

27. Woolf, "Professions for Women," speech at Women's Service League, 1931, reprinted in *Death of the Moth*, 235.

28. Gilbert and Gubar, "Infection in the Sentence," 79.

29. Cixous, "Laugh of the Medusa," 885.

30. Suleiman, *Subversive Intent*, 168.

31. Freud, *Jokes and Their Relation to the Unconscious*, 236. Freud further elaborates on his theory of humor in his 1928 essay "Humor."

32. Freud, *Jokes*, 105, 108–9 (emphasis added).

33. Bergson, *Laughter*, 117, 64.

34. Freud, *Jokes*, 143.

35. Morreall, *Comic Relief*, 10.

36. Aristotle, *Rhetoric* 3.2, qtd. in ibid., 11; Kant, *Critique of Judgment*, part I, div. 1, 54, reprinted in Morreall, *Philosophy of Laughter and Humor*, 47.

37. R. Martin, *Psychology of Humor*, 74.

38. Walker, *A Very Serious Thing*, xii.

39. Toth, "Female Wits," 783.

40. Walker, "Toward Solidarity," 57.

41. Walker, *Very Serious Thing*, 12, 137.

42. Sheppard, "Social Cognition," 39.

43. McGhee, "Role of Laughter," qtd. in Sheppard, "Social Cognition," 41.

44. Showalter, "Towards a Feminist Poetics," 217.

45. Gilbert and Gubar, "Infection in the Sentence," 73.

46. Little, "Humoring the Sentence," 20.

47. Bakhtin, *Problems of Dostoevsky's Poetics*, 106–37.

48. Bakhtin, *Rabelais and His World*, 18, 21.

49. Rowe Karlyn, *Unruly Woman*, 3; Russo, "Female Grotesques"; Davis, *Society and Culture*.

50. Rowe Karlyn, *Unruly Woman*, 119.

51. Hennefeld, "Abject Feminism," 98.

52. Hutcheon, *Irony's Edge*, 10.

53. Colebrook, *Irony*, 18–19.

54. Lakoff, *Language and Woman's Place*, 78.

55. Butler, *Gender Trouble*, 34.

56. Barreca, *They Used to Call Me Snow White*, 16.

57. Walker, *Very Serious Thing*, 20, 9–11.

58. Bunkers, "I Am Outraged Womanhood," 153.

59. Friedan, *Feminine Mystique*, qtd. in Walker, "Toward Solidarity," 58.

60. J. Gilbert, *Performing Marginality*, 172.

61. Barreca, introduction to *Untamed and Unabashed*, 18.

62. Kaufman, introduction to *Pulling Our Own Strings*, 13.

63. Walker, *Very Serious Thing*, 145–47.

64. J. Gilbert, *Performing Marginality*, 3, 65.

65. Ibid., 166–67.

66. See Dickinson et al., *Women and Comedy*.

67. Krefting, *All Joking Aside*, 2, 25, 110.

68. Highet, *Anatomy of Satire*, 240.

69. Seidel, *Satiric Inheritance*.

70. Abrams, *Glossary of Literary Terms*, 276–77.

71. Greenberg, *Cambridge Introduction to Satire*, 13.

72. Ibid., 24.

73. Griffin, *Satire*, 149, 158, 160 (emphasis added).

74. Caron, "Quantum Paradox of Truthiness," 156, 163. See also Caron, *Satire as the Comic Public Sphere*.

75. Krefting, "Hannah Gadsby," 99, 100.

76. Walker, *Very Serious Thing*, 118.

77. See Dickson-Carr, *Spoofing the Modern*; Lowe, "Hurston, Humor, and the Harlem Renaissance."

78. Weisstein, "Why We Aren't Laughing . . . Any More," 134.

79. Walker, "Toward Solidarity," 66.

80. Weisstein, "Why We Aren't Laughing . . . Any More," 137.

81. Rowe Karlyn, *Unruly Woman*.

82. Hitchens, "Why Women Aren't Funny."

83. Qtd. in Mizejewski, *Pretty/Funny*, 1–3.

84. Krefting, *All Joking Aside*, 107.

85. See Zeisler, *We Were Feminists Once*. Zeisler is the founder of Bitch Media.

CHAPTER 1

1. Taggard, "Her Massive Sandal," 12.

2. Atkins, *Edna St. Vincent Millay*, 70; S. Gilbert "Directions for Using the Empress," 170.

3. See S. Gilbert, "Female Female Impersonator"; Fried, "Andromeda Unbound"; Clark, "Unwarranted Discourse"; and Miller, *Making Love Modern*; Riviere, "Womanliness as a Masquerade."

4. For a discussion of modern magazine culture and the image of the New Woman in the 1920s, see Keyser, *Playing Smart*.

5. Fried, "Andromeda Unbound"; Clark, "Unwarranted Discourse."

6. Tate, "Miss Millay's Sonnets," 63.

7. Ransom, "Poet as Woman," 78.

8. Walker, *Very Serious Thing*; J. Gilbert, *Performing Marginality*.

9. S. Gilbert, "Directions for Using the Empress," 180.

10. Edna St. Vincent Millay to Norma Millay and Charles Ellis, November 10, 1922, in *Letters of Edna St. Vincent Millay*, 165–66.

11. Edna St. Vincent Millay to Arthur Davison Ficke, October 1919, ibid., 91.

12. Millay, *Distressing Dialogues*, vii.

13. Bruère and Beard, introduction to *Laughing Their Way*.

14. Walker, *Very Serious Thing*, 54.

15. Millay, *Distressing Dialogues*, 41. Subsequent quotations from Millay's sketches as Nancy Boyd refer to this source and are cited parenthetically in the text.

16. Lakoff, *Language and Woman's Place*.

17. In Dawn Powell's late novel *The Golden Spur*, she similarly satirizes Greenwich Village bohemian life in the 1920s and '30s with a popular bar among the artistic set modeled on a stable and inspired by the real-life Cedar Tavern.

18. Millay, "Barrel," 35. Subsequent quotations from this source are cited parenthetically in the text.

CHAPTER 2

1. Qtd. in Pollack, "Premium Swift," 200.

2. Barreca, introduction to *Complete Stories*, ix.

3. Walker, *Very Serious Thing*.

4. Barreca, introduction to *Complete Stories*, viii.

5. Capron, "Interview with Dorothy Parker," 355.

6. Toth, "Dorothy Parker," 140.

7. Capron, "Interview with Dorothy Parker," 359.

8. Ibid., 358.

9. Ibid., 359–60.

10. Parker, introduction to *Most of S. J. Perelman*, xii.

11. W. Cooper, "Whatever You Think," 57.

12. Meade, *Dorothy Parker*, 117.

13. Ibid., 15–16.

14. Capron, "Interview with Dorothy Parker," 358.

15. Regarding Parker's relationship with her father, see her story "The Wonderful Old Gentlemen," an ironic sketch that many critics consider to be semiautobiographical. While some early biographers (e.g., Frewin) portray Parker as having a negative relationship with her father, later biographers like Meade see the relationship as more complex. Meade refers to affectionate letters in which Parker and her father regularly exchanged light verse, a possible inspiration for Parker's own poetry. Regarding Parker's reading, see Frewin, *Late Mrs. Dorothy Parker*, 12–14; Kinney, *Dorothy Parker*, 10.

16. Capron, "Interview with Dorothy Parker," 362.

17. Meade, *Dorothy Parker*, 113, 203.

18. When asked if she was related to the elite Rothschild family, Parker is reported to have said, "My God, *no*,

dear! We'd never *heard* of *those* Roths-
childs." Ibid., 3.

19. Ibid., 41.

20. Miller, *Making Love Modern.*

21. Parker, "News Item," in *Portable Dorothy Parker*, 109.

22. See Frewin, *Late Mrs. Dorothy Parker*, 29; Pollack, "Premium Swift," 212.

23. Capron, "Interview with Dorothy Parker," 358.

24. See Helal, "Celebrity, Femininity, Lingerie."

25. Miller, *Making Love Modern*, 96.

26. Woollcott, "Our Mrs. Parker," 149.

27. W. Cooper, "Whatever You Think," 57.

28. Lansky, "Female Trouble," 250.

29. Woollcott, "Our Mrs. Parker," 149.

30. Miller, *Making Love Modern*, 104 (quoting Parker).

31. Woollcott, "Our Mrs. Parker," 149.

32. Kernan, introduction to *Modern Satire.*

33. Parker called Hemingway "the greatest living writer of short stories," though she added, "He is, also to me, not the greatest living novelist" ("A Book of Great Short Stories," *New Yorker*, October 9, 1927). She also wrote a laudatory personal reminiscence of him in "The Artist's Reward" (*New Yorker*, November 30, 1929). Their relationship was strained after what turned into a difficult trip to Paris and Spain with Benchley and Hemingway aboard the *Roosevelt* in 1926 (Meade, *Dorothy Parker*, 167). Hemingway skewered Parker in a poem he published after her death titled "To a Tragic Poetess— Nothing in her life became her like her almost leaving it" (Meade, *Dorothy Parker*, 173).

34. Capron, "Interview with Dorothy Parker," 361.

35. Walker, *Very Serious Thing*, 52.

36. Little, "Humoring the Sentence"; Bakhtin, *Problems of Dostoevsky's Poetics*, 106–37.

37. Parker, *Portable Dorothy Parker*, 50. Subsequent quotes from this story refer to this collection and are cited parenthetically in the text.

38. Lakoff, *Language and Woman's Place*, 78–79.

39. Critics like Sondra Meltzer go so far as to see it as a metaphor for rape (Melzer, *Rhetoric of Rage*).

40. Parker, *Portable Dorothy Parker*, 119. Subsequent quotes from this story refer to this collection and are cited parenthetically in the text.

41. Parker, *Complete Stories*, 99. Subsequent quotes from this story and from all the remaining stories discussed in this chapter, unless otherwise indicated, refer to this collection and are cited parenthetically in the text.

42. Capron, "Interview with Dorothy Parker," 361.

43. Ibid., 359.

44. Keats, *You Might as Well Live*, 90.

45. Meade, *Dorothy Parker*, 160–62.

46. Walker, *Very Serious Thing*, 12.

47. Parker, *Portable Dorothy Parker*, 187. Subsequent quotes from this story refer to this collection and are cited parenthetically in the text.

48. Meade, *Dorothy Parker*, 107.

49. Parker, *Portable Dorothy Parker*, 99.

50. Toth, "Dorothy Parker," 149–50.

51. Barreca, *They Used to Call Me Snow White*, 18, 21.

CHAPTER 3

1. *On Being Told That Her Second Husband Has Taken His First Lover and Other Stories* includes the novella *The*

Answer on the Magnolia Tree (1935), based on Slesinger's experience teaching at Briarcliff, an elite private school, which she later turned into a screenplay, *Girl's School* (1938).

2. See L. Trilling, "Young in the Thirties," 45.

3. See Sharistanian, afterword to *The Unpossessed*.

4. Schwartz, *Menorah Treasury*; Kallen, "Promise of the Menorah Idea"; Alter, "Epitaph for a Jewish Magazine"; Greene, *Jewish Origins of Cultural Pluralism*, 2. While IMA dissolved in the 1930s, it was a precursor to B'nai B'rith Hillel societies, which are still active on campuses today and share a similar pluralistic, inclusive outlook.

5. Hurwitz and Sharfman, *Menorah Movement*, 1.

6. Ibid., 4.

7. L. Trilling, "Young in the Thirties," 46.

8. See L. Trilling, *Sincerity and Authenticity*; L. Trilling, *Liberal Imagination*.

9. Kallen, "Promise of the Menorah Idea," 13.

10. See Korelitz, "Menorah Idea," 84, 81.

11. Kallen, "Promise of the Menorah Idea," 9–10.

12. Qtd. in Wald, *New York Intellectuals*, 36.

13. Kallen, "Promise of the Menorah Idea," 11.

14. Ibid., 12.

15. In the early 1930s, Columbia College was considered to be roughly 25 percent Jewish, NYU was 40 percent Jewish, and City College, self-ironically dubbed the "cheder [yeshiva] on the Hill," was 80–90 percent Jewish. See Grinberg, "Neither 'Sissy' Boy nor Patrician Man," 141.

16. See Kallen, "Culture and the Ku Klux Klan." Although Kallen may have known Locke at Harvard and later at Oxford, he does not address racial equity in his call for cultural pluralism. The application of ethnic diversity and cultural pluralism to racial diversity became more explicit in the 1970s with the multicultural movement. See Greene, *Jewish Origins of Cultural Pluralism*, 7–8.

17. L. Trilling, "Young in the Thirties," 45.

18. Ibid., 45, 46.

19. Wald, "Menorah Group Moves Left," 292.

20. L. Trilling, "Young in the Thirties," 45.

21. Wald, *New York Intellectuals*, 42–45.

22. See Hurwitz, foreword to *Menorah Journal*.

23. See Korelitz, "Menorah Idea," 94.

24. Qtd. in Biagi, "Forgive Me for Dying," 226.

25. Qtd. in Wald, "Menorah Group Moves Left," 318–19.

26. Biagi, "Forgive Me for Dying," 231.

27. Sharistanian, afterword to *The Unpossessed*, 359–86.

28. Wald, "Menorah Group Moves Left," 312; Biagi, "Forgive Me for Dying," 231; Teres, *Renewing the Left*, 181.

29. Teres, *Renewing the Left*, 181.

30. See Rudnick, "New Woman," 71.

31. Ibid., 78.

32. Slesinger, "Memoirs of an Ex-Flapper," 76.

33. L. Trilling, "Young in the Thirties," 49; D. Trilling, *Beginning of the Journey*, 137.

34. L. Trilling, "Young in the Thirties," 44.

35. D. Trilling, *Beginning of the Journey*, 138.

36. Rabinowitz, *Labor and Desire*, 137.

37. L. Trilling, "Young in the Thirties," 48.

38. Slesinger, *The Unpossessed*, 13. Subsequent quotations from this source are cited parenthetically in the text.

39. See Castro, "My Little Illegality."

40. L. Trilling, "Young in the Thirties," 44.

41. Gannett, review of *The Unpossessed*; Brickell, review of *The Unpossessed*.

42. Kempton, *Part of Our Time*, qtd. in L. Trilling, "Young in the Thirties," 49.

43. L. Trilling, "Young in the Thirties," 48–49.

44. Niebuhr, "Art of Fiction," 8.

45. Seaver, "Phony 'Intellectuals.'"

46. Rahv, "Storm over the Intellectuals."

47. Qtd. in Wald, *New York Intellectuals*, 40.

48. Qtd. in Abbott, "Are Three Generations of Radicals Enough?," 618.

49. See Sharistanian, afterword to *The Unpossessed*; Kessler-Harris and Lauter, introduction to *The Unpossessed*; Rabinowitz, *Labor and Desire*; Felski, *Gender of Modernity*; Rottenberg, "New Woman Ideal," 341–55; Goldsmith, "Strangers in the Village."

50. Qtd. in Biagi, "Forgive Me for Dying," 231.

51. L. Trilling, "Young in the Thirties," 44.

52. Rabinowitz, *Labor and Desire*, 137.

53. Slesinger, *On Being Told*, 5–6. Subsequent quotations from the stories refer to this collection and are cited parenthetically in the text.

CHAPTER 4

1. Fauset, "Gift of Laughter," 166.

2. Hughes, *Big Sea*.

3. See Du Bois, "Browsing Reader."

4. Locke, "Saving Grace of Realism," 9.

5. Braithwaite, "Novels of Jessie Fauset," 26.

6. McKay, *Long Way from Home*, 91; Wright qtd. in Gilbert and Gubar, "Ain't I a New Woman?," 126.

7. Fauset, "Gift of Laughter," 164.

8. Hughes, "Negro Artist and the Racial Mountain," 693.

9. Dickson-Carr, *African-American Satire*, 1, 3.

10. Haggins, *Laughing Mad*, 4.

11. Fuentes Morgan, *Laughing to Keep from Dying*, 7, 6.

12. Dickson-Carr, *African-American Satire*, 4.

13. Dickson-Carr, *Spoofing the Modern*, 93.

14. Finley, "Black Women's Satire," 242; Krefting, "Hannah Gadsby," 99.

15. Krefting, "Hannah Gadsby," 100.

16. Wall, *Women of the Harlem Renaissance*, 60.

17. Hughes, *Big Sea*.

18. Locke, "Harlem, Mecca of the New Negro."

19. Rampersad, introduction to *The New Negro*.

20. "New Negro Woman."

21. Welter, "Cult of True Womanhood."

22. Tillman, "Afro-American Women and Their Work," 286.

23. Lindsey, *Colored No More*, 23, 110.

24. B. Cooper, *Beyond Respectability*, 1–10.

25. Sylvander, *Jessie Redmon Fauset*.

26. Wall, *Women of the Harlem Renaissance*, 41–42.

27. Gilbert and Gubar, "Ain't I a New Woman?," 125.

28. Fauset, *Plum Bun*, iii. Subsequent quotes from the novel are cited parenthetically in the text.

29. McDowell, introduction to *Plum Bun*.

30. See Tomlinson, "Vision to Visionary"; Todd, *"New Woman" Revised*.

31. Tomlinson, "Vision to Visionary," 92–93.

32. Fauset, foreword to *The Chinaberry Tree*, ix, x.

33. See Simmons, *Making Marriage Modern*, 105–37; duCille, *Coupling Convention*; Chapman, *Prove It on Me*.

34. Fauset, foreword to *The Chinaberry Tree*, x.

35. See Carby, *Reconstructing Womanhood*.

36. Feeney, "Sardonic, Unconventional Jessie Fauset," 382.

37. Sylvander, *Jessie Redmon Fauset*, 184, 188.

38. Ibid., iii.

39. DuCille, *Coupling Convention*, 84.

40. Tomlinson, "Vision to Visionary," 90.

41. Rottenberg, "Jessie Fauset's *Plum Bun*," 267.

42. Keyser, *Playing Smart*, 105.

43. Mendelman, *Modern Sentimentalism*, 5.

44. Fuentes Morgan, *Laughing to Keep from Dying*, 3.

CHAPTER 5

1. Powell, *Diaries of Dawn Powell*, 419. Subsequent quotations from this source are cited parenthetically in the text with the abbreviation *D*.

2. Josephson, "Dawn Powell," 20.

3. D. Trilling, review of *A Time to Be Born*, 243.

4. Edmund Wilson, "Dawn Powell," 526.

5. Griffin, *Satire*, 4; Kernan, *Cankered Muse*, 35; see also Smith Rice, *Dawn Powell*.

6. Qtd. in Updike, "Ohio Runaway," 271.

7. D. Trilling, review of *Locusts Have No King*, 611–12.

8. Vidal, "Dawn Powell, the American Writer," 52.

9. Qtd. in Vidal, "Dawn Powell, the American Writer," 52.

10. Page, *Dawn Powell*, 7, 12–13.

11. Qtd. in Josephson, "Dawn Powell," 28.

12. Edmund Wilson, "Dawn Powell," 526–27.

13. Vidal, "Dawn Powell, the American Writer," 52.

14. Ibid.

15. Vidal, "Dawn Powell: Queen of the Golden Age," 16.

16. Like Hemingway, Fitzgerald, and Parker, Powell was a regular guest at art patrons Gerald and Sara Murphy's summer home, and she was close friends with Hemingway's third wife, Pauline Pfeiffer.

17. Wetzsteon, *Republic of Dreams*, 10–11.

18. Page, *Dawn Powell*, 12–14.

19. Updike, "Ohio Runaway," 271.

20. Vidal, "Dawn Powell, the American Writer," 52.

21. Wetzsteon, *Republic of Dreams*, 509–10.

22. Vidal, "Dawn Powell, the American Writer," 52–53.

23. Page, *Dawn Powell*, 60–66.

24. Updike, "Ohio Runaway," 271.

25. Josephson, "Dawn Powell," 24.

26. Qtd. in ibid., 23.

27. Ibid., 25.

28. Ibid., 23.

29. Ibid., 24; Wetzsteon, *Republic of Dreams*, 510; Palermo, *Message of the City*, 28.

30. Palermo, *Message of the City*, 28; Peters, "Travelers in Residence," 148.

31. Peters, "Travelers in Residence," 222, 211–12, 120.

32. Powell, *Wicked Pavilion*, 32.

33. Peters, "Travelers in Residence," 124. See also Wetzsteon, who describes the Golden Spur as "a kind of cross between the Cedar Tavern and the San Remo—one of the few places remaining from the Golden Age of the Village" (*Republic of Dreams*, 517). The Cedar Tavern has since been relocated.

34. Wetzsteon, *Republic of Dreams*, 514–15.

35. Wilson, "Dawn Powell," 531–32.

36. Ibid., 527.

37. Powell, *Turn, Magic Wheel*, 152. Subsequent quotes from the novel appear parenthetically in the text, with the abbreviation *TMW*.

38. Page, *Dawn Powell*, 231.

39. Powell, *Wicked Pavilion*, epigraph. Subsequent quotes from the novel appear parenthetically in the text, with the abbreviation *WP*.

40. Powell, *Golden Spur*, 1. Subsequent quotes from the novel appear parenthetically in the text, with the abbreviation *GS*.

CHAPTER 6

1. Qtd. in Grumbach, *Company She Kept*, 147.

2. Abrams, *Glossary of Literary Terms*, 276.

3. Qtd. in Grumbach, *Company She Kept*, 147.

4. Kernan, introduction to *Modern Satire*.

5. Lurie, "True Confessions," 19.

6. Kramer, "Mary McCarthy's Valentine to Fanny Farmer," 1; Podhoretz, *Making It*, 154; Mailer, "Mary McCarthy Case," 3.

7. Showalter, "Killing the Angel in the House"; W. Martin, "Satire and Moral Vision."

8. Brightman, "Mary, Still Contrary," 245.

9. McCarthy, introduction to *Mary McCarthy's Theatre Chronicles*, ix.

10. Niebuhr, "Art of Fiction XXVII," 14.

11. Podhoretz, *Making It*, 154.

12. Mailer, "Mary McCarthy Case," 1; Brower, "Mary McCarthyism," 60.

13. Gelderman, *Mary McCarthy*, 184.

14. Gross, "Our Leading Bitch Intellectual," 27–28.

15. Hardwick, *View of My Own*.

16. Smith, "Mary McCarthy Said," 60.

17. M. Gross, "World Out of Joint," 176; Brightman, "Mary, Still Contrary," 245.

18. Brightman, "Mary, Still Contrary," 244.

19. M. Gross, "World Out of Joint," 176.

20. Smith, "Mary McCarthy Said," 53, 56.

21. McCarthy, *The Company She Keeps*, 10. Subsequent quotes from the novel appear parenthetically in the text, with the abbreviation *CSK*.

22. McCarthy, *Intellectual Memoirs*, 62.

23. Kiernan, *Seeing Mary Plain*, 116.

24. Qtd. in Gelderman, *Mary McCarthy*, 170.

25. Barrett, *Truants*, 65.

26. Dickstein, "Glint of Malice," 19.

27. McCarthy, *How I Grew*, 16–17.

28. Niebuhr, "Art of Fiction XXVII," 8. Though McCarthy says the "Yale man" was based loosely on John Chamberlain, she clarifies that she never had an affair with him.

29. McCarthy, "Notes on *The Group*," ms. box 21 f.6, Mary McCarthy Papers, Special Collections, Vassar College Libraries, 1, qtd. in Fuchs Abrams, *Mary McCarthy*, 44.

30. See Kaufmann, review of *The Group*; Mailer, "Mary McCarthy Case."

31. McCarthy address at the Women's National Press Club in Washington, DC, qtd. in Gelderman, *Mary McCarthy*, 255.

32. Newman, "Conversation with Mary McCarthy," 76.

33. Mailer, "Mary McCarthy Case"; Newman, "Conversation with Mary McCarthy," 76.

34. Aldridge, "Mary McCarthy," 99.

35. McCarthy, "Letter to a Translator About *The Group*," 70, qtd. in Fuchs Abrams, *Mary McCarthy*, 45–46.

36. McCarthy, "Vassar Girl," 200.

37. Ibid., 210, 202.

38. McCarthy, *The Group*, 16. Subsequent quotes from the novel appear parenthetically in the text, with the abbreviation *TG*.

39. Smith, "Mary McCarthy Said," 61.

40. McCarthy, application for Guggenheim Fellowship, 1951, qtd. in Gelderman, *Mary McCarthy*, 252.

41. Brightman, *Writing Dangerously*, 174–77.

EPILOGUE

1. See Pershing, "There's a Joker," 194; Willett and Willett, *Uproarious*, 21–46.

2. Honig, "Toward an Agonistic Feminism," 227.

3. McRobbie, *Aftermath of Feminism*, 1.

4. Tasker and Negra, introduction to *Interrogating Postfeminism*, 12.

5. S. Douglas, *Rise of Enlightened Sexism*, 15.

6. Shifman and Lemish, "Between Feminism and Fun(ny)mism," 874, 887.

7. Douglas, *Rise of Enlightened Sexism*, 11.

8. Hitchens, "Why Women Still Don't Get It."

9. See George, *Hip Hop America*; Neal, *Soul Babies*.

10. Springer, "Divas," 251, 250, 254, 258.

11. Finley, "Black Women's Satire," 237.

12. Ibid., 247.

13. Guerrero, "Can I Live," 266, 276.

14. See Lockyer and Pickering, *Beyond a Joke*; Davies and Ilott, *Comedy and the Politics of Representation*.

15. Krefting, "Hannah Gadsby," 95.

Bibliography

Abbott, Philip. "Are Three Generations of Radicals Enough? Self-Critique in the Novels of Tess Slesinger, Mary McCarthy, and Marge Piercy." *Review of Politics* 53, no. 4 (1991): 602–26.

Abrams, M. H. *A Glossary of Literary Terms*. 7th ed. Boston: Heinle & Heinle, 1999.

Aldridge, John. "Mary McCarthy: Princess Among the Trolls." In *Time to Murder and Create: The Contemporary Novel in Crisis*, 95–132. New York: David McKay Co.

Alter, Robert. "Epitaph for a Jewish Magazine: Notes on the *Menorah Journal*." *Commentary* 39, no. 5 (1965): 51–55.

Atkins, Elizabeth. *Edna St. Vincent Millay and Her Times*. Chicago: University of Chicago Press, 1936.

Bakhtin, Mikhail. *Problems of Dostoevsky's Poetics*. Translated by Caryl Emerson. Minneapolis: University of Minnesota Press, 1984.

———. *Rabelais and His World*. 1965. Translated by Hélène Iswolsky. Bloomington: Indiana University Press, 1984.

Barreca, Regina. Introduction to *Complete Stories*, by Dorothy Parker, edited by Colleen Breese, vii–xix. New York: Penguin Books, 2003.

———. Introduction to *Untamed and Unabashed: Essays on Women and Humor in British Literature*, edited by Regina Barreca, vii–xx. Detroit: Wayne State University Press, 1994.

———, ed. *Last Laughs: Perspectives on Women and Comedy*. New York: Gordon and Breach, 1988.

———. *They Used to Call Me Snow White . . . But I Drifted: Women's Strategic Use of Humor*. New York: Viking/Penguin, 1991.

Barrett, William. *The Truants: Adventures Among the Intellectuals*. Garden City, NY: Anchor Press/Doubleday, 1982.

Bender, Thomas. *The Unfinished City: New York and the Metropolitan Idea*. New York: New Press, 2001.

Bergson, Henri. *Laughter: An Essay on the Meaning of the Comic*. Edited by Wylie Sypher. 1911. Reprint, Garden City, NY: Doubleday Anchor Books, 1956.

Biagi, Shirley. "Forgive Me for Dying." *Antioch Review* 35, no. 2/3 (1977): 224–36.

Braithwaite, William Stanley. "The Novels of Jessie Fauset." *Opportunity* 13 (January 1934): 24–28.

Brickell, Herschel. Review of *The Unpossessed*, by Tess Slesinger. *New York Evening Post*, May 12, 1934, 11.

Brightman, Carol. "Mary, Still Contrary." *The Nation*, May 19, 1984, 611–18. Reprinted in Gelderman, *Conversations*, 234–49. Page numbers in the notes refer to the Gelderman volume.

———. *Writing Dangerously: Mary McCarthy and Her World.* New York: Random House, 1992.

Brower, Brock. "Mary McCarthyism." *Esquire,* July 1962, 60–65.

Bruère, Martha Bensley, and Mary Ritter Beard. Introduction to *Laughing Their Way: Women's Humor in America,* edited by Martha Bensley Bruère and Mary Ritter Beard. New York: Macmillan, 1934.

Bunkers, Suzanne L. "'I Am Outraged Womanhood': Dorothy Parker as Feminist and Social Critic." In Pettit, *Critical Waltz,* 152–65.

Butler, Judith. *Gender Trouble: Feminism and the Subversion of Identity.* 1990. Reprint, New York: Routledge, 2006.

Capron, Marion. "An Interview with Dorothy Parker." 1956. Reprinted in Pettit, *Critical Waltz,* 355–63.

Carby, Hazel V. *Reconstructing Womanhood: The Emergence of the Afro-American Woman Novelist.* New York: Oxford University Press, 1987.

Caron, James E. "The Quantum Paradox of Truthiness: Satire, Activism, and the Postmodern Condition." *Studies in American Humor* 2, no. 2 (2016): 153–74.

———. *Satire as the Comic Public Sphere: Postmodern "Truthiness" and Civic Engagement.* University Park: Penn State University Press, 2021.

Carpio, Glenda. *Laughing Fit to Kill: Black Humor in the Fictions of Slavery.* New York: Oxford University Press, 2008.

Castro, Joy. "'My Little Illegality': Abortion, Resistance, and Women Writers on the Left." In *The Novel and the American Left: Critical Essays on Depression-Era Fiction,* edited by Janet Galligani Casey, 16–34. Iowa City: University of Iowa Press, 2004.

Chapman, Erin D. *Prove It on Me: New Negroes, Sex, and Popular Culture in the 1920s.* Oxford: Oxford University Press, 2012.

Cixous, Hélène. "The Laugh of the Medusa." Translated by Keith Cohen and Paula Cohen. *Signs* 1, no. 1 (1976): 875–93.

Clark, Suzanne. "The Unwarranted Discourse: Sentimental Community, Modernist Women, and the Case of Millay." In Thesing, *Critical Essays,* 248–65.

Cohen, Sarah Blacher, ed. *Comic Relief: Humor in Contemporary American Literature.* Urbana: University of Illinois Press, 1978.

Colebrook, Claire. *Irony.* London: Routledge, 2004.

Cooper, Brittney C. *Beyond Respectability: The Intellectual Thought of Race Women.* Urbana: University of Illinois Press, 2017.

Cooper, Wyatt. "Whatever You Think Dorothy Parker Was Like, She Wasn't." *Esquire,* July 1968, 56–57, 61, 110–14.

Davies, Helen, and Sarah Ilott, eds. *Comedy and the Politics of Representation: Mocking the Weak.* London: Palgrave Macmillan, 2018.

Davis, Natalie Zemon. *Society and Culture in Early Modern France.* Stanford: Stanford University Press, 1975.

Dean, Michelle. *Sharp: The Women Who Made an Art of Having an*

Opinion. New York: Grove Press, 2018.

Dell, Floyd. *Love in Greenwich Village*. New York: George H. Doran, 1926.

Dell, Jerri. *Blood Too Bright: Floyd Dell Remembers Edna St. Vincent Millay*. Warwick, UK: Glenmere Press, 2017.

Dickinson, Peter, Anne Higgins, Paul Matthew St. Pierre, Diana Solomon, and Sean Zwagerman, eds. *Women and Comedy: History, Theory, Practice*. Madison: Fairleigh Dickinson University Press, 2013.

Dickson-Carr, Darryl. *African-American Satire: The Sacredly Profane Novel*. Columbia: University of Missouri Press, 2001.

Dickstein, Morris. "A Glint of Malice." In *Twenty-Four Ways of Looking at Mary McCarthy*, edited by Eve Stwertka and Margo Viscusi, 17–26. Westport, CT: Greenwood Press, 1996.

———. *Spoofing the Modern: Satire in the Harlem Renaissance*. Columbia: University of South Carolina Press, 2015.

———. "Womb Versus World." Review of *The Unpossessed*. *Bookforum* 13 (June–September 2006).

Douglas, Ann. *Terrible Honesty: Mongrel Manhattan in the 1920s*. New York: Farrar, Straus and Giroux, 1996.

Douglas, Susan J. *The Rise of Enlightened Sexism: How Pop Culture Took Us from Girl Power to Girls Gone Wild*. New York: St. Martin's Press, 2010.

Dresner, Zita. "Heterodite Humor: Alice Duer Miller and Florence Guy Seabury." In Morris, *American Women Humorists*, 311–26.

Du Bois, W. E. B. "The Browsing Reader." Review of *Plum Bun* by Jessie Fauset. *The Crisis* 36, no. 4 (1929): 125, 138.

duCille, Ann. *The Coupling Convention: Sex, Text, and Tradition in Black Women's Fiction*. New York: Oxford University Press, 1993.

"Editorial Statement." *Vanity Fair*, March 1914.

Elliott, Robert C. "The Satirist and Society." *ELH* 21, no. 3 (1954): 237–48.

Fass, Paula S. *The Damned and the Beautiful: American Youth in the 1920s*. New York: Oxford University Press, 1979.

Fauset, Jessie Redmon. Foreword to *The Chinaberry Tree: A Novel of American Life*, ix–x. 1931. Reprint, Mineola, NY: Dover, 2013.

———. "The Gift of Laughter." In Locke, *The New Negro*, 161–67.

———. *Plum Bun: A Novel Without a Moral*. 1929. Reprint, Boston: Beacon Press, 1990.

———. "The Symbolism of Bert Williams." *The Crisis* 24, no. 5 (1922): 12–15.

Feeney, Joseph J. "A Sardonic, Unconventional Jessie Fauset: The Double Structure and Double Vision of Her Novels." *CLA Journal* 22, no. 4 (1979): 365–82.

Felski, Rita. *The Gender of Modernity*. Cambridge: Harvard University Press, 1995.

Finley, Jessyka. "Black Women's Satire as (Black) Postmodern Performance." *Studies in American Humor* 2, no. 2 (2016): 236–65.

Finney, Gail. Introduction to *Look Who's Laughing: Gender and Comedy*, edited by Gail Finney, 1–16. New York: Routledge, 1994.

Freedman, Diane P., ed. *Millay at 100: A Critical Reappraisal.* Carbondale: Southern Illinois University Press, 1995.

Freud, Sigmund. "Humor." *International Journal of Psycho-Analysis* 9 (1928): 1–6.

———. *Jokes and Their Relation to the Unconscious.* Translated and edited by James Strachey. 1905. Reprint, New York: W. W. Norton, 1960.

Frewin, Leslie. *The Late Mrs. Dorothy Parker.* New York: Macmillan, 1987.

Fried, Debra. "Andromeda Unbound: Gender and Genre in Millay's Sonnets." In Thesing, *Critical Essays,* 229–47.

Friedan, Betty. *The Feminine Mystique.* New York: W. W. Norton, 1963.

Fuchs Abrams, Sabrina. *Mary McCarthy: Gender, Politics, and the Postwar Intellectual.* New York: Peter Lang, 2004.

———, ed. *Transgressive Humor of American Women Writers.* New York: Palgrave Macmillan, 2017.

Fuentes Morgan, Danielle. *Laughing to Keep from Dying: African American Satire in the Twenty-First Century.* Urbana: University of Illinois Press, 2020.

Gannett, Lewis. Review of *The Unpossessed,* by Tess Slesinger. *New York Herald Tribune,* May 10, 1934, 10.

Gates, Henry Louis, Jr. and Gene Andrew Jarrett. Introduction to Gates and Jarrett, *New Negro,* 1–20.

———, eds. *The New Negro: Readings on Race, Representation, and African American Culture, 1892–1938.* Princeton: Princeton University Press, 2007.

Gelderman, Carol, ed. *Conversations with Mary McCarthy.* Jackson: University Press of Mississippi, 1991.

———. *Mary McCarthy: A Life.* New York: St. Martin's Press, 1988.

George, Nelson. *Hip Hop America.* New York: Viking, 1998.

Gilbert, Joanne R. "Lesbian Stand-Up Comics and the Politics of Laughter." In Dickinson et al., *Women and Comedy,* 185–96.

———. *Performing Marginality: Humor, Gender, and Cultural Critique.* Detroit: Wayne State University Press, 2004.

Gilbert, Sandra M. "'Directions for Using the Empress': Millay's Supreme Fiction(s)." In Freedman, *Millay at 100,* 163–81.

———. "Female Female Impersonator: Millay and the Theatre of Personality." In Thesing, *Critical Essays,* 293–312.

Gilbert, Sandra M., and Susan Gubar. "Ain't I a New Woman? Feminism and the Harlem Renaissance." In *No Man's Land: The Place of the Woman Writer in the Twentieth Century,* vol. 3, *Letters from the Front,* 121–65. New Haven: Yale University Press, 1994.

———. "Infection in the Sentence: The Woman Writer and the Anxiety of Authorship." In *The Madwoman in the Attic: The Woman Writer and the Nineteenth-Century Literary Imagination,* 2nd ed., 45–92. New Haven: Yale University Press, 2000.

Gillette, Meg. "Modern Abortion Narratives and the Century of Silence." *Twentieth-Century Literature* 58, no. 4 (2012): 663–87.

Goldsmith, Meredith. "Strangers in the Village: Greenwich Village and the Search for Alternative Space in Ethnic Women's Fiction of the

1920s and 1930s." In *Black Harlem and the Jewish Lower East Side: Narratives Out of Time*, edited by Catherine Rottenberg, 43–64. Albany: State University of New York Press, 2013.

Grant, Thomas. "A Feminist Humorist of the 1920s: The 'Little Insurrections' of Florence Guy Seabury." In *New Perspectives on Women and Comedy*, edited by Regina Barreca, 157–68. Philadelphia: Gordon and Breach, 1992.

Greenberg, Jonathan. *The Cambridge Introduction to Satire*. Cambridge: Cambridge University Press, 2019.

Greene, Daniel. *The Jewish Origins of Cultural Pluralism: The Menorah Association and American Diversity*. Bloomington: Indiana University Press, 2011.

Griffin, Dustin. *Satire: A Critical Reintroduction*. Lexington: University Press of Kentucky, 1994.

Grinberg, Ronnie. "Neither 'Sissy' Boy nor Patrician Man: New York Intellectuals and the Construction of American Jewish Masculinity." *American Jewish History* 98, no. 3 (2014): 127–51.

Gross, Beverly. "Our Leading Bitch Intellectual." In *Twenty-Four Ways of Looking at Mary McCarthy*, edited by Eve Stwertka and Margo Viscusi, 27–34. Westport, CT: Greenwood Press, 1996.

Gross, Miriam. "A World Out of Joint." *The Observer* 14 (October 1979): 35. Reprinted in Gelderman, *Conversations*, 170–78. Page numbers in the notes refer to the Gelderman volume.

Grumbach, Doris. *The Company She Kept: A Revealing Portrait of Mary McCarthy*. New York: Coward-McCann, 1967.

Guerrero, Lisa. "Can I Live? Contemporary Black Satire and the State of Postmodern Double Consciousness." *Studies in American Humor* 2, no. 2 (2016): 266–79.

———. *Crazy Funny: Popular Black Satire and The Methods of Madness*. New York: Routledge, 2019.

Haggins, Bambi. *Laughing Mad: The Black Comic Persona in Post-Soul America*. New Brunswick: Rutgers University Press, 2007.

Hardwick, Elizabeth. *A View of My Own*. New York: Farrar, Straus and Cudahy, 1962.

"Harold Ross' Vision for *The New Yorker*." American Studies at the University of Virginia, September 1, 2009. http://xroads.virginia.edu/~ug02/newyorker/prospectus.html.

Helal, Kathleen M. "Celebrity, Femininity, Lingerie: Dorothy Parker's Autobiographical Monologues." *Women's Studies* 33, no. 1 (2004): 77–102.

Hennefeld, Maggie. "Abject Feminism, Grotesque Comedy, and Apocalyptic Laughter on *Inside Amy Schumer*." In *Abjection Incorporated: Mediating the Politics of Pleasure and Violence*, edited by Maggie Hennefeld and Nicholas Sammond, 86–114. Durham: Duke University Press, 2020.

Highet, Gilbert. *The Anatomy of Satire*. Princeton: Princeton University Press, 1962.

Hitchens, Christopher. "Why Women Aren't Funny." *Vanity Fair*, January 2007, 54.

———. "Why Women Still Don't Get It." *Vanity Fair*, March 3, 2008.

http://www.vanityfair.com/culture/
features/2008/04/hitchens200804.

Honig, Bonnie. "Toward an Agonistic
Feminism: Hannah Arendt and the
Politics of Identity." In *Feminists
Theorize the Political*, edited by
Judith Butler and Joan W. Scott,
215–35. New York: Routledge, 1992.

Hughes, Langston. *The Big Sea: An
Autobiography*. 1940. Reprint, New
York: Hill and Wang, 1993.

———. *Laughing to Keep from Crying*.
New York: Henry Holt, 1952.

———. "The Negro Artist and the
Racial Mountain." *The Nation*, June
23, 1926, 692–93.

Hurwitz, Henry. Foreword to *Menorah
Journal* 14, no. 1 (1928): 1–4.

Hurwitz, Henry, and I. Leo Sharfman.
*The Menorah Movement: For the
Study and Advancement of Jewish
Culture and Ideals; History,
Purposes, Activities*. Ann Arbor,
MI: Intercollegiate Menorah Asso-
ciation, 1914.

Hutcheon, Linda. *Irony's Edge: The
Theory and Politics of Irony*. New
York: Routledge, 1994.

Jerkins, Morgan. "The Forgotten Work
of Jessie Redmon Fauset." *New
Yorker*, February 18, 2017.

Josephson, Matthew. "Dawn Powell: A
Woman of 'Esprit.'" *Southern
Review*, January 1, 1973, 18–52.

Kallen, Horace M. "Culture and the Ku
Klux Klan." 1924. In *Culture and
Democracy in the United States*,
1–35. Reprint, New Brunswick, NJ:
Transaction Publishers, 1998.

———. "The Promise of the Menorah
Idea." *Menorah Journal* 49, no. 1/2
(1962): 9–16.

Kant, Immanuel. *Critique of Judgment*.
Translated by J. H. Bernard.
London: Macmillan, 1892.

Kaufman, Gloria. Introduction to *Pull-
ing Our Own Strings: Feminist
Humor and Satire*, edited by Gloria
Kaufman and Mary Kay Blakely,
13–21. Bloomington: Indiana
University Press, 1980.

Kaufmann, Stanley. Review of *The
Group*, by Mary McCarthy. *New
Republic*, August 31, 1963, 25–28.

Keats, John C. *You Might as Well Live:
The Life and Times of Dorothy
Parker*. New York: Simon & Schus-
ter, 1970.

Kempton, Murray. *Part of Our Time:
Some Ruins and Monuments of the
Thirties*. New York: New York
Review of Books, 1955.

Kernan, Alvin. *The Cankered Muse:
Satire of the English Renaissance*.
New Haven: Yale University Press,
1959.

———. Introduction to *Modern Satire*,
edited by Alvin Kernan. New York:
Harcourt, Brace & World, 1962.

Kessler-Harris, Alice, and Paul Lauter.
Introduction to *The Unpossessed*,
by Tess Slesinger, vii–xvi. 1932.
Reprint, Old Westbury, NY: Feminist Press, 1984.

Keyser, Catherine. *Playing Smart: New
York Women Writers and Modern
Magazine Culture*. New Brunswick:
Rutgers University Press, 2010.

Kiernan, Francis. *Seeing Mary Plain: A
Life of Mary McCarthy*. New York:
W. W. Norton, 2000.

Kinney, Arthur F. *Dorothy Parker*. New
York: Twayne, 1979.

Korelitz, Seth. "The Menorah Idea:
From Religion to Culture, from
Race to Ethnicity." *American Jewish
History* 85, no. 1 (1997): 75–100.

Kramer, Hilton. "Mary McCarthy's
Valentine to Fanny Farmer."
Review of *Birds of America* by

Mary McCarthy. *Washington Post*, May 23, 1971, 1.

Krefting, Rebecca. *All Joking Aside: American Humor and Its Discontents*. Baltimore: Johns Hopkins University Press, 2014.

———. "Hannah Gadsby: On the Limits of Satire." *Studies in American Humor* 5, no. 1 (2019): 93–102.

Lakoff, Robin Tolmach. *Language and Woman's Place*. Edited by Mary Bucholtz. 1975. Reprint, New York: Oxford University Press, 2004.

Lansky, Ellen. "Female Trouble: Dorothy Parker, Katherine Anne Porter, and Alcoholism." In Pettit, *Critical Waltz*, 246–66.

Levy, Ariel. *Female Chauvinist Pigs: Women and the Rise of Raunch Culture*. New York: Free Press, 2005.

Lindsey, Treva B. *Colored No More: Reinventing Black Womanhood in Washington, D.C.* Urbana: University of Illinois Press, 2017.

Little, Judy. *Comedy and the Woman Writers*. Lincoln: University of Nebraska Press, 1983.

———. "Humoring the Sentence: Women's Dialogic Comedy." In Sochen, *Women's Comic Visions*, 19–32.

Locke, Alain, ed. "Harlem, Mecca of the New Negro." Special issue. *Survey Graphic* 53, no. 11 (March 1925).

———, ed. *The New Negro: Voices of the Harlem Renaissance*. 1925. Reprint, New York: Macmillan, 1992.

———. "The Saving Grace of Realism." *Opportunity* 13 (January 1934): 8–11, 30.

Lockyer, Sharon, and Michael Pickering, eds. *Beyond a Joke: The Limits of Humor*. New York: Palgrave Macmillan, 2009.

Lowe, John. "Hurston, Humor, and the Harlem Renaissance." In Morris, *American Women Humorists*, 341–81.

Lurie, Alison. "True Confessions." *New York Review of Books*, June 11, 1987, 19–20.

Mailer, Norman. "The Mary McCarthy Case." Review of *The Group*, by Mary McCarthy. *New York Review of Books*, October 17, 1963, 1–3.

Martin, Rod A. *The Psychology of Humor: An Integrative Approach*. London: Elsevier, 2007.

Martin, Wendy. "The Satire and Moral Vision of Mary McCarthy." In Cohen, *Comic Relief*, 187–206.

McCarthy, Mary. *The Company She Keeps*. New York: Dell, 1942.

———. *The Group*. New York: Harcourt, Brace & World, 1963.

———. *How I Grew*. New York: Harcourt Brace Jovanovich, 1987.

———. *Intellectual Memoirs: New York, 1936–1938*. New York: Harcourt Brace Jovanovich, 1992.

———. "Letter to a Translator About *The Group*." *Encounter* 23, no. 5 (1964): 70. Reprint of "Letter to Mr. Hertel," ms. box 22 f.8, Mary McCarthy Papers, Special Collections, Vassar College Libraries.

———. *Mary McCarthy's Theatre Chronicles: 1937–1962*. New York: Farrar, Straus, 1963.

———. "The Vassar Girl." *Holiday*, May 1951. Reprinted in *On the Contrary*, 193–214.

McDougald, Elise Johnson. "The Task of Negro Womanhood." In Gates and Jarrett, *New Negro*, 369–82.

McDowell, Deborah. Introduction to *Plum Bun: A Novel Without a Moral*, by Jessie Redmon Fauset, ix–xxxiii. Boston: Beacon Press, 1990.

McGhee, Paul. "The Role of Laughter and Humor in Growing Up Female." In *Becoming Female: Perspectives on Development*, edited by Claire B. Kopp, 33–56. New York: Plenum Press, 1979.

McKay, Claude. *A Long Way from Home*. 1937. Reprint, New Brunswick: Rutgers University Press, 2007.

McRobbie, Angela. *The Aftermath of Feminism: Gender, Culture and Social Change*. Los Angeles: Sage, 2009.

Meade, Marion. *Dorothy Parker: What Fresh Hell Is This?* New York: Penguin Books, 1987.

Melzer, Sondra. *The Rhetoric of Rage: Women in Dorothy Parker*. New York: Peter Lang, 1997.

Mendelman, Lisa. *Modern Sentimentalism: Affect, Irony, and Female Authorship in Interwar America*. New York: Oxford University Press, 2019.

Millay, Edna St. Vincent. "The Barrel: Showing That to a Woman a Man, Even a Philosopher, Is Always a Little Ridiculous, and That to a Man, Any Man, a Woman Is Something More than a Nuisance." *Vanity Fair*, July 1922, 35–36.

——— [pseud. Nancy Boyd]. *Distressing Dialogues*. New York: Harper and Brothers, 1924.

———. *Letters of Edna St. Vincent Millay*. Edited by Allan Ross Macdougall. New York: Harper & Brothers, 1952.

Miller, Nina. *Making Love Modern: The Intimate Public Worlds of New York's Literary Women*. New York: Oxford University Press, 1998.

Mizejewski, Linda. *Pretty/Funny: Women Comedians and Body Politics*. Austin: University of Texas Press, 2014.

Morreall, John. *Comic Relief: A Comprehensive Philosophy of Humor*. Foreword by Robert Mankoff. Malden, MA: Wiley-Blackwell, 2009.

———, ed. *The Philosophy of Laughter and Humor*. Albany: State University of New York Press, 1987.

Morris, Linda A., ed. *American Women Humorists: Critical Essays*. New York: Routledge, 1993.

———. *Women's Humor in the Age of Gentility: The Life and Works of Frances Miriam Whitcher*. Syracuse: Syracuse University Press, 1992.

Neal, Mark Anthony. *Soul Babies: Black Popular Culture and the Post-Soul Aesthetic*. New York: Routledge, 2002.

"The Negro in Art: How Shall He Be Portrayed?" Symposium. *The Crisis*, 1926. Reprinted in Gates and Jarrett, *New Negro*, 190–203.

Newman, Edwin. "A Conversation with Mary McCarthy." WNBC-TV, New York, filmed and recorded in Paris, December 4, 1966. Reprinted in Gelderman, *Conversations*, 68–87.

"New Negro Woman, The." In "The New Negro Woman's Number." Special issue. *The Messenger* 5, no. 7 (1923): 757.

Niebuhr, Elizabeth. "The Art of Fiction XXVII: Mary McCarthy—An Interview." *Paris Review* 27 (Winter–Spring 1962): 59–94. Reprinted in Gelderman, *Conversations*, 3–29. Page numbers in the notes refer to the Gelderman volume.

Page, Tim. *Dawn Powell: A Biography*. New York: Henry Holt, 1998.

Palermo, Patricia E. *The Message of the City: Dawn Powell's New York Novels, 1925–1960*. Athens, OH: Swallow Press, 2016.

Parker, Dorothy. *Complete Stories*. Edited by Colleen Breese. New York: Penguin Books, 2003.

———. Introduction to *The Most of S. J. Perelman*, xi–xiv. New York: Simon & Schuster, 1958.

———. *The Portable Dorothy Parker*. New York: Penguin Books, 1976.

Patterson, Martha H. *Beyond the Gibson Girl: Reimagining the American New Woman, 1895–1915*. Urbana: University of Illinois Press, 2008.

Pershing, Linda. "There's a Joker in the Menstrual Hut: A Performance Analysis of Comedian Kate Clinton." In Sochen, *Women's Comic Visions*, 193–235.

Peters, Ann M. "Travelers in Residence: Women Writing New York at Mid-Century." PhD diss., CUNY, 2005.

Peterson, Anne Helen. *Too Fat, Too Slutty, Too Loud: The Rise and Reign of the Unruly Woman*. New York: Plume, 2017.

Pettit, Rhonda S., ed. *The Critical Waltz: Essays on the Work of Dorothy Parker*. Madison: Fairleigh Dickinson University Press, 2005.

———. *Sentimentalism and Modernism in Dorothy Parker's Poetry and Fiction*. Madison: Fairleigh Dickinson University Press, 2000.

Podhoretz, Norman. *Making It*. New York: Random House, 1967.

Pollack, Ellen. "Premium Swift: Dorothy Parker's Iron Mask of Femininity." In Pettit, *Critical Waltz*, 200–218.

Powell, Dawn. *The Diaries of Dawn Powell: 1931–1965*. Edited by Tim Page. South Royalton, VT: Steerforth Press, 1995.

———. *The Golden Spur*. 1962. Reprint, South Royalton, VT: Steerforth Press, 1999.

———. *Selected Letters of Dawn Powell: 1913–1965*, edited by Tim Page. New York: Henry Holt, 1999.

———. *Turn, Magic Wheel*. 1936. Reprint, South Royalton, VT: Steerforth Press, 1999.

———. *The Wicked Pavilion*. 1954. Reprint, South Royalton, VT: Steerforth Press, 1996.

Rabinowitz, Paula. *Labor and Desire: Women's Revolutionary Fiction in Depression America*. Chapel Hill: University of North Carolina Press, 1991.

Rahv, Philip. "Storm over the Intellectuals." *New Masses*, May 29, 1934, 26–27.

Rampersad, Arnold. Introduction to *The New Negro: Voices of the Harlem Renaissance*, edited by Alain Locke, ix–xxiii. 1925. Reprint, New York: Macmillan, 1992.

Ransom, John Crowe. "The Poet as Woman." *Southern Review* 2 (Spring 1937): 783–806.

Riviere, Joan. "Womanliness as a Masquerade." *International Journal of Psycho-Analysis* 9 (1929): 303–13.

Rottenberg, Catherine. "Jessie Fauset's *Plum Bun* and the City's Transformative Potential." *Legacy: A Journal of American Women Writers* 30, no. 2 (2013): 265–86.

———. "The New Woman Ideal and Urban Space in Tess Slesinger's *The Unpossessed*." *Women's Studies* 45, no. 4 (2016): 341–55.

Rowe Karlyn, Kathleen. *The Unruly Woman: Gender and the Genres of Laughter.* Austin: University of Texas Press, 1995.

Rudnick, Lois. "The New Woman." In *1915, the Cultural Moment: The New Politics, the New Woman, the New Psychology, the New Art and the New Theatre in America*, edited by Adele Heller and Lois Rudnick, 69–81. New Brunswick: Rutgers University Press, 1991.

Russo, Mary. "Female Grotesques: Carnival and Theory." In *Feminist Studies, Critical Studies*, edited by Teresa de Lauretis, 213–39. Bloomington: Indiana University Press, 1986.

Schwartz, Leo W., ed. *The Menorah Treasury: Harvest of Half a Century.* Philadelphia: Jewish Publication Society, 1964.

Seaver, Edwin. "Phony 'Intellectuals.'" *Menorah Journal* 22 (1934): 188–89.

Seidel, Michael. *Satiric Inheritance: Rabelais to Sterne.* Princeton: Princeton University Press, 1979.

Sharistanian, Janet. Afterword to *The Unpossessed*, by Tess Slesinger, 359–86. Old Westbury, NY: Feminist Press, 1984.

Sheppard, Alice. "Social Cognition, Gender Roles, and Women's Humor." In Sochen, *Women's Comic Visions*, 33–56.

Sherrard-Johnson, Cherene. *Portraits of the New Negro Woman: Visual and Literary Culture in the Harlem Renaissance.* New Brunswick: Rutgers University Press, 2007.

Shifman, Limor, and Dafna Lemish. "Between Feminism and Fun(ny) mism." *Information, Communication and Society* 13, no. 6 (2010): 870–91.

Showalter, Elaine. "Killing the Angel in the House: Autonomy of Women Writers." *Antioch Review* 32, no. 3 (1973): 339–53.

———. "Towards a Feminist Poetics." In *Twentieth-Century Literary Theory: A Reader*, edited by K. M. Newton, 216–19. New York: Palgrave Macmillan, 1997.

Simmons, Christina. *Making Marriage Modern: Women's Sexuality from the Progressive Era to World War II.* Oxford: Oxford University Press, 2009.

Slesinger, Tess. "Memoirs of an Ex-Flapper." *Vanity Fair*, December 1934, 26–27, 74, 75.

———. *On Being Told That Her Second Husband Has Taken His First Lover and Other Stories.* 1935. Reprint, Chicago: Quadrangle Books, 1971.

———. *The Unpossessed: A Novel of the Thirties.* 1934. Reprint, Old Westbury, NY: Feminist Press, 1984.

Smith, Peter Duval. "Mary McCarthy Said: 'Men Have More Feeling, Women Have More Intelligence.'" *Vogue*, October 1963. Reprinted in Gelderman, *Conversations*, 52–61.

Smith Rice, Marcel. *Dawn Powell.* New York: Twayne, 2000.

Smith-Rosenberg, Carroll. *Disorderly Conduct: Visions of Gender in Victorian America.* New York: Oxford University Press, 1985.

Sochen, June. Introduction to Sochen, *Women's Comic Visions*, 9–18.

———. *The New Woman: Feminism in Greenwich Village, 1910–1920.* New York: Quadrangle Books, 1972.

———, ed. *Women's Comic Visions.* Detroit: Wayne State University Press, 1991.

Springer, Kimberly. "Divas, Evil Black Bitches, and Bitter Black Women:

African American Women in Post-feminist and Post-Civil Rights Popular Culture." In *Interrogating Postfeminism*, edited by Yvonne Tasker and Diane Negra, 249–76. Durham: Duke University Press, 2007.

Stanley, Alessandra. "Who Says Women Aren't Funny?" *Vanity Fair*, April 2008, 185–91, 251.

Stwertka, Eve, and Margo Viscusi, eds. *Twenty-Four Ways of Looking at Mary McCarthy*. Westport, CT: Greenwood Press, 1996.

Suleiman, Susan Rubin. *Subversive Intent: Gender, Politics, and the Avant-Garde*. Cambridge: Harvard University Press, 1990.

Sylvander, Carolyn Wedin. *Jessie Redmon Fauset: Black American Writer*. Troy, NY: Whitston, 1981.

Taggard, Genevieve. "Her Massive Sandal." *Measure*, April 1924, 12.

Tasker, Yvonne, and Diane Negra. Introduction to *Interrogating Postfeminism*, edited by Yvonne Tasker and Diane Negra, 1–26. Durham: Duke University Press, 2007.

Tate, Allen. "Miss Millay's Sonnets." *New Republic* 66 (May 6, 1931): 335–36. Reprinted in Thesing, *Critical Essays*, 61–64. Page numbers in the notes refer to the Thesing volume.

Teres, Harvey. *Renewing the Left: Politics, Imagination, and the New York Intellectuals*. Oxford: Oxford University Press, 1996.

Thesing, William B., ed. *Critical Essays on Edna St. Vincent Millay*. New York: G. K. Hall, 1993.

Tillman, Katherine. "Afro-American Women and Their Work." 1895. Reprinted in Gates and Jarrett, *New Negro*, 277–86.

Todd, Ellen Wiley. *The "New Woman" Revised: Painting and Gender Politics on Fourteenth Street*. Berkeley: University of California Press, 1993.

Tomlinson, Susan. "Vision to Visionary: The New Negro Woman as Cultural Worker in Jessie Redmon Fauset's *Plum Bun*." *Legacy* 19, no. 1 (2002): 90–97.

Tomsett, Ellie. "Twenty-First Century Fumerist: Bridget Christie and the Backlash Against Feminist Comedy." *Comedy Studies* 8, no. 1 (2017): 57–67.

Toth, Emily. "Dorothy Parker, Erica Jong, and New Feminist Humor." In Pettit, *Critical Waltz*, 137–51.

———. "Female Wits." *Massachusetts Review* 22, no. 4 (1981): 783–93.

———. "A Laughter of Their Own: Women's Humor in the United States." In *Critical Essays on American Humor*, edited by William Bedford Clark and W. Craig Turner, 199–215. Boston: G. K. Hall, 1984.

Treichler, Paula A. "Verbal Subversion in Dorothy Parker: 'Trapped Like a Trap in a Trap.'" In Pettit, *Critical Waltz*, 1166–186.

Trilling, Diana. *The Beginning of the Journey: The Marriage of Diana and Lionel Trilling*. New York: Harcourt Brace, 1993.

———. Review of *A Time to Be Born*, by Dawn Powell. *The Nation*, September 19, 1942, 243–44.

———. Review of *The Locusts Have No King*, by Dawn Powell. *The Nation*, May 29, 1948, 611–12.

Trilling, Lionel. *The Liberal Imagination*. New York: Harcourt, 1979.

———. *Sincerity and Authenticity*. Cambridge: Harvard University Press, 1972.

———. "Young in the Thirties." *Commentary* 41 (May 1966): 43–51.

Updike, John. "An Ohio Runaway." *New Yorker*, February 20, 1995, 262–63, 266–71.

Vidal, Gore. "Dawn Powell: Queen of the Golden Age." *New York Review of Books*, March 21, 1996. Reprinted in *The Last Empire: Essays 1992–2000*, 16–29. New York: Vintage, 2002.

———. "Dawn Powell, the American Writer." *New York Review of Books*, November 5, 1987, 52–60.

Wald, Alan M. "The Menorah Group Moves Left." *Jewish Social Studies* 38, nos. 3–4 (1976): 289–320.

———. *The New York Intellectuals: The Rise and Decline of the Anti-Stalinist Left from the 1930s to the 1980s*. Chapel Hill: University of North Carolina Press, 1987.

Walker, Nancy A. "'Fragile and Dumb': The 'Little Woman' in Women's Humor, 1900–1940." *Thalia* 5, no. 2 (1982–83): 24–29.

———. "Toward Solidarity: Women's Humor and Group Identity." In Sochen, *Women's Comic Visions*, 57–81.

———. *A Very Serious Thing: Women's Humor and American Culture*. Minneapolis: University of Minnesota Press, 1988.

Walker, Nancy A., and Zita Dresner, eds. *Redressing the Balance: American Women's Literary Humor from Colonial Times to the 1980s*. Jackson: University Press of Mississippi, 1988.

Wall, Cheryl A. *Women of the Harlem Renaissance*. Bloomington: Indiana University Press, 1995.

Weisstein, Naomi. "Why We Aren't Laughing . . . Any More." *Ms.* 2, no. 2 (1973): 49–51, 88–90. Reprinted in Morris, *American Women Humorists*, 131–40. Page numbers in the notes refer to the Morris volume.

Welter, Barbara. "The Cult of True Womanhood: 1820–1860." *American Quarterly*, Summer 1966, 151–67.

West, Lindy. *Shrill: Notes from a Loud Woman*. New York: Hachette Books, 2016.

Wetzsteon, Ross. *Republic of Dreams: Greenwich Village: The American Bohemia, 1910–1960*. New York: Simon and Schuster, 2002.

White, E. B. *Here Is New York*. 1949. Reprint, New York: Little Book Room, 1976.

Whitehead, Colson. *The Colossus of New York*. New York: Anchor Books, 2003.

Willett, Cynthia, and Julie Willett. *Uproarious: How Feminists and Other Subversive Comics Speak Truth*. Minneapolis: University of Minnesota Press, 2019.

Williams, Raymond. *The Country and the City*. New York: Oxford University Press, 1973.

Wilson, Edmund. "Dawn Powell: Greenwich Village in the Fifties." In *The Bit Between My Teeth: A Literary Chronicle of 1950–1965*, 526–33. New York: Farrar, Straus and Giroux, 1965.

———. *I Thought of Daisy*. 1929. Reprint, Iowa City: University of Iowa Press, 2001.

———. *The Shores of Light: A Literary Chronicle of the 1920s and 1930s*. 1952. Reprint, Boston: Northeastern University Press, 1985.

Wilson, Elizabeth. *The Sphinx in the City: Urban Life, the Control of*

Disorder, and Women. Berkeley: University of California Press, 1991.

Woodard, Deborah. "'I Could Do a Woman Better than That': Masquerade in Millay's Potboilers." In Freedman, *Millay at 100*, 145–62.

Woolf, Virginia. *The Death of the Moth and Other Essays*. New York: Harcourt Brace and Company, 1942.

Woollcott, Alexander. "Our Mrs. Parker." In *While Rome Burns*, 142–52. New York: Grosset & Dunlap, 1936.

Worcester, David. *The Art of Satire*. New York: Russell and Russell, 1960.

Wright, Richard. "Blueprint for Negro Writing." 1937. Reprinted in Gates and Jarrett, *New Negro*, 268–76.

Wurtzel, Elizabeth. *Bitch: In Praise of Difficult Women*. New York: Anchor Books, 1998.

Yaross Lee, Judith. *Defining New Yorker Humor*. Jackson: University Press of Mississippi, 2000.

Zeisler, Andi. *We Were Feminists Once: From Riot Grrrl to Covergirl, the Buying and Selling of a Political Movement*. New York: Public Affairs, 2016.

Zeitz, Joshua. *Flapper: A Madcap Story of Sex, Style, Celebrity, and the Women Who Made America Modern*. New York: Broadway Books, 2007.

Index

McCarthy, Mary (*continued*)
  The Oasis, 26, 99, 102, 175, 177
  and *Partisan Review*, 3
  physical persona, 174–75
  on satire, 173
  sexual liberation, 178–79, 181
  social commentary, 26
  "The Vassar Girl," 185
McCarthy, Mary, stories
  "Cruel and Barbarous Treatment," 178
  "Ghostly Father, I Confess," 182–83
  "The Man in the Brooks Brothers
    Shirt," 91, 178, 180–81
  "Portrait of the Intellectual as a Yale
    Man," 91, 178, 181
McGhee, Paul, 14–15
McGinley, Phyllis, 19
McKay, Claude, 116, 119, 120
McMein, Neysa, 55
McRobbie, Angela, 194
Meade, Marion, 53
Medusa figures, 9, 137
Mendelman, Lisa, 139
Menippean satire, 15, 141
Menorah Journal (magazine), 3, 55, 78,
  79–80, 82–83, 100
Menorah Movement, The, 80
Menorah Society, 79–80
Mercury (magazine), 82
Messenger, The (magazine), 3, 119,
  120–21
Midtown Manhattan, 3, 82, 127, 142, 147,
  151, 156, 160–61
Millay, Edna St. Vincent
  background and overview, 2, 6,
    29–30
  cult of personality, 31
  Distressing Dialogues, 33–48
  A Few Figs from Thistles, 30, 50
  gender roles and identity, 30–31,
    34–35
  Mine the Harvest, 50
  Nancy Boyd satires, 32–33, 50
  satire regarding male-female rela-
    tions, 33–34, 50

  Second April, 30
  subversive voice of, 31–32
Millay, Edna St. Vincent, poems
  "First Fig," 31
  "Renascence," 30, 50
  "Thursday," 31–32
  "What lips my lips have kissed, and
    where, and why," 31
Millay, Edna St. Vincent, satirical
  sketches
  "Art and How to Fake It," 34, 45–47
  "The Barrel," 48–50
  "For Winter, for Summer," 34, 44–45
  "The Implacable Aphrodite," 34,
    35–37
  "Knock Wood," 34
  "Madame a Tort!," 34, 37–38
  "No Bigger than a Man's Hand," 34,
    42–44
  "Powder, Rouge, and Lipstick," 34,
    40–42
  "Tea for the Muse," 34, 47–48
  "Two Souls with but a Single
    Thought," 38–40
Miller, Alice Duer, 13, 55
Miller, Nina, 30, 56
minstrel performances, 117
Mitchell, Joseph, 149
Mizejewski, Linda, 10, 16, 20, 28
Modern Quarterly (magazine), 83
Modern Satire (Kernan), 173
Modernism, 2, 5, 101, 122
Modern woman, 8, 34, 39, 41, 78, 91, 99,
  103–5, 122, 129, 148, 171, 187
  See also New Woman
Money for Love (Herbst), 96
Morgan, Danielle Fuentes, 118, 139
Morningside Heights, 3, 82
Morris, Linda A., 10
Morrow, Felix, 3, 82–83
Moscow Trials (1936-1938), 84
Moses, Robert, 4, 148, 150
Motion Picture Guild, 84
Munsey's (magazine), 141
Murphy, Gerald, 54, 159

Murphy, Sara, 54, 159
Murray, Pauli, 122

names
  maiden *vs.* married, 54
  pseudonyms, 32
National American Woman Suffrage
  Association (NAWSA), 7
National Association for the Advance-
  ment of Colored People (NAACP),
  115, 119
National Association of Colored
  Women, 8
Negra, Diane, 194
"Negro Artist and the Racial Mountain,
  The" (Hughes), 117
"Neither 'Sissy' Boys nor Patrician Man"
  (Grinberg), 87
New Critical approach, 23, 32
New Masses (magazine), 2, 55, 100
New Negro, The (Locke), 117, 120
New Negro Movement, 3, 115, 120
New Negro Woman , 8, 116, 119, 120–21
  contrasted with New Woman,
    121–22, 132–33
  in Jessie Fauset's fiction, 124, 127–28
New Woman (see also Modern
    woman), 2, 4–9, 29–30, 31, 35–36,
    85, 119, 121–22
  and childbearing, 96–98
  and Dorothy Parker, 55–56
  and Edna St. Vincent Millay, 29–31, 34
  contrasted with New Negro Woman,
    121–22, 132–33
  and divorce, 39, 52, 78, 184, 185
  emergence of, 122
  in Dawn Powell's fiction, 171
  in Dorothy Parker's fiction, 73
  in Edna St. Vincent Millay's fiction,
    34–35, 39, 45
  in Jessie Fauset's fiction, 116, 124, 127,
    128–30, 132–33
  in Tess Slesinger's fiction, 79, 85,
    90–92, 93–94, 101, 104
  shift during 1920s, 55–56

New York City
  Algonquin Hotel, 55
  Brevoort Hotel, 148, 150
  bohemian life, 147–51
  café culture, 4, 140, 147–51, 164–65
  cultural milieu early 20th century,
    2–5
  Harlem contrasted with Greenwich
    Village, 130–32
  Lafayette Hotel, 4, 148–150, 159
  neighborhoods, 2–3, 127–29
  urban renewal, 148
  See also Greenwich Village; Harlem;
    Midtown Manhattan; Morning-
    side Heights
New Yorker (magazine), 3, 7, 33, 55, 122,
    141
New York Review of Books, 145
Nineteenth Amendment, 85, 122
Noah, Trevor, 21
Norris, Kathleen, 70
North American Review (magazine), 6

Oliver, John, 21
open marriage, 148–49
  See also sexual freedom
Opportunity (magazine), 3, 119
Orteig, Raymond, 150
Orwell, George, 22
"Our Leading Bitch Intellectual"
  (Gross), 176

Page, Tim, 140, 145, 156
Parker, Dorothy
  Algonquin Round Table, 3
  background and overview, 51–56
  childhood and education, 53–54
  contrasted with Dawn Powell, 141
  double entendre and wordplay, 58
  dual persona, 56–58
  gender roles and identity, 19, 51,
    52–53, 56–57, 70
  as Hollywood scriptwriter, 84
  Jewish identity, 25, 53–54
  Mongrel (projected memoir), 53

Shores of Light, The (Wilson), 35
Showalter, Elaine, 15
Shuffle Along (Broadway musical), 117
Silverman, Sarah, 16, 196
Sincerity and Authenticity (Trilling), 80
"skits" and sketches, 58–59
slavery, legacy of, 8, 115, 117–18, 121, 138
Slesinger, Tess
    on abortion, 96--98
    childhood and education, 79
    comparisons with Parker and McCarthy, 102
    as Hollywood scriptwriter, 84
    Jewish identity, 25
    marriage to Herbert Solow, 79, 82, 83–84
    "Memoirs of an Ex-Flapper," 85–86
    Menorah Journal, 3
    modernist fiction techniques, 87–88, 90–91
    and New Woman figure, 6
    On Being Told That Her Second Husband Has Taken His First Lover, 78–79, 101
    overview, 78–79
    socialist themes and social protest stories, 106
    social/political commentary, 26, 102–3
    Time: The Present, 78, 83, 101–2
    The Unpossessed, critical response, 99–101
    The Unpossessed: A Novel of the Thirties, 26, 78, 83, 84–85, 86–99
Slesinger, Tess, stories
    "The Friedmans' Annie," 103, 110–12
    "Jobs in the Sky," 103, 106–7
    "Mother to Dinner," 102, 105–6
    "The Mouse-trap," 103, 108–10
    "On Being Told That Her Second Husband Has Taken His First Lover," 102
    "White on Black," 103, 112–14
Smart Set (magazine), 3, 7
Smith, Bessie, 3, 122

Smith, Betty, 84
Snappy Stories (magazine), 141
Sochen, June, 10
"Social Cognition, Gender Roles, and Women's Humor" (Sheppard), 14
socialist themes, 106–7
social justice, 195–96
    "satiractivism," 24
    social protest fiction, 78–79
Solow, Herbert, 3, 79, 82–83, 86
Sontag, Susan, 175
Soyer, Raphael, 128
Spencer, Niles, 150
Sphinx in the City, The (Wilson), 5, 139
Springer, Kimberly, 197–98
stand-up comedy, 21, 199
Stanley, Alessandra, 196, 197
Stein, Gertrude, 58
stereotypes
    "Angel" contrasted with "Monster" figures, 9
    "bitch" image, 2, 28, 174, 175–76
    Black women, 121–22, 197–98
    gendered, 18–19, 27, 44–45, 92–93, 146–47
    subversion of, 20, 196–97
    "unruly women," 16–17
    women in Dorothy Parker's "Big Blonde," 73–77
Stewart, John, 21
Story (magazine), 83, 101, 141
stream-of-consciousness style, 91
suicide, 76–77
Suleiman, Susan Rubin, 9
superiority theory of humor, 10, 11–12
Survey Graphic (magazine), 120
Swift, Jonathan, 22
Swope, Herbert, 54
Swope, Maggie, 54
Sykes, Wanda, 16, 185, 193, 196
Sylvander, Carolyn Wedin, 138

Taggard, Genevieve, 29, 140
Tasker, Yvonne, 194
Tate, Allen, 32

Printed in the USA
CPSIA information can be obtained
at www.ICGtesting.com
LVHW091040151123
763629LV00001B/1